"May be the beginning of a new, and healthier, trend . . . After grasping at the straws of Asian culture, American business is going back to Deming. . . . Gabor's book is the most exhaustive and gives the best picture of Deming as a man and in his historical setting."

— *The Los Angeles Times Book Review*

"*The Man Who Discovered Quality* provides an invaluable, permanent record of Dr. Deming's many contributions. He is proof . . . that one person can still make a difference."

— H. Ross Perot

"The stuff of dramatic literature . . . Ms. Gabor's book is impressive. Her analyses of companies that have tried to introduce Demingism . . . highlight key principles while offering readers a scenic tour through the thickets of corporate decision making. . . . Ms. Gabor's book is certainly a good place to start on the search for useful ideas."

— *The New York Times Book Review*

"Andrea Gabor offers not only a comprehensive review of the influence Deming has had to date in America and Japan, but also an acute assessment of how his theories might best be implemented in the future."

— Yotaro Kobayashi,
president of Fuji Xerox

"A fascinating account of the man as well as of his methods and influence"

— *USA Today*

"This insightful and hopeful book shows how America has finally begun to use Deming's ideas."

— Robert B. Reich,
author of *The Next American Frontier* and
The Work of Nations

PENGUIN BOOKS

THE MAN WHO DISCOVERED QUALITY

Andrea Gabor was a senior editor for business at *U.S. News and World Report*. She is currently at work on a new nonfiction book for Viking. She lives in New York City.

The MAN WHO DISCOVERED QUALITY

HOW
W. EDWARDS DEMING
BROUGHT THE QUALITY
REVOLUTION TO AMERICA—
THE STORIES OF
FORD, XEROX, AND GM

ANDREA GABOR

PENGUIN BOOKS

PENGUIN BOOKS
Published by the Penguin Group
Penguin Books USA Inc.,
375 Hudson Street, New York, New York 10014, U.S.A.
Penguin Books Ltd, 27 Wrights Lane, London W8 5TZ, England
Penguin Books Australia Ltd, Ringwood, Victoria, Australia
Penguin Books Canada Ltd, 10 Alcorn Avenue,
Toronto, Ontario, Canada M4V 3B2
Penguin Books (N.Z.) Ltd, 182–190 Wairau Road, Auckland 10, New Zealand

Penguin Books Ltd, Registered Offices:
Harmondsworth, Middlesex, England

First published in the United States of America by
Times Books, a division of Random House, Inc., 1990
Reprinted by arrangement with Times Books
Published in Penguin Books 1992

7   9   10   8

THE LIBRARY OF CONGRESS HAS CATALOGUED THE HARDCOVER AS FOLLOWS:
Gabor, Andrea.
The man who discovered quality: how W. Edwards Deming brought the quality
revolution to America—the stories of Ford, Xerox, and GM / by Andrea Gabor.
p.   cm.
ISBN 0-8129-1774-X (hc.)
ISBN 0 14 01.6528 2 (pbk.)
1. Quality control—United States.   2. Deming, W. Edwards (William Edwards).
1900–   .   I. Title.
TS156.G3   1990
658.5'62—dc20   89–40788

Printed in the United States of America
Designed by Jenny Vandeventer

For Jose and my parents,
Clara and Andre Gabor

ACKNOWLEDGMENTS

This book was in the works for nearly five years. It wouldn't have made it without Flip Brophy, my tireless agent. I also want to give a special thank-you to Dr. Deming for his time and trust, and for introducing me to the world of quality management and a unique insight into the way companies work. Beth Brophy and Arthur Karlin offered advice and a home-away-from-home (Ariel deserves credit here too) during my numerous trips to Washington, D.C. I am grateful to all the folks from Random House who, at various times, helped midwife this book, including Kathleen Becker, Sandee Brawarsky, Derek Johns, Susan Luke, Hugh O'Neill, and Steve Wasserman. Several colleagues and editors at *U.S. News & World Report* lent their help and support, including Peter Bernstein and Chris Ma, who approved the leaves of absence I needed to finish the book. This project also owes much to the cooperation of many at Xerox, Fuji Xerox, Ford, GM, Florida Power & Light, and Nashua. Several people reviewed the manuscript and lent advice during its various stages of incompletion, including Susan Adler, Dr. Lloyd Nelson, Gipsie Ranney, Dr. Harold Hansen, Ron Moen, Hamish Norton, Larry Sullivan, Bill Cook, Cathy Harris, Maryann Keller, Kent Sterett, Marta Mooney, and Joyce Orsini, the last two from Fordham University's business school, and John Whitney of Columbia University's B-School. Other Columbia faculty members who were very helpful include Martin Starr and Peter Kolesar, who let me audit his class on quality management. Michael Berger helped with some excellent reporting in Japan. The quality and productivity of my first trip to Japan owe much to the introductions provided by Jeff Kennard, as well as the time and help lent me by several people at JUSE, Fuji Xerox, and Toyota Motor Company. Thank you, too, to my sister Tony Gabor for her help with some of the charts in the book. Finally, hugs for my husband, Jose, who has lived with this book during our entire marriage, showing a remarkable capacity for endurance, support, and humor.

CONTENTS

INTRODUCTION

C O N T E N T S

THE
MAN WHO
DISCOVERED
QUALITY

AMERICA REDISCOVERS
W. EDWARDS DEMING

"I have never known a concern to make a decided success that did not do good, honest work, and even in these days of the fiercest competition, when everything would seem to be a matter of price, there lies still at the root of great business success the very much more important factor of quality. The effect of attention to quality upon every man in the service, from the president of the concern down to the humblest laborer, cannot be overestimated."

—Andrew Carnegie

The name and reputation of W. Edwards Deming first came to the attention of a few Detroit auto executives in 1978, when they began taking fact-finding missions to Japan to figure out how the Japanese automakers were outclassing them in car quality and design. In January 1981 Donald E. Petersen, the new president of Ford, made an urgent appeal to Deming. Would Dr. Deming be willing to come to Ford and help the company lick its quality problems? It appeared to be a highly unusual SOS, to say the least. Half a world away, Deming's name had become almost synonymous with Japanese quality. In the United States, however, he was virtually unknown in executive suites and boardrooms. Moreover, the octogenarian's professional life had been spent as a statistician and academic. He had never held a full-time job in a corporation, never built a company, never even bothered to market his services.

Ford, it turned out, was one of the first major U.S. companies to "discover" Deming's expertise in quality management. The association between Detroit's second-largest automaker and America's forgotten quality pioneer would change history for both of them. Less than a decade after their first encounter, Ford would be hailed as a model of American management, and Petersen would lay much of the credit at Deming's feet. "We are moving toward building a quality culture at Ford, and the many changes that have been taking place here have their roots directly in Dr. Deming's teachings," says Petersen, who was CEO until 1990.[1] Meanwhile, Ford's success would help turn Deming into the most sought-after quality expert in America, his ideas serving as an inspiration to hundreds of companies.

Deming swooped into Detroit like a tornado that had spent eighty-one years gathering strength. He ripped the lid off prevailing assumptions about the reasons for the United States' competitiveness problems, which had long focused on Japan's manufacturing advantages. First, the theory went, Japan was beating the United States because of low labor rates. But when Japanese wages began to reach parity with U.S. paychecks, nervous Japan watchers pointed to the country's spanking-new factories and its state-of-the-art manufacturing equipment. Then, when General Motors spent close to $70 billion on new technology and acquisitions and *still* lost market share, the nervous Japan watchers seized on the soft yen, certain that the competition's advantage lay in cheap exports. But even before the yen reached an all-time high against the dollar in the late 1980s, cooler heads were beginning to wonder whether they'd been looking at the right symptoms at all.

The day thirty Ford executives gathered, on a chilly February afternoon in 1981, for their first meeting with Deming, they were still convinced their problems lay somewhere between John Doe's paycheck and Cincinnati Milacron's machine tools. They were expecting to hear about cars, about how to transform manufacturing plants that were turning out automobiles with at least 4.5 "things gone wrong" per car, according to one of Ford's traditional quality indices, into operations that could produce trouble-free vehicles.[2] Deming, they knew, had made a name for himself forty years before by popularizing a method of statistical analysis that could help minimize variation and control the quality and consistency of manufacturing output. Although this system, known as statistical process control (SPC), had enjoyed a brief popularity in the United States, American companies had somehow never gotten the hang of it. Deming, the Ford executives thought, would help them apply such techniques properly.

The Ford men couldn't have been further off the mark. While the guru touched on the importance of statistical theory and statistical thinking in that first meeting, he didn't want to talk about cars or the reject rates on the production line. Nor did he deliver conventional bromides about quality, such as that everything would be okay if everyone just worked a little harder. Instead, what Deming really wanted to know about were processes and people and how they were managed at Ford. He wanted to know about the executives sitting in the room, and what they understood their responsibilities to be—to the company, to their employees, and to the customer. Deming has developed a philosophy of quality management that is rooted in an understanding of the power and pervasiveness of variation and how it affects the process, that delicate interaction of people, machines, materials, and the environment. All systems are subject to some amount of variation that leads to inconsistency and, eventually, to an erosion of both process and product quality. Inconsistency makes it difficult for management to predict how its systems and strategies will perform, and the degradation of quality inevitably results in a loss to the organization. Deming's teachings on variation give management the vital knowledge it needs to recognize when a problem is the result of an isolated glitch in an otherwise well-run organization and when it is the result of deep-rooted systemic problems. Thus, an understanding of variation is vital to managing change.

Deming started out looking at processes through the lens of the scientist, studying the effects of variation on a multitude of individual processes. This unique perspective ultimately led him to develop an all-encompassing quality blueprint that helps management hone the focus of the company and, ultimately, improve and optimize the organization as a whole. Deming's system, known as the Fourteen Points, ties together disparate process-oriented management ideas into a single, holistic vision of how companies can anticipate and meet the desires of the customer by fostering a better understanding of "the process" and by enlisting the help of every employee, division, and supplier in the improvement effort.

Deming and his ideas about variation have revived, and rede-fined, SPC, a way of determining whether a process is producing predictable results and a basic tool for identifying both immediate systemic problems and opportunities for improvement. One of the most powerful characteristics of this methodology is that, if used properly, data derived through SPC can literally be used to predict how a process will function in the future, thereby making it possible to avoid quality problems before they happen. Consider a simple example on a production line: By monitoring the minute fluctuations over time in the dimensions of supposedly identical parts produced by a machine, SPC can in many cases predict *when* the machine's tool bit is likely to wear out, *before* it begins producing faulty prod-ucts. Ultimately, an understanding of variation can give manage-ment a powerful predictive tool that it can use to help manage change in almost every business process.

Today, at companies such as Ford, General Motors, and Florida Power & Light, which have all come under the influence of Dem-ing, traditional SPC has given way to a kind of analysis, variation control, and improvement methodology that embraces far more than just manufacturing. Achieving major improvements in the quality of a part coming off the assembly line can rarely be accomplished by upgrading *only* the production process. It generally requires improve-ments in design, which in turn call for more detailed market research and close coordination with suppliers—in other words, process op-timization throughout the organization.

TUNING IN TO THE CUSTOMER

To Deming, America's quality crisis is symptomatic of a fundamen-tally outdated management system that focuses on short-term results at the expense of the process, the customer, and, ultimately, long-term achievements. What worked in the "days of free land and rugged individualism," as Deming, who grew up on a homestead in Wyoming, is fond of saying, won't work in the era of intense foreign competition. In other words, he is calling for a more systematic approach to pursuing customers and product strategies to replace the mentality of planned obsolescence that worked in the seller's market of the 1950s and 1960s but has come to hobble American business since the 1970s. The importance Deming attaches to controlling and reducing variation has led him to a holistic view of leadership that casts management in a very different role from the one prevailing in American companies since the end of World War II. Deming rejects the model of the modern American manager, who can "manage anything" based on a company's balance sheet.[3] Instead, he advocates a process-obsessed management culture that is capable of harnessing the know-how and natural initiative of its employees and fine-tuning the entire organization to higher and higher standards of excellence and innovation.

Deming and his followers believe that under the influence of beancounters, corporate goals have fallen out of step with the heartbeat of the marketplace and with objective assessments of companies' capabilities. In a finance-minded company, the shareholders replace the customer as the principal focus of management. And many American managers delegate the responsibility for achieving objectives to subordinates without ever fully examining their feasibility. What's more, goals and strategies often are based not on the long-term needs of the company but on reactions to financial results and on wishful thinking. Another problem is that legally mandated financial statements are little more than "a fuzzy approximation of a distant past," notes Professor John Whitney of Columbia University Business School, a former chief operating officer of Pathmark, who has joined Deming's inner circle. That they have no predictive value is made starkly evident by the fact that most of the largest bankruptcies, including those of Penn Central, Baldwin United, and several Savings & Loan institutions, were preceded by an auditor's "clean opinion."[4]

In Deming's view, the traditional financial mentality is the greatest impediment to quality management in the United States, because it deflects attention from the long-term interests of a company's operations and because traditional financial and accounting measures offer managers few of the insights they need to plan for the future. In 1983 Deming addressed a group of students at Utah State University and tried to explain why numbers were of little use when it comes to satisfying customers: "Some of you are students of finance. You learn how to figure and how to run a company on figures. If you run a company on figures alone you will go under. How long will it take the company to go under, get drowned? I don't know, but it is sure to fail. Why? Because the most important figures are not there. Did you learn that in the school of finance? You will, 10 or 15 years from now, learn that the most important figures are those that are unknown or unknowable.

"What about the multiplying effects of a happy customer, in either manufacturing or in service? Is he in your figures? What about the multiplying effect of an unhappy customer? Is that in your figures? Did you learn that in your school of finance? What about the multiplying effect of getting better material to use in production? What about the multiplying effect that you get all along the production line? Do you know that figure? You don't! If you run your company without it, you won't have a company. What about the multiplying effect of doing a better job along the line?"[5]

In companies that have embraced Deming's vision, management's job is to "work on the system" to achieve continual product and process improvement.[6] The Deming-style manager must ensure a system's consistency and reliability, by bringing the level of variation in its operations within predictable limits, then by identifying opportunities for improvement, by enlisting the participation of every employee, and by giving his subordinates the practical benefit of his experience and the help they need to chart improvement strategies. The Deming-style manager learns to probe behind the numbers, knowing that numbers don't give you the answers, only the questions that need to be asked, and understanding that in the short term figures can be dressed up to suit almost any occasion. He also understands that in the long run, if his products and processes improve, the measures of corporate health will follow. When objectives are finally established, they are based on careful analysis of both a company's own products and capabilities and those of the competition, as well as an assessment of the future needs of the customer. The analysis never ceases, and the objectives are amended systematically as new information emerges about the system or the requirements of the marketplace.

Deming maintains that to lose touch with the process is also to risk losing touch with the customer. The widening gulf between the customer and the company has led to a major misunderstanding of the meaning of quality in U.S. industry, where, since the 1950s, it has typically been associated with fancy features and high prices. More recently it has come to mean the absence of defects or conformance to specifications. Deming is a critic of quality approaches that emphasize "zero defects" because they confuse the crucial difference between product quality and process quality.[7] The existence of variation simply doesn't allow for the mass production of goods over a reasonable length of time without any defects at all. Indeed, focusing on zero defects is like demanding the end of variation—which is asking for the impossible. Even the most inefficient, problem-prone operation can turn out *some* "zero-defect" products if the company is willing to pay a high enough price to cull out the faulty items. Thus, companies would do better to focus on constant improvement rather than the elusive goal of zero defects. Moreover, Deming contends that companies can go out of business producing defect-free products because being defect-free doesn't, in and of itself, guarantee that a product is what the customer wants. Deming uses the example of an expensive fountain pen and an inexpensive, disposable ballpoint pen: While they appear to have similar uses, they are in fact vastly different products that conjure up vastly different customer expectations and definitions of "quality."

Quality, according to Deming, has no meaning except as defined by the desires and needs of customers. Ever since the 1950s, when he began lecturing to the Japanese about improving quality, Deming has stressed the importance of conducting incisive market research. "A satisfied customer is not enough," says Deming. "Business is built on the loyal customer, one who comes back and brings a friend."[8] Deming goes one step further: While market research is important, he contends, it isn't enough because the research measures past demand and doesn't predict what the customer will want in the future. The most productive and successful companies focus on increasing a market by staying one step ahead of the customer and coming up with brand-new product innovations that will inspire his imagination, rather than by battling for market share in an already crowded arena. Deming goes so far as to postulate that the traditional pursuit of market share can be a trap, in that it shifts the focus of the company from the customer to the competition. Notes Peter Drucker, the management expert who followed Deming to

Japan in the late 1950s, "Japanese managers do not start out with a *desired* profit, that is, with a financial objective in mind. Rather, they start out with *business* objectives and especially with *market* objectives . . . the purpose of a business is to create a customer and to satisfy a customer."[9] Quality, then, means anticipating the needs of the customer, translating those needs into a useful and dependable product, and creating a system that can produce the product at the lowest possible price, so that it represents "good value" to the consumer and profits for the enterprise. Quality and profitability become synonymous when quality concepts suffuse the entire organization.

Thus, the Deming philosophy has come to encompass every function and discipline within the corporation. Controlling variation, eliminating the corresponding impediments to quality, such as waste and defects, and improving production processes are merely the price of entry in the competitiveness challenge. Equally important is the systematic search for new product (and process) characteristics that will best serve to *enhance* quality on an ongoing basis. Ultimately, management's job is to hone the entire system so that it is capable of making the leap from continual improvement to continual innovation in whole new product categories the customer has never even contemplated. "No advance is made by the customer," Deming repeatedly tells the gatherings at his four-day seminars. "None asked for electricity, or the automobile, the camera, pneumatic tires, or the copying machine. The consumer can think only in terms of what you and the competition offer . . . improvement is important, but it's not enough."[10]

MAKING THE LEAP FROM IMPROVEMENT TO INNOVATION

A company that has a well-defined customer focus and that successfully manages the knowledge gained through incremental improvements is much more likely to trigger innovation than is an organization that is satisfied with the status quo. America's inability to best the Japanese in product innovation, even though we continue to lead in basic science and invention, points directly to the fact that U.S. companies lag far behind the Japanese in mastery of "the process." Just as SPC helps employees analyze, understand, and improve individual processes, so companies that harness such knowledge throughout an organization are more likely to come up with innovations and less likely to squander the seeds of creativity within their ranks. C. K. Prahalad and Gary Hamel refer to this process as recognizing and developing "core competencies"; it was, for example, Honda's ability to exploit its strength in designing lightweight, powerful engines that made it possible for the upstart motorcycle manufacturer to break into the auto business with a unique, winning product. By contrast, the failure of both Xerox and Procter & Gamble to capitalize on potential blockbuster inventions in the 1970s was attributable in large part to their failure to manage institutional knowledge or "core competencies." Although Xerox did some of the earliest work in personal computers, it was unable to translate its inventions into leadership in the computer business because top management didn't understand the significance of the innovations made by its computer scientists (see Chapter 7). And P&G began to commercialize sucrose polyester (SPE), a low-calorie fat substitute that could be used to make everything from low-cal cookies to ice cream, only some twenty years after researchers first discovered the substance. In what was then a relatively rigid organizational structure at P&G, which thought of itself as a maker of foods, not food ingredients, SPE became an "orphan." As a result, Olestra, as the commercial version of SPE became known, would still be wending its way through the FDA in 1990, when NutraSweet won approval for its fat substitute, Simplesse, and years after its first patent had expired.[11] It's noteworthy that the top management at both companies came from marketing and financial backgrounds, and thus lacked the knowledge to make difficult decisions about R & D. Their organizations failed at least one crucial test of Demingism: making sure *all* the key corporate disciplines are represented in the decision-making process. As the pace of product development quickens, there is less and less margin for sloppiness in innovation. Both companies have since begun to adopt a holistic approach to quality management that is modeled, to a great extent, on Deming's teachings.

Significantly, an understanding of variation and its effects on an organization can serve as a common language for bridging communications barriers and what often seem like the antithetical interests of different departments within the same company. By contrast, accounting, America's primary corporate language today, more often than not excludes nonfinancial employees and is of little use when it comes to understanding manufacturing's concern over operations, the marketing department's analysis of the customer's needs, or R & D's interest in a new avenue of research.[12]

Deming's philosophy and the single-minded dedication with which he has pursued it have been instrumental in giving a much needed impetus to a process-oriented management movement that began to make some inroads into the United States during the 1980s. A man whose desire to constantly learn and improve himself is legendary, Deming sprinkles his speeches and books with ideas of both famous and obscure experts who have influenced him. While Deming's ideas have been embraced by countless corporate executives and academics, he is privately criticized by some contemporary quality and management experts, who resent his transformation in the United States from a relatively obscure statistical expert to a widely respected management guru. Most significantly, his teachings on variation were based originally on the work of Walter Shewhart, a physicist at Bell Laboratories, who became Deming's mentor in the 1930s and who developed a groundbreaking approach to improving manufacturing systems by studying the variation produced by each process. He is a contemporary of both Peter Drucker, who was for a time a colleague of Deming's at New York University, and Joseph Juran, who went to Japan a few years after Deming; Deming's ideas on the need to foster interdepartmental cooperation, for example, were undoubtedly influenced by them. Most important, perhaps, Deming has returned to Japan almost every year for forty years, so that Japan's great American *sensei* has himself become one of the preeminent students of prominent Japanese quality experts, including the late Kaoru Ishikawa and Genichi Taguchi, leading lights of Japan's Total Quality Control (TQC) movement, as well as the contemporary management practices of Japanese companies.

In addition, Deming's philosophy borrows from, and informs, the theories on human motivation that were put forth years ago by such experts as Frederick Herzberg, Abraham Maslow, and Douglas Mc-

Gregor. Although Deming doesn't recall reading the works of these theorists, he has surrounded himself with psychologists and organizational behaviorists who would have exposed him to their ideas. Deming fervently believes in the "intrinsic motivation" of mankind, and that it is management's policies that often serve to demotivate employees. Instead of helping workers develop their potential, he asserts, management often prevents them from making a meaningful contribution to the improvement of their jobs, robs them of the self-esteem they need to foster motivation, and blames them for systemic problems beyond their control.

Equally important for Americans laboring in the corporate jungle, Deming's teachings on variation give management the tools to clearly distinguish between the kinds of systemic problems that individual employees can influence and those that only management can solve. They offer new insight into the reason for fluctuations in the performance of everything from people to machines; in so doing, they highlight the inaccuracy and unfairness of relying on short-term numerical quotas and results, the measures by which management often judges performance. They also provide the analytical tools any employee can use to help pinpoint problems and opportunities for improvement, in the process helping to enrich their jobs. As Peter Drucker puts it, "Deming supplied the scientific methodology for analyzing the process. . . . [T]he concept of the worker as a resource rather than as a 'cost' was 'philosophy' rather than [an] 'operational' " concept until Deming refined and popularized the statistical methods that could be used to root out process variation. Marta Mooney and Marek Hessel of Fordham University, in their interpretation of Deming's work, note, "Firms cannot expect to tap the creative intelligence and productivity of their employees without first breaking long-standing habits of treating work-teams as elements of process costs rather than key resources and valued investment opportunities."[13]

Demings insights give a new sense of urgency to the need for a genuinely democratic partnership in the workplace. Moreover, based on the contention that 75 to 85 percent of the problems in an organization are caused by the system and not by individual employees, Deming calls for a dramatic reappraisal of the way corporations judge the performance of individuals (see Chapter 9).

*　　*　　*

In Deming's eyes, the ultimate victim of traditional American management isn't the consumer, who can always cross the street to buy a Toyota, but the American employee, whose job is jeopardized by mismanagement and who is often blamed for management's mistakes. That is one reason Deming has become notorious for publicly insulting executives; his attack on Jim McDonald, the former president of GM, at an industry conference in the early 1980s, is among his more infamous tantrums (see Chapter 8). That is also why Deming is most eloquent (and most patient) when he is addressing a group of hourly workers. Indeed, contrary to what many executives assume, hourly workers are almost always receptive to Deming's message—in part because he understands their powerlessness to change the system without management's support and because he believes in their good faith. But they also believe in Deming because an organization that is managed for continuous quality improvement is one that can make their jobs more interesting and fulfilling, and often easier.

Deming's suspicion that American management hasn't sufficiently grasped the importance of his message has led him to develop a style that sometimes resembles a maddening, mischievous mixture of Huey Long and *enfant terrible*. He demands absolute loyalty from his followers and brooks no dissent. He is willing to take on only a few clients—companies in which top management has demonstrated its willingness to adopt his philosophy. While he remains eager to learn from respected colleagues and experts, he has encapsulated that philosophy in a set of commandments that his followers must accept without question, on pain of banishment from his circle.

For the vast majority of corporate executives, the four-day seminars Deming gives as often as thirty times a year are about the only chance to see the guru in action. Executives from leading companies around the country flock to the seminars like Holy Rollers to a revival meeting. Each of Deming's one-man shows, which boast little in the way of props or visual aids, attracts five hundred to a thousand managers. He introduces his audience to his Fourteen Points, which are the blueprint of his philosophy. And for four straight days Deming stands at a lectern hammering away at the importance of anticipating the desires of customers, winning the trust and involvement of employees, reducing variation, and constantly improving both processes and products.

The Fourteen Points, which range from working closely with suppliers to eliminating numerical quotas, represent the key components of quality management that Deming believes a company must follow in order to achieve continuous improvement and to "get the customer to come back and bring a friend." There are several reasons why Deming and his Fourteen Points deserve a prominent place in the annals of American management.

First, Deming was extremely influential in shaping what the United States has come to think of as the Japanese management method. He initially went to Japan in 1947, at the behest of General Douglas MacArthur's occupying government, to help conduct a census and to assess the needs of the war-torn country. In the following years he returned repeatedly to lecture on quality and statistical theory, and in 1951 the Japanese created the Deming Prize, an award for quality that has been influential in shaping Japanese business practices. Although experts have long assumed that his principal influence was in teaching the Japanese about statistics, far broader themes emerge from his early lecture notes. Deming talked about the importance of market research, working closely with suppliers, and the need to control variation in every process of a business (see Chapter 2). Moreover, as will be seen in later chapters, by gaining broad acceptance in Japan, Deming's teaching and the Deming Prize criteria helped institutionalize TQC and an approach to quality management known as "policy deployment" or *kaizen*; the two concepts created the framework for Japan's quality revolution.

There was also something about the way Deming approached the Japanese. When he stood before the recently vanquished enemy of the United States, Deming spoke not as a conquerer but as a man who had grown up poor, the son of Wyoming pioneers, and who understood the hardships involved in building something from nothing. He would, for example, buy out the American PXs and distribute food and sweets to the Japanese he met during his travels, many of whom were homeless and living on the streets. Deming bridged the cultural divide as few other Americans at that time did. Tatsuro Toyoda, executive vice president of Toyota Motor Corporation and scion of the family that founded the company, remembers Deming best for his sensitivity to the unique needs of other countries and cultures.[14]

Deming also has become by far the most influential proponent of quality management in the United States. While both Joseph Juran and Armand V. Feigenbaum have strong reputations and advocate approaches to quality that in many cases overlap with Deming's ideas, neither has achieved the stature of Deming. One reason is that while these experts have often taken a very nuts-and-bolts, practical approach to quality improvement, Deming has played the role of a visionary, distilling disparate management ideas into a compelling new philosophy. While his knowledge and technical expertise are beyond dispute, he believes it is more useful to ask questions than to give answers, an approach that has gained popularity as executives of troubled companies grow wary of easy solutions. Amid the growing din of consultants who have come to profess expertise in everything from "leadership" to "quality" during the 1980s, Deming's voice has emerged as the country's most legitimate and trusted source of advice. And he has been sought out by companies around the world. His four-day seminars attract hundreds of managers from such companies as AT&T, P&G, and Xerox. Executives at a division of Dow Canada credit Deming with helping to stanch the flow of red ink at their company in the early 1980s.[15] The former head of Nashua Corporation, a New Hampshire maker of office paper and equipment, says Deming's ideas saved some of Nashua's most troubled product lines from the ravages of foreign competition. After watching its market share being eroded throughout the 1980s, GM seized on a quality management strategy that it modeled on Deming's philosophy. Several business schools, including those of Fordham and Columbia universities in New York, have revised their curricula or updated existing courses to include a heavier emphasis on quality and process management. Even the Department of Defense has called on Deming to conduct seminars for generals and top Pentagon officials, and is fashioning a new quality management strategy that draws on Deming's philosophy.

Deming's enormous legitimacy also stems from the messianic zeal and total commitment with which he pursues his vision of management. Deming works out of a basement office in his Washington home, where his only employee is Ceil Kilian, his secretary of more than thirty years. Deming has never solicited a single client. Yet the demands on Deming's time and his dedication are so great that through the long months of his wife Lola's illness, before her death in 1987, Deming continued to spend most weekdays on the road, frequently interrupting client meetings to phone home. Well into his eighties, Deming's usual business itinerary includes a visit to at least three cities each week. He spends weekends working at home in Washington and Mondays in New York City, where he frequently teaches a seminar at Columbia University in the mornings, then takes the subway to NYU. Then he spends three or four days either visiting a client company or conducting a four-day seminar. And while he lavishes time on his students, often taking groups of them out for an Indian meal in Greenwich Village, where he maintains a small, sparsely furnished studio apartment, getting on Deming's client roster is almost impossible.[16] Deming, who was knifed in the ribs one evening when he refused to give his wallet to a mugger on his way to mailing a letter in Greenwich Village, has become a virtual legend among students and followers.[17]

Deming works closely with only a handful of companies—Chrysler Corporation is one he was forced to turn away for lack of time.[18] Client companies are ones Deming has agreed to visit every month because the top executives have demonstrated their commitment to his philosophy and because they are willing to meet regularly with him, answer his questions, and take his advice. Client companies must send their executives to Deming's four-day seminars. And they must hire a master statistician of Deming's choosing to help train both workers and management in the proper use of statistical theory and methods and to help guide them through his philosophy.

DEMING'S FOURTEEN POINTS

Deming's modest goal in formulating the Fourteen Points was to create the management equivalent of the Ten Commandments. They do, in fact, crystallize the key quality management practices that have come to be accepted at most high-quality companies in the United States and Japan. None of the commandments stands on its own. Each is part of a holistic guide to building customer awareness, to reducing variation, and to nurturing constant change and improvement throughout a corporation. The Fourteen Points lead to detailed analysis of everything from customers' desires to the decision-making process itself, which is often fraught with erroneous assumptions.

While analysis is unquestionably a staple of most businesses, that which increasingly distinguishes the winners from the losers in our information-laden world is the incisiveness of the analysis. In the competition for global markets, the Japanese outanalyzed the United States, then mustered the corporate willpower to find better and more efficient ways of acting on their conclusions. They were able to do this in part because an understanding of variation and the concept of continuous improvement gave every member of the company a common focus when discussing problems and changes.

The Fourteen Points are, in fact, based on the following six principal ideas that will be illustrated in the upcoming chapters:

1. Quality is defined by the customer. Improvement in products and processes must be aimed at anticipating customers' future needs. Quality comes from improving the process, not from "inspecting out" the shoddy results of a poorly run process.

2. Understanding and reducing variation in every process is a must.

3. All significant, long-lasting quality improvements must emanate from top management's commitment to improvement, as well as its understanding of the means by which systematic change is to be achieved. Improvement *cannot* come merely from middle managers' and workers' "trying harder." Neither quality improvement nor long-term profitability can be achieved through wishful thinking and arbitrary goals set without consideration for how they are to be achieved within the context of an organization's process capabilities.

4. Change and improvement must be continuous and all-encompassing. It must involve every member in an organization, including outside suppliers.

5. The ongoing education and training of all the employees in a company are a prerequisite for achieving the sort of analysis that is needed for constant improvement.

6. Performance ratings that seek to measure the contribution of

individual employees are usually destructive. Given a chance by management, the vast majority of employees will take pride in their work and strive for improvement. But performance-ranking schemes can impede natural initiative. For one thing, by their very nature they create more "losers" than "winners" and thus batter morale. And since they don't take into account natural variation, they are inaccurate and unfair, and are perceived as such by employees.

In this rendering of Deming's Fourteen Points, the points themselves have been reordered in the interest of highlighting some of the synergies between them. For example, in Deming's book, his exhortation to "improve constantly . . . the system of production and service" is number five. However, it appears here right after Deming's point number one, constancy of purpose, both because these two ideas are very closely linked and because Deming's definition of constant improvement is central to his philosophy.

Establish constancy of purpose.

Constancy of purpose, on a macro level, entails an unequivocal long-term commitment to invest in, and adapt to, the challenging requirements of the marketplace. It is the antithesis of managing for short-term financial gain. Constancy of purpose, on a micro level, entails the systematic fine-tuning of every function in a corporation around the changes in company strategy and product line that are needed to meet long-term market needs.

Deming's concept of constancy begins and ends with the customer. While U.S. companies initially turned to Deming because they had lost control of their processes and discovered that they were producing far more faulty products than the competition was, they soon discovered that eliminating defects isn't enough to capture markets. Success depends on how well a company evaluates the processes, products, and markets of today to figure out what the customer will want tomorrow, and whether a company has the management conviction to change accordingly. It requires a commitment to long-term strategies and the analytical know-how to accurately gauge where organizational changes need to be made.

U.S. companies may think this obvious. But the evidence of the marketplace shows that many have become so sidetracked by short-term interests that even if they do have a long-term strategy it often lacks commitment from top management and is frequently undermined by contradictory policies and actions. Chapter 9 will show how GM's lack of a consistent vision led the company to spend some $70 billion on acquisitions and new technology as a way to help stem its market share erosion and to improve quality, while at the same time it pinched pennies on product development projects like the Fiero. This lack of constancy undermined the Fiero and GM's need to build cars of distinction, while at the same time it diminished the value of the company's technology investments.

Once top management has correctly identified its problems, it must figure out the best way to deploy its improvement strategy in such a way as to make certain that the entire company stays on course and maintains its constancy of purpose. Florida Power & Light learned this lesson, and Chapter 6 will show how even the best-laid quality management plans were nearly derailed when FP&L left middle management out of the planning process.

Improve constantly and forever every system of production and service.

During his early trips to Japan, Deming introduced an approach to process analysis and improvement that the Japanese applied to the development of products, and ultimately to the establishment and execution of strategic plans. The device is known in Japan as the Deming cycle, even though it was originally developed by Walter Shewhart, a Bell Laboratories physicist who was Deming's friend and mentor. The Deming cycle has become both a metaphor for constancy of purpose and a principal method used to achieve continual improvement.

The Deming cycle involves constantly defining and refining the wishes of customers, and is at the same time a vehicle for rallying every function in the business around these desires. Thus, the Deming cycle hinges on the constant cooperation of different departments, including research, design, production, and sales, so that the corporate eye never wavers from either the customer or any part of the process that might affect the integrity of the product being built for the customer. As applied to product development, the Deming cycle, which has also become widely known as the PDCA cycle, for "plan, do, check, act, and analyze," works something like this:

1. Plan the product with the help of consumer research, and design it.
2. Make the product and analyze it.
3. Market the product.
4. Test how the quality, price, and features of the item are received by consumers, both those who buy the product and those who choose not to buy it.[19]

The final step inevitably leads to redesign and improvement. At leading Japanese companies and a few U.S. pioneers in quality management, the process of analysis behind the Deming cycle has permeated every level of decision making from product development to strategic planning. The chapters on Ford and FP&L will show how these two U.S. companies have gradually shifted their corporate cultures and processes to pursue constant improvement.

The Deming cycle is conceptually the mirror opposite of the traditional U.S. approach, which could be described as follows: Design, make, and sell, sell, sell.

Eliminate numerical goals and quotas, including management by objective.

The problem with management by objective (MBO), as it is generally practiced, is that an organization can usually achieve almost any objective it wishes to, in the short term, by paying a high enough price, including, in extreme cases, destroying the system itself. By definition, MBO focuses on the end goal rather than the process. For example, almost any company that is losing money can show a profit if it juggles the books and sells off its healthiest operations. Long-term, however, that company has probably made its situation worse. As Deming puts it, "A quota is a fortress against improvement of quality and productivity. I have yet to see a quota that includes any trace of a system by which to help anyone to do a better job."[20]

Similarly, Deming argues that workers should never be subjected to a quota because they can work only as well as the system permits—assuming it is in control. Deming uses one of his students at NYU and her job as a telephone reservations clerk for an airline as an example. "She must take 25 calls per hour. She must be courteous. . . . She is continually plagued by obstacles: (a) the computer is slow in delivery of information that she asks for; (b) it sometimes reports no information, whereupon she is forced to use directories and guides. Christine, what is your job? Is it: To take 25 calls per hour? Or to give callers courteous satisfaction? . . . It cannot be both."[21]

Deming cites a litany of even more absurd examples. Take, for instance, the city of Alexandria, Virginia, where police officers are given outstanding ratings for issuing twenty-five or more traffic tickets and twenty-one or more parking tickets per month. The obvious conclusion is that whether or not a driver gets written up may depend as much on how close an officer is to filling his unofficial quota as it does on the driver's driving and parking habits. Then there is the federal mediator who is rated on the number of meetings he attends annually. Deming likes to cite a U.S. Postal Service buyer who is rated on the basis of the number of contracts she negotiates during the year—the system clearly discourages complex, long-term agreements that might be in the better interest of the Postal Service.[22]

Drive out fear so that everyone may work effectively for the company.

"Our managers aren't interested in good news, they only want to know the bad news."[23] No one familiar with U.S. business culture could ever mistake this statement as being typical of the attitude of American management. In fact, it was used by a Japanese quality expert, Ichiro Miyauchi, to describe a crucial difference between management as it is practiced in Japan and in the United States. A Japanese manager, well versed in quality management, isn't interested in "good news" because it is unlikely to reveal opportunities for improvement. He is interested only in "bad news," which offers a gold mine of improvement possibilities.

American management must learn to appreciate the opportunities in bad news. But first it must begin to change a business culture that has grown used to killing the messenger of bad tidings. "No one can put in his best performance unless he feels secure. *Secure* means without fear, not afraid to express ideas, not afraid to ask questions. . . . A common denominator of fear in any form, anywhere, is loss from impaired performance and padded figures," writes Deming in *Out of the Crisis*.[24]

Institute leadership.

Leadership is a natural corollary of managing *without* fear. "The aim of leadership should be to help people, machines and gadgets to do a better job."[25]

Leadership, by Deming's definition, involves transforming the role of both the manager and the production supervisor from that of cop to coach. Thus, management reviews at companies such as Xerox and FP&L have shifted away from their earlier, virtually exclusive focus on the results of financial performance. Today, management reviews at these companies involve a discussion of problems and potential solutions.

At the most quality-oriented companies, rigorous management reviews focus almost exclusively on the capabilities of the process. Chapters 2, 6, and 7 will show how the management reviews at Japanese companies that have won the coveted Deming Prize, as well as the ones conducted by FP&L, the first U.S. company to win the award, are the culmination of an ultra-process-oriented approach to management. These companies bring in outside experts to grill top management about every facet of their operations in a review that is designed to reveal the *weaknesses* of a company's products and processes. Out of this assessment of the company's weaknesses, as well as an evaluation of the competition and customers' future needs, emerges a framework for fine-tuning the firm's near- and long-term strategies.

End the practice of awarding business largely on the basis of price.

No division or company works in a vacuum. Variability can creep into the process through the parts shipped by suppliers, adding inspection and correction costs. Therefore, continual improvement to a system can only be accomplished if the suppliers, whose output constitutes as much as 80 percent of many finished products, are able to deliver at a predictable, and continuously improving, level of quality. Therefore, Deming calls on companies to "move toward a single supplier for any one item on a long-term relationship of loyalty and trust."[26] While Deming acknowledges that it is not always practical to use a single supplier, he insists that the customer company work closely with suppliers in order to convey their needs effectively and to help the vendor improve the quality of its goods while reducing overall cost to the buyer. When quality and consistency are the most important objectives, this often means abandoning the practice of awarding supplier contracts to the lowest bidder. "Price has no meaning without a measure of the quality being purchased," says Deming. In this regard he points out that, for example, the United States, by awarding contracts for the purchase of mass transit equipment to the lowest bidder, has acquired a slew of erratic equipment and "retarded by a generation expansion of mass transit in the U.S."[27]

Moreover, companies that want to move to just-in-time inventory control procedures as a way to hold down costs have no choice but to adopt Deming's supplier directive. Eliminating just-in-case inventories means that a manufacturer must be able to rely on his supplier to deliver top-quality goods precisely on time.[28] Indeed, the point of working closely with suppliers is to get total low cost, rather than just a low purchase price.

Under Deming's influence, many major companies, including Ford and GM, have winnowed their base of suppliers and forged much closer relationships with those that remain. Chapter 5 will explore the importance to the auto industry of forging close ties with suppliers by focusing on the relationship between Ford and a small vendor of engine covers in Sheboygan, Wisconsin. Similarly, the chapter on GM will show how an unusually rigorous hunt for just the right suppliers helped make the company's new Quad 4 engine a huge success. In Detroit, the realization that component parts from suppliers are the single most important variable in the production of complex products such as automobiles has also spawned the establishment of the American Supplier Institute (ASI). A spin-off of Ford, ASI has become something of a quality management clearinghouse for auto industry suppliers.

Break down the barriers between departments.
Ford chairman Don Petersen refers to this process as "dismantling chimneys." It involves the mobilization of individual corporate fiefdoms to cooperate on common objectives as defined by customer needs and the company's improvement priorities. The need to dis-

mantle chimneys is born of the realization that just as outside suppliers hold enormous sway over a customer company's ability to meet its own quality objectives, various divisions and functions within a corporation—its internal customers and suppliers—affect one another's ability to maintain consistency and control. This logic is behind Xerox's recent reorganization of its sales, service, and administrative functions, as can be seen in Chapter 7.

Institute training on the job.

Controlling a process requires a detailed understanding of the system in question and how variation can affect it. Therefore, it is useful to train as many members of the corporation as possible to recognize when a system is in control or drifting out of control. Workers can do this even more efficiently than quality engineers. In addition, workers and managers need to be trained to identify problems and improvement opportunities. However, learning to understand the effects of variation is just the first step in the training process. Most companies find they must also teach employees who for years have worked in functional fiefdoms how to operate in multidisciplinary teams. "Industry desperately needs to foster teamwork. The only training or education on teamwork our people receive in school is on the athletic field. Teamwork in the classroom is called cheating."[29]

For companies that want to pursue this holistic approach to quality management, the biggest hurdle often involves convincing most of the personnel in nonmanufacturing disciplines that they too create and are affected by variation. Employees in such areas as marketing and product development often believe that training in the use of statistics to spot different kinds of variation applies only to manufacturing. Similarly, subjecting workers to months of training sessions, as many companies do, is useless unless managers go through the same training process.[30] That has certainly been the experience of FP&L and Xerox, as will be seen in the chapters on those companies.

People also tend to overestimate their ability to analyze and pinpoint the information they need to make decisions and to solve problems. Deming talks at great length about the importance of developing operational definitions. Percy Williams Bridgman, a physicist whose book *Reflections of a Physicist* Deming admires, puts it this way: "One of the chief purposes of an operational analysis is to recover the complexities of the primitive situation. . . . Einstein recognized that such apparently simple concepts as length and time have multiple meanings, so that there are different kinds of length for example optical length and tactual length, and that the precise meaning involves the procedure used in obtaining lengths or times in concrete instances. This attitude toward meanings is what I have called 'operational.' . . . A thoroughgoing application of the operational analysis of meanings puts in our hands, I believe, the possibility of eventually eliminating failure of agreement on meanings as a source of friction in human affairs. No more potent instrument of good will can be imagined."[31]

Another reason Deming focuses so heavily on training is that achieving consistency in the output of employees is as important as reducing the variation in the items produced by two different machines or delivered by two different suppliers. As with everything else in a Deming-oriented process, the goal is to bring workers into statistical control—that is, to have their work be as uniform and predictable as possible. Deming argues that once a work group is performing in a stable and predictable manner, defects and problems that occur are the fault not of workers, but rather of the system. Once the performance of the work force is under control, management and workers can begin to search for more efficient ways to perform a job.

Eliminate the annual rating or merit system.
Corporate America loves to reward achievement. Deming believes, however, that rating and merit systems are unfair and counterproductive. This is the most controversial and intriguing of his Fourteen Points. It seems to repudiate the American promise that anyone can be a star if only he works hard enough. While it dovetails with the belief in "intrinsic motivation" put forth by other management theorists, it is also a direct outgrowth of the theory of variation.

Deming contends that the time-honored system of performance appraisals, bonuses, and other reward systems that brand a few employees winners and encourage constant competition in the ranks is fundamentally unfair and ultimately harmful to the interests of both companies and employees. He believes that if the system in which people work is predictable—and if management has done its job well in selecting employees—then over time most employees will perform at about the same level, and that only a very few will perform exceptionally well or poorly. Moreover, the influence of variation is such that it is impossible to accurately measure the overall performance of individuals within a variable process. While Deming has been attacked for his views on the subject, he has also begun to attract followers in some surprising places. As the following chapters will detail, both American Cyanamid and GM recently abolished appraisal systems that required managers to rate their employees on a bell curve. In addition, both companies have moved toward systems in which employee evaluations are not ranked numerically at all. Compensation at both companies is increasingly based on the assumption that although there is variation in people, it is impossible to separate the performance of the individual from that of the system, and that employees should therefore be paid on the basis of their experience and responsibilities rather than according to some numerical ranking. Both companies based their new appraisal and compensation schemes on research done within their own companies showing that long-term corporate success often accrues to organizations that foster teamwork and an environment in which an entire group of employees is encouraged to shine, rather than just a select few. As will be seen in Chapter 9, GM and American Cyanamid found that ratings, because they are often based on quotas and can almost never be administered fairly, frequently discourage future performance to the detriment of the entire company.

Institute a vigorous program of education and self-improvement.

Deming's views on training stem from his understanding of variation and his conviction that training is linked directly to a company's ability to maintain and improve processes. While his ideas about education and self-improvement seem to follow directly from the logic of training, they also represent a far more personal view of the nature of work and motivation. A human being deserves to take pride in his work, Deming often says, quoting from Ecclesiastes. A devout Protestant, Deming believes that this pride, or "joy" as he often refers to it, comes from self-improvement and that it is the company's job to offer opportunities for continuous education.

Similarly, Deming believes that a mutual covenant is established between a company and its employees. Just as the employee accepts the responsibility of performing a job to his or her best ability, the company has an obligation to make sure the individual is given meaningful work to do. Deming may have been influenced in his views by the Japanese concept of "lifetime employment," but his sensitivity to the plight of the worker has been evident ever since his days as a student intern at AT&T's Hawthorne plant in the 1920s, which happened to coincide with the beginning of the famous Hawthorne Experiments.

Eliminate slogans and exhortations.

Since workers alone can do little to change the system, the burden of improvement rests with management. Slogans and exhortations, on the other hand, are at best misleading because they imply that improving quality depends on added effort by individual employees, rather than on a well-functioning system. "Such exhortations only create adversarial relationships, as the bulk of the causes of low quality and low productivity belong to the system and thus lie beyond the power of the work force."[32]

Cease dependence on mass inspection.

Deming calls on management to stop depending on inspection. "Routine 100 percent inspection to improve quality is equivalent to planning for defects, acknowledgement that the process has not the capability required for specifications."[33] Deming often quotes Feigenbaum, who estimates that 15 to 40 percent of the manufacturer's cost of U.S.-made products pays for the "waste embedded in it." Of that cost, handling damage alone can equal 5 to 8 percent.[34] By spotting problems in the system early, you can nip them in the bud. Huge savings can be achieved if a system is functioning as it should—if it isn't creating faulty products, if it isn't generating waste, and if the inspection function can be radically reduced. Chapter 3, on Nashua Corporation, will show how manufacturing workers trained in statistics helped improve the processes the company uses to make paper products. Deming advocates working toward the virtual elimination of inspection in all but a few critical cases, such as the production of semiconductor chips, in which the production of one or two faulty products is likely, but letting them get into customers' hands is intolerable. Similarly, some inspection is needed to study variation.

However, quality experts point out that as international competition has raised quality standards, many Japanese companies that have honed their processes so that they produce virtually no defects have, nevertheless, reestablished inspection systems in the unlikely event that a faulty product goes down the line.

Adopt the new philosophy.

While many companies have come to understand that they must conduct their businesses differently, few have grasped the enormity of the task that faces them. Some companies adopt SPC in their manufacturing operations only to discover that marketing and sales have been left out of the improvement loop. For example, Ford Motor Company didn't realize a jump in customer satisfaction until it matched advances in manufacturing quality with better product features that were the result of the marketing department's involvement in an overall quality improvement effort.[35] Yet other companies spend millions retraining their workers, but neglect to educate managers about their new role in the process. Quality management, Deming style, is a holistic philosophy that must be adopted in its entirety if it is to work at all.

Deming's philosophy has been widely hailed throughout corporate management, yet in the United States it has rarely been adopted in its totality because of the magnitude of change it requires. "It can be very difficult to make significant changes, especially when you have been in the habit of doing things differently for decades, and especially when the very success that brought you to the positions you now hold is rooted in doing some things, frankly, the wrong way," Deming told a gathering of Ford executives in 1982. "It is going to be hard for you to accept . . . that you were promoted for the wrong reasons a time or two."[36]

Create a structure in top management to accomplish the transformation.

Every job in an organization is part of a process. And only by understanding the role each job plays in the company's customer-driven strategy can the process be improved. Thus, to achieve transformation, companies must be committed to analyzing every project and every step of a process with a view to constantly bettering it, along the lines of the Deming cycle described earlier.

Since 1981, when he made his Detroit debut, Deming has attracted an enormous management following in the United States. Hardly a single major U.S. company exists that has not been touched by his ideas, either because the companies have themselves learned from them or because their competitors have. Some companies, including Ford, GM, Nashua Corporation, and FP&L, as well as dozens of Japan's Deming Prize winners, have been profoundly affected by Deming's theories concerning the interaction of people, processes, and variation.

Yet nationally, the transformation brought about by Deming's evangelism has been more evolutionary than revolutionary. U.S. companies have been far slower to accept the new management agenda than their Japanese counterparts have. Most U.S. firms have assiduously avoided turning for help to the Japanese themselves. And so, for the most part, the progress of the United States in adopting the quality management principles espoused by Deming was for a long time only as rapid as the stamina and travel schedule of Deming himself would allow.

This relatively slow rate of change, plus Deming's belief that people must continuously work at learning and improving their performance, leads him to contend that there is no model Deming company. However, the case studies cited in the following chapters exemplify the most positive quality management practices now at work in the United States, as well as the most common mistakes made by American companies trying to improve quality, productivity, and their competitive position. The best practices of these companies, taken together, represent the sum of Deming's management philosophy.

THE STATISTICAL
FOUNDATION OF
DEMINGISM

T o Deming's followers, the belief that variation must be minimized has dictated a fundamental change in management methods. At the vanguard of the struggle to contain and ultimately to minimize variation are a new breed of experts, the process-minded statisticians. Corporations are increasingly hiring statisticians to design tests and take mathematical readings of both processes and products to determine whether they are functioning predictably, whether they need special attention, and how they might be improved.

By statistical Luddites, Deming is often dismissed as a "mere" statistician who has usurped the role of management expert. In fact, both the strength and the uniqueness of Deming's contribution to the practice of quality management stem, in large part, from the theories and methods that he advocates for collecting and using data to analyze processes and make predictions about how they will function in the future. Statistical theory is the leitmotif of Deming's Fourteen Points of Management. And to understand Deming's philosophy, one must first understand its statistical underpinnings.

The Deming management philosophy emanates from a profoundly simple statistical observation about how processes work: All processes, Deming points out, are subject to some level of variation that is likely to diminish quality. Variation is the enemy of quality, and it is as inevitable and ubiquitous as gravity. What makes variation a particular nuisance is that the culprit comes in two distinct guises that if confused will lead only to more trouble and loss. Yet they are difficult to distinguish. Statisticians refer to the two types of variation as "common" and "special" causes. Special causes are the product of special circumstances, a temporary glitch in a system—the malfunctioning of a single piece of machinery or the use of unusual materials, for instance. These special causes, because of their relatively discrete nature, can often be identified and eliminated by workers who have been properly trained to analyze the process.

Common causes, on the other hand, are more difficult to spot because they are inherent in the system and represent the greatest opportunity for long-term improvement. And precisely because common causes are part and parcel of the system that *management created*, only management can reduce the variation and thus improve the system.

To simply illustrate these two causes, consider the case of a production line that is turning out a defective tin can, one with blemishes or indentations. If the blemish is being produced because of relatively minor wear and tear on the production machinery, workers can reduce or eliminate the problem by adjusting or replacing parts of the machine. If, however, the can is blemished because management is purchasing inferior grades of tinplate—perhaps as the result of an effort to cut costs—then there is nothing workers can do about the problem. Only management can change the purchasing policy.

There is another important lesson in the case of the defective tin can, one that leads to a central tenet of Demingism: Decisions made by management or workers must be based on data and the theoretical knowledge needed to know how to use it, not on instinct. When a defective can rolls down the assembly line, "gut reaction" might lead a worker to adjust the machinery. If, however, the problem resides in the material and not the machine, the adjustment may throw the system off kilter, which could eventually lead to new and more severe problems. In the meantime the actual source of trouble would go undetected.

Deming's reputation in both Japan and the United States was initially based on his knowledge of statistics and how to distinguish between the two types of variation and thus to improve production processes. But Deming's approach to management derives in large part from his conviction that management has the unique opportunity—and responsibility—constantly to work at reducing common causes of variation. Deming goes so far as to argue that for managers one of the most important jobs is the identification and reduction of variation in everything from the production floor to the finance department. "The central problem of management in all its aspects, including planning, procurement, manufacturing, research, sales, personnel, accounting, and law, is to understand better the meaning of variation," to analyze the process, and to extract the clues it offers to better its processes, says Deming.[1] An important goal of Deming's philosophy and statistical teachings is to achieve predictable results in processes and to pinpoint weaknesses that, if corrected, will lead to ever higher standards of uniformity and productivity and to continuous process improvement. Only by reducing variation can management identify the best opportunities for improvement and create an environment that is ripe for creative and constructive change.

Over the years, the champion of process improvement has become obsessed with the idea that cooperation among firms, industries, and nations is essential to achieving prosperity and peace on a global scale, especially in a world of dwindling natural resources. Deming contends that the U.S. government hampers constructive cooperation because its chief liason with industry, the regulatory bodies, "have never understood their jobs to involve optimization of a system of suppliers and customers." As a result, problems with the regulatory process have led Washington to seize blindly on the mantra of competition with few positive results. Certainly, in the case of the airline industry, deregulation has failed to appreciably improve prices or service for customers, while it may be hastening the demise of several airlines.[21]

George Kuper, former director of the National Commission on Productivity (NCP), had an interesting insight into what Deming refers to as "the new economics of win/win": In the mid 1970s, the NCP was asked to help halt the spiraling price of food, brought on by a transportation system that took two weeks to deliver produce from western farms to eastern cities, with much of it rotting en route. The NCP got shippers and growers together to analyze the process and to agree on several compromises. For example, to meet shipping schedules, growers would pick crops at times that might be inconvenient for them. West Coast shippers would replace the haphazard arrangement of railcars with a LIFO system in which only the last car would need to be unhooked at each stop across the country; ironically, a LIFO system had been pioneered by railroads in the 1860s for the shipment of single commodities. The new system slashed shipping time in half, delivered fresher produce to consumers, and lowered costs, creating a win/win situation for all. However, the NCP was ultimately disbanded, in large part because it couldn't take credit for its role in such efforts; had it done so, the NCP would never have won the cooperation of the various players in the system. Although NCP wasn't a regulatory body, its role in the food crisis offers insights into how a different type of government initiative—one that need involve little spending at all—could play a more productive role in industry. "Regulators need to get off of their pedestal and become more subject to challenges from industry when it comes to issues of economic efficiency," says Kuper. The problem for both government and industry in the U.S. is to understand "where we need to cooperate, where we need to compete, and whether we know the difference," he says. "[So far] we don't."[3]

Within companies, statisticians are the diagnosticians who can help determine which symptoms point to which systemic illnesses. They study the output of a process over time and develop tests to determine whether a system is in control and, if it isn't, to help pinpoint the nature of the abnormalities. Take the case of a bottling company that uses machines to fill twelve-ounce soda bottles. The company may wish to test whether its machinery is indeed pouring the requisite amount of soda pop into each bottle. The nature of variation is such that no two bottles will ever contain exactly the same amount of soda. But the job of management is to make sure that its machines consistently produce as close to twelve ounces per bottle as possible. To do so, management might hire a statistician to devise a series of tests that will gauge the consistency of the process. Typically, the statistician may decide to sample the first three or four out of every hundred bottles coming off the assembly line. One bottle may yield 11.98 ounces, another 12.01 ounces, and so forth.

By plotting the values on a chart that shows both the amount of beverage in the bottle and the point in time at which the sample was taken, the statistician, using a mathematical formula, can determine "the boundaries of the system" and ascertain whether the variation around the target value, in this case twelve ounces, is predictable and "in control." If it is, management can safely assume that the particular machine being tested will, in the future, consistently vary no more than, say, plus or minus .03 ounce from the twelve-ounce target.

Given a stable, predictable process, management has two options: It may decide that a variation of .03 ounce in the level of soda pop is acceptable and leave the process alone, continuing to monitor it periodically to make sure it doesn't stray from those limits; or it may decide that it wishes to improve the process so that the level of variation falls within, say, plus or minus .01 ounce. In that case, it would have to study every aspect of the process carefully to determine how to achieve a higher level of precision. Management might conclude that achievement of this higher level of precision could require new capital equipment; they would have to weigh this cost against the increase in benefit.

But let's suppose the process is unstable and unpredictable. The statistician samples dozens of bottles and comes out with a pattern of variation that is mostly but not always within the range of .03 ounce. If management wishes to stabilize the variation, it must discover exactly what is causing the erratic output. Perhaps the solution is as simple as a worn part, a stuck lever, or a new employee who's unsure of how to operate the machinery.

As Deming points out, it doesn't take a genius to plot the results of process samples on a chart and to see whether the pattern created signals a stable or unstable process. Nevertheless, the way statisticians go about the design of surveys and the collection of data can mean the difference between useful information or utterly useless paperwork.

It is in their powers of prediction, or—more precisely—the lack thereof that statisticians and companies run into problems. While sampling sounds simple, Deming, who is an expert on the subject, points out that the business of applying statistical theorems to real-world problems often produces grossly inaccurate results. The reason is that the mathematical models used by statisticians often fail to account for the variation that exists in the real world. One typical mistake companies make is to sample products of what are essentially two or more different processes and to mix up the data. For example, let's assume the soda pop factory has three separate machines pouring soda into twelve-ounce bottles. It would not be unusual for a traditional quality control engineer to take samples off all three machines, mix up the data, and try to improve the process based on the data he has collected. The data may show a "stable process." In fact, the results of this test would be of no help at all in improving the system, because each machine is likely to be subject to a different level of variation; a remedy that would work for one machine might throw another off kilter. The correct thing to do would be to sample each machine individually, because the only way to reduce the overall variation is to understand how it affects each machine individually.

One of the most vivid misuses of statistics has been perpetrated in the auto industry for years. Engineers at the proving grounds of U.S. auto companies run sample cars around a test track until they reach the 100,000-mile limit—the distance the company would like its automobiles to go without a breakdown. By applying their theoretical models to the test results, the companies' statisticians predict a 90 percent probability that at least 90 percent of the population driving its cars will run 100,000 miles without failure. In fact, the experience of customers turns out to be *three times* worse than what the tests would indicate because neither the test nor the statistician's prediction has any way of factoring in a variety of real-life circumstances that can degrade the test results. For example, there might be so much variation in the quality of the cars rolling off the final production lines that the test results of one car will have little to do with how another car will perform, even if it comes from the same factory; only plants with the highest levels of consistency in their finished output are likely to avoid this problem. In addition, these tests do not do a good job of gauging the effects of the aging process on belts, hoses, and so forth. While a good engineer can pick up the limitations of such predictions, companies like to fall back on what is sometimes thought to be the limitless ability of statisticians to predict future performance. One of Deming's major contributions has been to teach his disciples the limits of their craft and to find better ways to improve the way data is collected and analyzed in the real world so as to enhance the integrity and usefulness of statistical predictions.[4]

That is why when Deming is asked by a prospective client to give one of his four-day seminars, the company must first make a commitment to hire an in-house statistician from Deming's list of statistically trained disciples. And when he gathers his disciples around him several times a year over dinner at Washington's venerable Cosmos Club, the conversation often digresses into a discussion about how to train more statisticians. Finally, it is his obsession with controlling variation that lies at the root of his most controversial ideas, including his abhorrence of management by numbers, merit pay, and bonuses.

While statistical theory has shaped the intellectual foundation of Deming's work, the near-religious zeal with which he pursues it was created nearly a century ago by the pioneer values on which he was raised. During his childhood, Deming was weaned on the struggle and dreams of his parents, who had left behind their roots in the Midwest to build a new life as homesteaders in the sagebrush- and cactus-covered desert of Wyoming. In his youth, he was initiated into corporate life at Western Electric, the manufacturing arm of AT&T, coincidentally at the very same time that the company became a laboratory for one of the greatest industrial experiments of the twentieth century. And as an aging guru, he has experienced the frustration of finding intellectual kinship abroad while being ignored at home until it was almost too late.

Deming was born on October 14, 1900, in Sioux City, Iowa, to William and Pluma Irene Edwards Deming. He was heir to an old and politically eclectic American tradition. Deming's maternal grandmother was Elizabeth Grant, a relative of General Ulysses S. Grant.[5] On his father's side, however, Deming's earliest American ancestor was Major Jonathan Deming, who served as an officer in the British army during the American Revolution. Jonathan Deming was a prosperous merchant, and the parlor of his house, which he built in Colchester, Connecticut, was transported to the American Museum in Bath, England, where it stands today as an image of colonial bourgeois comfort.[6]

Deming, however, spent his formative years in modest circumstances. Until his second birthday, the Demings lived in Sioux City
in a house on Bluff Street, overlooking the Missouri River. But soon
after the birth of Deming's brother Robert, the family moved to his
grandfather's 300-acre farm, known as the Edwards Farm, near Polk
City, Iowa. Those were simple, lean years. Deming recalls that he
and his brother, Bob, "wore on the farm, in the summer, one piece
suits like pajamas, contrived by my mother for simplicity, and we
went barefoot in those suits all over the farm." Although the family
had a telephone, Deming didn't see his first automobile until he was
about four years old, when a doctor was called to the farm to treat
Deming for a case of diphtheria. He had caught the disease when he
stepped on a nail while running barefoot around the farm.[7]

While Deming was still a toddler, his father headed out for Wyoming in pursuit of free land. In 1906 Deming, his brother, and his
mother made the long trip west by train, through Omaha, Burling-
ton, Alliance, and Tuluka. Deming would maintain a connection to
railroads for the rest of his life. He would come to count among his
most faithful clients the Interstate Commerce Commission, railroads, and freight companies, for whom he used statistical methods
to help establish rates. And when the railroads began to merge in the
1950s, Deming helped sort out the routes each railroad would retain.

In those early days, however, the railroads were the main arteries
of the country, channeling homesteaders to the western states. Many
of these early pioneers, including the Demings, got off the train in
Cody, a town named after Colonel William Frederick ("Buffalo
Bill") Cody, the army scout, buffalo hunter, and founder of Buffalo
Bill's Wild West Show. Cody was a lively place in those days, boasting at least eleven saloons. Buffalo Bill's sister Irma ran a hotel of the
same name, and he was a frequent visitor there. Both Deming and
his little brother knew Buffalo Bill by sight. The Demings moved
into a boardinghouse while William Deming, who had studied the
law in Iowa, worked as a law clerk for a man named Simpson, whose
son Milward and grandson Alan would both become senators from
Wyoming. Deming's mother supplemented the family income by
giving piano lessons, sometimes traveling with her children to neighboring towns.[8]

Ed, as he was called to distinguish him from his father, developed a love of music from his mother that would remain an important part of his life. He learned to play the piano, organ, piccolo, and flute. Although Deming developed into a shy and bookish young man, his ear for music served him well in Japan, where sing-alongs would break the ice during late-night dinners and parties at bars and geisha houses with his Japanese hosts. And well into his eighties, when music remained one of his only respites from a seven-days-a-week work schedule, you could sometimes spot liturgical music he had composed mixed in among his lecture notes.

The Demings spent two years in Cody before moving twenty-two miles away to a town that would come to be known as Powell, after John Wesley Powell. A Civil War veteran and anthropologist who had explored the West, Powell became known as the "father of reclamation" for advocating the development, by the federal government, of irrigation water that would attract homesteaders to barren lands in places like Wyoming.[9] Deming's family was among the first group of settlers who moved to Powell. At the time, 15,237 acres of land were being parceled out to pioneering families; William Deming received a forty-acre plot near what was yet to become the town.[10]

The early years in Powell were difficult ones. The Demings spent their first five or so years in a tar-paper shack, where Deming's sister, Elizabeth, was born in 1909. The farm was never much of a success. William Deming continued to bring in some free-lance legal work, and Pluma Deming helped support the family with music lessons, but their best efforts, a vegetable garden, a few chickens, and a cow weren't always enough to keep food on the table. Winters, when snow would seep through the cracks and accumulate inside the house, were especially harsh.[11]

As Powell began to grow, William Deming built houses on his property and sold them for profit, but the family's circumstances improved only marginally. William Deming became something of an entrepreneur, selling insurance, making loans to farmers, drawing up wills, and selling land. Deming's mother continued to give music lessons at fifty cents a class. Nevertheless, Deming recalls that when his father was off to Saskatchewan and Alberta on one of his land-selling expeditions his mother would read the Cody papers expecting to see that, for failure to pay taxes, the family farm had been put up for sale.[12] As a result, Deming made contributions to the family's finances. The $1.25 he earned after school hauling kindling and coal at Judson's Hotel and the few extra dollars he got for lighting Powell's gasoline street lamps sometimes went to buy household necessities.[13]

Deming's abhorrence of waste, his diligence, and his frugality took root during his childhood and lasted the rest of his life. Although he would eventually collect anywhere from $30,000 to $120,000 annually from each of about half a dozen clients and between $40,000 and $100,000 for the four-day seminars he held each year, he and his wife, Lola, remained in the modest Washington home near the Maryland border that they had bought during the Depression.[14] It was in the basement of this brick house that Deming kept his office and ran his global quality practice. Deming's youngest daughter, Linda, even recalls her father dating the eggs in the refrigerator with a felt-tipped pen to make sure the older ones were eaten first, so none would go to waste.[15]

As a young man, Deming continued to lead a studious and sheltered existence. Even after he left Powell, his life continued to revolve around his studies and odd jobs, and only when he was well into his twenties did Deming begin to broaden his horizons. In 1917 he made the train trip to Laramie, where he attended the University of Wyoming and would earn a B.S. in engineering. Initially he supported himself with working as a janitor, shoveling snow in the winter, and hustling customers for a local cleaner. His mother died before he finished school, and two years later he married his first wife, Agnes. They spent their early married years in Golden and Boulder, Colorado, where Deming attended the Colorado School of Mines and the University of Colorado, from which he received a master's degree in mathematics and physics.[16]

Between his studies in Colorado and getting his doctorate in physics from Yale in 1928,[17] Deming landed two summer jobs in a row that would make up one of the most formative experiences of his early career. His work at Western Electric's Hawthorne plant in Chicago was the only time in his career that he was employed full time by a corporation. And what he saw at Hawthorne, a plant that employed 46,000 people assembling telephone equipment, left a lasting impression on him. While Hawthorne has been described as a relatively progressive place to work—it offered higher-than-average wages, a restaurant that dished out the same food to both workers and executives, and various savings plans—it was no utopia.[18] The work, much of it performed by women, was monotonous. Assembling telephone relays, for example, entailed "putting together a coil armature, contact springs, and insulators in a fixture and securing the parts in position by means of four machine screws," a job that took about sixty seconds and had to be repeated endlessly throughout the day. Workers regularly complained of smoke, fumes, and extreme temperatures.[19] Deming himself described the place as "hot" and "dirty."[20]

Such Dreiseresque conditions were completely foreign to the impressionable twenty-five-year-old. While he had experienced his share of hardship, he was influenced by the frontier spirit and pioneer experience of his parents and his childhood, a life of unpredictable adventure in which each man could shape his own destiny. Deming had no frame of reference for the demeaning drudgery the workers had to endure at the Hawthorne plant. While Deming's statistical work still echoes Walter Shewhart's early experiments with control charts at the same plant, Deming's ideas about job incentives and management's responsibilities to its workers grew out of the work conditions he saw at the Western Electric plant and, indirectly, from the results of another failed Hawthorne venture.

It was during Deming's stay in Chicago that Hawthorne became the setting for the now famous Hawthorne Experiments. A group of academicians and AT&T managers were making the Hawthorne Works the location of one of the most famous industrial studies of the century. Elton Mayo, a professor of industrial research at the Graduate School of Business Administration at Harvard during the 1920s, and a group of researchers undertook a controversial study on the effects of working conditions on workers, their morale, and their productivity. The studies, which were conducted from 1924 to 1932, indicated that output jumps when there is improvement in the resources provided workers, when trust and cooperation between workers and supervisors are fostered, when fear in the workplace is eliminated, and when monotony is reduced. The study also showed that paying workers according to a "bogey" or piecework system is counterproductive—workers will never exceed a certain level of productivity for fear that the standard on which their pay is based will continuously be ratcheted upward.

The findings and the spirit of the Hawthorne studies ran counter to the popular "scientific industrial management" ideas that had been embraced by the great industrialists of the day such as Henry Ford. Developed by Frederick Winslow Taylor, "scientific management" called for specialists and engineers to set work and technical standards, which generally broke jobs into their simplest rote functions. This system seemed ideally suited to mass production and to a transient and ill-educated work force.[21] Taylor's defenders contend that his ideas were misinterpreted by both management and the press; even Deming notes that Taylor avoided the term "scientific management."[22] Yet Taylor's famous time-and-motion studies were used to wring machinelike efficiency out of workers. The studies, for example, determined how much time it would take a worker to perform a given task and even established the optimum number of movements for getting the job done. Right up to the 1980s, companies expected workers to "check their brains at the door" when they arrived for work in the mornings—robbing working men and women of self-respect and the corporation of its most valuable source of knowledge and input about production processes.

Deming insists that during his stint at Hawthorne, he knew nothing about the experiments being conducted there. However, decades later, when the methodology of the experiments came under attack, Deming defended the conclusions of the study. Indeed, Deming had used statistical theory to arrive at conclusions very similar to those of the Hawthorne studies. Deming's exhortation to eliminate numerical quotas for workers, for example, number ten of his Fourteen Points, dovetails with some of the evidence gathered at Hawthorne. "Rates of production are often set to accommodate the average worker," writes Deming. "Naturally, half of them are above average, and half below. What happens is that peer pressure holds the upper half to the rate, no more."[23] That Deming's career took the turn it did is in large part due to the fact that some sixty years after the Hawthorne studies were concluded, most U.S. corporations still draw more from the Taylor model than from the results gathered at Hawthorne.

*   *   *

Beginning in the 1930s, Deming participated in a statistical revolution that would dramatically alter the process of data collection in all spheres of research. The statistical mavericks were instrumental in perfecting the quality control techniques and production systems without which America's groundbreaking telephone system would not have been possible.[24] Deming and his colleagues were responsible for developing the statistical sampling methods that not only helped make modern quality management possible, but also led to modern polling techniques, market research, and census taking. It was during the 1930s that probability sampling first began to gain legitimacy outside scientific circles. The technique was applied in 1937 to the gathering of information for a pioneering survey conducted by the Census Bureau in 1937 that sought to measure the level of unemployment during the Great Depression. A year earlier, the Gallup organization had used a method that approximated probability sampling to determine the outcome of the 1936 presidential election in which Franklin D. Roosevelt trounced Alfred E. Landon. By correctly predicting the outcome, the Gallup and Roper polls eclipsed *Literary Digest* magazine's role as the country's premier poll taker—the magazine having predicted a Landon victory. Although Gallup's methods weren't up to the strict modern methods of probability sampling, its success would help establish the validity of scientific sampling.[25]

Throughout the early twentieth century, the period in which Deming was in school, the study and understanding of statistics were in their most formative stages. Statistics was still considered somewhat of a black art, and Deming's own degrees were not in statistics at all, but in mathematics and physics.

Deming, however, was a leader in bringing probability sampling into the mainstream of research by helping to pioneer the use of this survey technique in the 1940 census. That census, which was planned during the Depression, included questions on wages, salary income, and other questions that had not previously been asked.[26] A few years before the 1940 census, Deming organized a lecture series on statistics at the newly formed Graduate School of Agriculture in Washington, which would become a popular forum for the latest statistical ideas and a major influence on the work of the U.S. Bureau of the Census. While Deming wasn't directly involved with the 1937 unemployment survey, many of the Census Bureau statisticians who participated in it had attended the lecture series organized by Deming at the Graduate School of Agriculture.

In 1937 unemployment estimates varied wildly from three million to fifteen million—there was no way to know for sure. Because of the urgency of the situation and the economic and logistical difficulties of attempting to survey every household in the country, the unemployment census was to be based on a survey of only 2 percent of the population. At the time it was probably the largest survey based on probability sampling that had ever been undertaken; that is, it marked the first time the Census Bureau had relied on the canvassing of so small a portion of the population to calculate the makeup of the entire population. Both the Census Bureau leadership and Congress were initially suspicious of the effort. "They were afraid they'd lose accuracy," recalls Morris Hansen, who worked at the Census Bureau at that time and helped direct the unemployment survey. He remains one of Deming's best friends.[27]

To ensure accuracy, the census takers based the sample survey on a representative cross section of the U.S. population. The job led the Census Bureau to team up with the Postal Service, which, more than any other government agency, including the Internal Revenue Service, knew the addresses of the vast majority of Americans. The bureau was going to survey only a tiny portion of the population. So, to get a representative cross section, the survey had to be designed in such a way that every household in America had an equal chance of being chosen. Hansen divided the nation into 93,728 residential postal routes and grouped them into blocks of fifty each. To select the routes that would make up the ultimate sample, one route in each block of fifty was selected. On November 19, 1937, John Garner, the vice president of the United States, helped make the final selection by picking a number from one to fifty. The number he chose, forty-seven, became the designated postal route in each block of fifty that would be surveyed. Postal workers were charged with the final house-to-house canvassing of the addresses on those routes. In the end, the Census Bureau determined that eleven million Americans had been out of work during the week following Thanksgiving, and of these, two thirds were men.[28]

When Deming began working on the 1940 census, he introduced

methods that improved the accuracy of the results. In particular, he pioneered the use of SPC techniques at the Census Bureau's Washington offices, where a vast number of questionnaires were received, processed, and summarized in a system seething with variation. As the questionnaires poured into the Census Bureau from the census districts, it was the job of some 1,750 keypunch operators and verifiers to make sure the information was entered correctly onto millions of punch cards. The process was fraught with both systemic and special-cause quality problems. The operators, who were given one to three weeks of training, weren't all well prepared. Moreover, in what one of Deming's friends (Lloyd Nelson of Nashua Corporation) refers to as the "perversity principle,"[29] the punch cards underwent a costly inspection process that was designed to ensure quality by inspecting every single punch card, but that actually served to undermine it! For one thing, the pay of inspectors was linked to the volume of punch cards they processed, which encouraged speedy work but not careful inspection. And because some of the inspectors were friendly with the keypunch operators, they would often overlook errors for fear of getting their friends in trouble.[30]

Deming concluded that 100 percent inspection was neither useful nor necessary. Instead, he would sample the output of 5 percent of the operators and analyze the results to find out which ones, if any, were out of control. Those who were out of control were retrained. He reserved 100 percent inspection only for new operators, until they had gained enough practice that their performance was on a par with the more seasoned workers. In the course of changing the approach to inspection, the Census Bureau also concluded that the practice of putting the best employees in charge of inspection was a waste of talent. Instead, the better inspectors were moved into jobs where they would replace the less-qualified keyers who made mistakes.[31]

Deming first became interested in the application of statistics to manufacturing, and in the weaknesses of management processes such as inspection, when he became the protégé of Walter Shewhart, a researcher at Bell Laboratories during the early 1930s. Shewhart, who worked at Bell, had helped lead a quality revolution at AT&T in the 1920s by pioneering the use of statistics to control manufacturing quality at Western Electric, the phone company's manufacturing arm. While Western Electric is given credit around the world for implementing the quality methods pioneered by Shewhart, Deming contends that Shewhart was disappointed with the rate at which his own company adopted SPC. Deming contends that AT&T continued to rely heavily on inspection for many years after Shewhart invented the control chart, and was slow to adopt this innovation throughout its operations. Yet clearly by the end of World War II experts from Western Electric were well versed in SPC and began to teach it to the Japanese.[32] This groundbreaking effort had been prompted by the unique demands of building a telephone network and the difficulty of achieving process reliability and uniformity using standard production methods, the limitations of which were already becoming evident in the late nineteenth century. As early as 1882, it became apparent that "building a nationwide telephone network was to demand quality and reliability previously unheard of for manufactured products. Even the very first telephone networks were going to be series systems of such complexity that exacting specifications and tolerances would have to be met by each piece of the system."[33]

The birth of high-technology products and manufacturing systems drove the early twentieth century's revolution in quality control. For centuries, standardization and end-of-the-line inspection had been the methods used to produce large-volume products with specific quality characteristics. The Egyptians were said to have used interchangeable bows and arrows as long ago as 3000 B.C. But standardization did not become a global phenomenon until the beginning of mass production. By the end of World War I, standard-setting organizations around the globe were writing specifications aimed at achieving specific quality characteristics.[34] The same need for uniform, interchangeable parts also gave rise to a new cadre of production experts, the inspectors. These inspectors were charged with ensuring that no matter how many problems occurred during the manufacturing process, defective parts would be weeded out at the end and only those items that met specifications would be shipped to customers.[35]

But it quickly became clear that end-of-the-line inspection wouldn't meet the demands of the modern age. The advent of new, complex products and services such as the telephone system made it crucial to develop a better way to achieve high quality. The components that made up the equipment in a telephone plant, for example, were made up of more than 100,000 pieces that came from all over the world. To inspect all this componentry was virtually impossible. Moreover, tests for some quality characteristics, such as the blowing time of a fuse, were impractical because they were inherently destructive. By the 1920s and 1930s, the concept of developing systems that were capable of building large quantities of products correctly from the beginning began to emerge. In 1922 G. S. Radford broke new ground with his book *The Control of Quality in Manufacturing,* which identified quality as a distinct management responsibility and even advocated the need for different departments in a company to coordinate their efforts and the importance of making quality a consideration early in the design phase.[36]

The most crucial breakthrough in the modern quality movement came in 1931 with the publication of Shewhart's *Economic Control of Quality of Manufactured Product.* Shewhart became the first "to recognize that variability was a fact of industrial life and that it could be understood [and managed] using the principles of probability and statistics." Shewhart gave the quality movement its theoretical underpinnings when he defined the problem of managing quality as one of differentiating between acceptable variation, or common causes, and unacceptable variation, or special causes.[37] Both kinds of causes produce variation. But Shewhart recognized that it is possible to live with common causes because, while they can never be fully eliminated, they allow the process to function with a *predictable* level of variation. Thus, a company that has only common causes to contend with in its processes will produce products of a predictable level of quality to which it can peg warranties, product claims, and prices. Special causes, however, are by definition unpredictable, can wreak havoc with a process, and offer management no basis on which to predict the quality level of its products or manage change.

Shewhart determined that what was needed was a way to simplify the inspection process and eventually make it redundant. In 1924 he gave his boss at AT&T, George Edwards, a short note and a diagram that would eventually be responsible for sparking a new wave in manufacturing and quality control. The note contained the methodology for creating a so-called control chart.

Shewhart's simple diagram showed whether a process was stable and measured the capability of the process over time. To use a control chart, a worker or technician would sample a production process at regular intervals and plot the results on a chart. Using a mathematical formula devised by Shewhart, he could establish boundaries of variation for a given process within which it was considered stable, predictable, in control. Outside those boundaries—in the case of the soda pop bottles described earlier, more than .03 ounce per bottle—the process is deemed unstable, unpredictable, and out of control. Samples that fall outside the boundaries of the control chart signal a problem, or special cause of variation.

Think of a driver rolling along a highway. While he may be steering a "straight" course, there will be tiny variations—an inch to the right, two inches to the left. But essentially his performance is acceptable because he is driving within the control boundaries of the system—his car and his driving ability—which together roughly coincide with the two lines that define his lane. (The widths of traffic lanes are roughly analogous to control boundaries because they are based on how close to a straight line the average automobile and driver can remain over time, assuming the car has passed registration requirements and the driver is sober and knows how to drive. If automotive technology were to improve so that all cars on the highway had far less sway to the right or left, a statistician measuring this improved system would find a narrower control boundary and might recommend that the width of traffic lanes be narrowed by a few inches.)[38] If, however, he suddenly started to careen outside the two lines of his lane, his car would be "out of control." The special causes might be drunkenness or sleepiness on the part of the driver, a flat tire, or some other mechanical malfunction that needs immediate attention.

It's important to note that the boundaries of stability are *not* arbitrary; they are dictated by the system itself. In other words, the boundaries are only as wide or as narrow as the system permits: Wide boundaries indicate a lot of variation; narrow boundaries signal less variation. To achieve better control, the level of variation must be reduced *by improving* the system, which *de facto* narrows the control boundaries.

Thus, with Shewhart's control chart as a guide, a worker in a factory would have to inspect only a sample of each batch of items being manufactured and would be able to draw conclusions about the capability of the entire system with great accuracy. Eventually control charts would be used farther and farther upstream—not to weed out defects, but to help keep the system in control from the beginning of the production process. "Where inspection had focused much of its efforts on finding and removing bad products or lots of products before shipment to the customer, Shewhart saw how statistical techniques could be used to increase the amount of good product being manufactured."[39]

However, while Shewhart and some others saw the importance of amending the role of inspectors, it would be many decades before American industry began to wean itself away from an "inspect out" approach to bad quality and to adopt a "build in" approach to good quality. Indeed, inspectors had become part and parcel of the new "scientific" approach to production that fragmented factory jobs and separated workers from a sense of responsibility and involvement in the products they manufactured. Only in the latter half of the century would management experts such as Deming begin to advocate more involvement and responsibility for workers.

One reason for the prevalence of inspectors in U.S. companies well into the 1980s is that in the United States, manufacturing quality continued to be associated with the idea of building products "to specifications." Typically, a U.S. engineer would design a product with an ideal performance level in mind. But for the benefit of the manufacturing department, he would circumscribe that "optimum target" with specification limits based on the *range* within which he thought the product would not fail. Thus, in designing a gear, for example, an engineer might determine the critical dimension of the gear's shaft bore to be one inch in diameter; that is, it would function best at a diameter of precisely one inch. But in the specifications he sent to manufacturing, the engineer would bracket that target so that the specs might call for one inch in diameter, plus or minus .005 inch. The limits were picked because the shaft bore would function as long as it fell anywhere within that continuum. And according to the conventional definition of quality, there was no qualitative difference among a gear with a .995-inch shaft bore, one with a one-inch shaft bore, and one with a 1.005-inch shaft bore because all fell within the specification limits. Conventional wisdom held that the gear would function equally well as long as the shaft bore fell anywhere within that range.[40]

In fact, makers of such sophisticated machinery as robotics would learn that precision is crucial to performance. The more parts in a product, the greater the risk of so-called "tolerance stack-up"; that is, enough parts produced off target, even if they are, technically speaking, within the specification limits, will create a defective final product. Thus the more sophisticated an item, the less tolerable *any* variation in production becomes.

In the early 1980s, a Ford field trip to Japan determined that one of the reasons Japanese companies had been able to improve quality while doing away with inspection was that they were constantly reducing variation instead of relying on specifications and inspection. Ford found that performance variation in systems designed to approach optimum targets was smaller by orders of magnitude than the variation in systems organized merely to meet specifications (see Chapter 5 for more details). This realization prompted Larry Sullivan, who was then the manager of reliability, warranty, and supplier quality assurance at Ford, to observe that there were two problems with the U.S. adherence to specifications: "First, you can never improve. You'll keep meeting specifications, but you won't improve. Second, as long as you control [systems] to meet specifications, you will always have to inspect, you will always have to cull out the defectives."[41]

To illustrate his point, Sullivan described a quality improvement effort he had witnessed in Japan. Visiting a maker of cigar lighters, the Ford team ran across a group of Japanese workers who were trying to improve the process that makes detents, one of the lighter's mechanical parts. In one room, eight workers hovered around an eleven-foot-long control chart spread across the table. "I figured they must be having problems in the field or with customer complaints," observed Sullivan. When he looked more closely at the control chart, he realized that the process was not only within specification limits, but that, on average, the process performed within less than one third of the range of the specification limits![42] That is, the system for producing the cigar lighter part was already performing at a far higher level of accuracy and quality than what had been specified in the product blueprints (see Chart 1).

Cigar Lighter Socket Detent
How One Japanese Company Aims for the Process Target

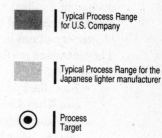

Typical Process Range for U.S. Company

Typical Process Range for the Japanese lighter manufacturer

Process Target

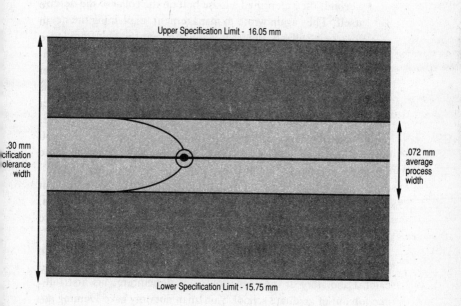

Upper Specification Limit - 16.05 mm

.30 mm specification tolerance width

.072 mm average process width

Lower Specification Limit - 15.75 mm

Diagram: Antonia Gabor

So what were the workers doing? They were trying to improve the process capability still further, to bring it even closer to the optimal design target. Judging by the control chart, which tracked the production of the lighter detent over a twenty-month period, the process had gone out of control four times. The workers were trying to identify the causes in order to prevent them from cropping up again. They identified the following problems and corresponding solutions:

- First, the process had gone out of control because a tool wore out. They wrote a letter to management explaining the problem and suggesting that the tool be replaced every four months, instead of every eight. Management delivered on their request.
- Second, they identified a loose bolt on the collar of the detent itself. They again wrote to management, explaining the need for a new collar design that would prevent the bolt from loosening.
- Third, they identified a problem with the steel that was being used for the detent. It would require work with the steel supplier.

This experience gave the visiting Ford executives a new insight into the nature of processes. Upon returning from Japan Sullivan remarked to a group of Ford executives, "It's important that we study statistical methods, but it is also important that we understand statistical concepts," that is, the effects of variation on every part of a business.[43]

In 1927 Deming was introduced to Shewhart by his boss, Charles Kunzman. Deming worked for Kunzman at the Fixed Nitrogen Research Laboratory of the Department of Agriculture, his first full-time job out of graduate school. Kunzman not only gave Deming an entree to Bell Laboratories circles but also encouraged him to travel to London to study under one of the leading lights of statistical theory, Sir Ronald A. Fisher.[44] A geneticist and pioneer of modern statistical analysis, Fisher broke new ground in how to use statistics to design more efficient and accurate experiments, especially in agricultural research; Fisher's research methods would influence thinking in the sampling methods used in industrial production.[45] Over the years, Deming came to be a regular visitor at Mountain Lakes, New Jersey, where Shewhart lived. And in the mid-1930s, Deming took a one-year leave of absence from the Agriculture Department to study statistical theory under Fisher at the University of London.

By the time Deming returned from London, he was already a respected statistician in his own right, known especially for his leadership role in statistical education at the Graduate School of Agriculture. And it was Deming who would help disseminate the work of Shewhart—who was little known outside AT&T at the time—by introducing his mentor to the Washington community in about 1937. At the time, Deming was teaching a course in statistics at the Graduate School of Agriculture, one of the first in the country to offer evening courses. He had taken the job two years earlier, shortly after returning from his trip to London, and quickly turned it into a *Who's Who* of statistical theory, inviting leading scholars from all over the world to lecture. Shewhart was one of the lesser-known statisticians invited by Deming.[46] The Bell Laboratories guru delivered a four-part lecture, which Deming helped compile into a book. The resulting *Statistical Method from the Viewpoint of Quality Control* became for many years the bible of manufacturing quality control.

The lectures also put Deming on the map. It was through the lecture series that members of the Census Bureau first became acquainted with him, and later they would invite him to help plan the use of sampling on a large scale in the 1940 census. Milton Friedman, the renowned economist, and W. Allen Wallis, who would become assistant secretary of state in the Reagan administration, were among those who attended the lectures.[47]

When World War II erupted, Deming and other statisticians suddenly came into demand. The most famous group of statisticians—excluding Deming—was gathered at the War Department's Office of Statistical Control, which was established to manage the massive logistical task of coordinating and dispatching men, materiel, and supplies for tactical missions all around the globe. The group of young men recruited for the job eventually became known as the Whiz Kids and included Robert S. McNamara, who later served as president of Ford and secretary of defense in the Kennedy administration. These military beancounters handled such daunting questions as how to get 100,000 tons of equipment from San Francisco to Australia in the most efficient and cost-effective way possible. They calculated, for example, that it would take 10,022 planes and 120,765 fliers to perform the task that a mere forty-four freighters and 3,200 seamen could accomplish.[48] The Whiz Kids are particularly notable in this context because their work at Ford (see Chapter 4) after the war would prove that a scientific approach to management systems, without a clear understanding of variation and its effects on complex manufacturing operations, can do more harm than good. Ultimately, the quality management era introduced to Detroit by Japanese competition and by Deming would come to supplant the legacy of the Whiz Kids.

During the war, Deming was among a different group of statistical experts who were sought out by the government. He was called on to help improve wartime production. At the beginning of World War II, Wallis and Friedman joined the Statistical Research Group at Columbia University. Their job was to use their knowledge of statistics to advise the military and its suppliers on everything from the best settings for proximity fuses to methods for conducting sampling inspections of rocket propellant. On April 17, 1942, Walllis wrote to Deming to ask for his help in training statisticians in the special requirements of the war: "Those of us teaching statistics in various departments here are trying to work out a curriculum adapted to the immediate statistical requirements of the war. It seems probable that a good many students with research training might by training in statistics become more useful for war than in their present work or might increase their usefulness within their present fields."

Deming responded a few days later with a characteristic sense of urgency: "Here is my idea. Time and materials are at a premium, and there is no time to be lost. There is no royal short-cut to producing a highly trained statistician, but I do firmly believe that the most important principles of application can be expounded in a very short time to engineers and others. I have done it, and have seen it done. You could accomplish a great deal by holding a school in the Shewhart methods some time in the near future. I would suggest a concentrated effort—a 'short' course followed by a 'long' course. The short course would be a two day session for executive and industrial people who want to find out some of the main principles and advantages of a statistical program in industry. It would be a sort of popularization, four lectures by noted industrial people who have seen statistical methods used, and can point out some of their advantages. The long course would extend over a period of weeks, or, if given evenings, over a longer period. It would be attended by the people who actually intend to use statistical methods on the job. In many cases they would be delegated by the men who had attended the short course.

"I would suggest that both courses be thrown open to engineers, inspectors and industrial people with or without mathematical or statistical training. Naturally, any person who has had considerable statistical training would be in a position to get much more out of the course, but few would be in this fortunate position. . . ."[49]

Within a period of months a national program of eight- and ten-day courses had been established, based on Deming's specifications, to teach statistical techniques in quality control to executives and engineers of the companies that were supplying the war effort. The program, which ultimately was headed by Holbrook Working, a statistician and economist at Stanford University, took the form of a traveling road show. Classes were held in conference centers and motels around the country. Many of the classes were taught by Deming, who estimates that some ten thousand engineers were trained in SPC techniques. The courses taught control charting techniques and the revolutionary four-step "Shewhart cycle."[50] Many who attended these seminars became America's early converts to quality control; the study groups they formed at Deming's behest eventually evolved into the American Society for Quality Control.

The Shewhart cycle, another idea Deming adopted from his mentor, is one that has become a central theme of quality management at leading companies. It is more often referred to today as the "Deming cycle" because of the way it was popularized by Deming in Japan. The original aim of Shewhart's model was to create a preventive system of checks, improvements, and analysis that would produce products correctly with relatively little trial and error and predict the effects of changes. Deming would apply the idea to a customer-driven product planning process designed to continuously improve products and services in *anticipation* of the changing needs of the marketplace.

Deming's interpretation of the Shewhart cycle was the antithesis of traditional U.S. marketing techniques, which could be said to rest on a "sell, sell, sell" mentality, in which the marketer's job is to convince the customer to buy no matter what his needs, no matter what the suitability of the product. As John Z. DeLorean has said of General Motors, instead of preparing an "overall marketing strategy which scientifically ascertains consumer needs, designs products to fill those needs and then merchandises these products to bring the need, the product and the consumer together, GM relied on little more than rah-rah sales pitches and hard-sell techniques."[51] Deming, by contrast, called for a cycle that emphasized market testing both before and after a product was put on sale with a view to continuously improving it based on the test results and to better serving the needs of customers.[52] The Deming cycle was his vision for getting at the *desires,* both conscious and subconscious, of the consumer, and of devising products that would meet those needs and bring the customer running: design it, *test* and build it, market it, and *retest* it.

In about 1949, Deming was invited by members of Japanese industry to deliver lectures on quality as part of their effort to rebuild the country. He based his lectures on Shewhart's teachings and the classes he had given during World War II. To these he added another crucial business function: the use of statistical tests and surveys to enhance market research. "The terms 'good' quality and 'quality control' have no meaning except with reference to the consumer's needs," Deming told his Japanese students.[53] In other words, you can create a process only after you have defined the product you're going to build and the customer for whom you are building it. A typical Ford automobile, for example, will have different product *and* process requirements than a typical Mercedes-Benz. And it was the Japanese who carried the pioneering efforts of Shewhart and Deming to their logical conclusion: the harnessing of all business processes involving both people and machines to define customer needs, to translate those needs into product strategies with the optimum features and price, and to control and constantly improve both the product and the process.[54] In fact, the Japanese would adopt the Deming cycle as the principal model for establishing and carrying out quality management strategies throughout an entire organization.

This process also has come to be known as *kaizen* in Japan. It calls for continuous improvement for every strategy, product, and process in an organization. "This means that management must first establish policies . . . and procedures for all major operations and then see to it that everybody follows [these standard operating procedures]. . . . If people are *unable* to follow the standard, management must either provide training or review and revise the standard so that people can follow it."[55] Thus even management's standards and directives must be tested continuously to ensure their validity and workability and must ultimately be improved.

While Deming and his process-oriented approach to quality management were embraced by the Japanese, in America's postwar economy, quality control was relegated to the back burner. What little progress had been made during the war to introduce SPC methods to industry began to dissipate. Even at AT&T the control charts disappeared virtually overnight during the late 1950s, according to Myron Tribus, a former director of the MIT Center for Advanced Engineering Study.[56]

After World War II, U.S. industry couldn't produce goods fast enough to satisfy consumer needs around the world. With a seller's market for American-made products, there clearly was no urgency to improve products and services. It is a little more difficult to explain why the gradual encroachment of high-quality foreign products in the 1960s and 1970s—ones that were often superior to domestic versions—didn't rekindle an appreciation of statistical methods. Hubris was partly to blame. In addition, business schools, which after the war became increasingly influential, championed the finance function and traditional approaches to cost accounting, which tended to equate improved quality with increased costs.[57]

Another reason for the neglect of variation control and the lack of appreciation for the benefits of continuous improvement is the decline in standards of the U.S. educational system, which led to a national aversion to mathematics and statistics. One U.S. executive, on returning from a visit to Japan in the 1980s, estimated that the average Japanese worker, once he got through the Japanese public school system and a company-sponsored training program, had "a more in-depth understanding of statistical methods than the average American engineer."[58] Says Hal Tragash, a human resources exec-

utive at Xerox, of the company's efforts to introduce statistical methods as part of its quality control efforts in the 1980s: "The resistance
to statistics is beyond belief."[59]

Nevertheless, with the growing evidence of Japan's performance
superiority, Deming and his theories of management gradually came
to be recognized during the 1980s. With Deming's arrival and the
debut of quality management in the United States, companies are
beginning to train their employees in the use of statistics. Statistics
is also entering a new phase in academia. During the mid-1980s, a
few universities, including Columbia and Fordham, began to make
statistics, as it pertains to production and management questions,
part of their fledgling quality management curricula. Unlike in the
old days, when statistics was the exclusive domain of mathemati-
cians and theoreticians, these schools are beginning to heed Deming
and a few other experts who advocate an approach to the teaching of
statistics based on more practical applications.

Undoubtedly the most profound effect of the evolution of SPC
has been its role in debunking the assumptions that have governed
the use of Taylor's time-honored "scientific management" techniques. SPC, as Deming envisioned it, has helped redefine the
interaction of blue-collar workers and management in the manufacturing sector. Deming's theories create a scientifically reasoned jus-
tification for reenlisting the brains of workers to solve production
problems. In addition, in one of its most provocative and controversial contentions, it challenges such time-honored management practices as performance ratings, payment of commissions, and bonus
plans.

Deming argues that quotas, performance ratings, and bonus systems are generally unfair and arbitrary—and that they demoralize
workers who perceive them as such. "Some leaders forget an important mathematical theorem: that if twenty people are engaged on
a job, two will fall at the bottom ten percent, no matter what," says
Deming.[60] Take the top performers at the top ten business schools
in the country, the top skiers in ten states, the top scientists in ten
countries. If you give them each a test in their common field of
expertise, one of them will always have to be on the bottom of the
list, and one always on top. Deming argues that if you readminister

the test several times, the winners and losers will very likely change. But for the individuals who ended up at the bottom, for any reason, the experience will always be devastating.

Control charts can introduce some rationality to this system. By monitoring the performance of a group over time, and by plotting each individual's performance on the chart, a pattern will develop that will show a variety of information that is far more valuable than rating individuals on some kind of bell curve. In particular:

1. If one individual is outside the limits because of exceptionally high performance, it is worth studying her work habits to determine if she is using a method that could improve the system overall, if applied by all the workers.
2. If an individual is outside the limits, showing exceptionally poor performance, she needs either retraining or a new job.
3. If there are several people outside the control limits, there is something wrong either with the system or with the tests used to measure the system.

An important point, however, is that the performance of the workers will *always* vary because they are human and because it is in the nature of all worldly things to be variable. The first objective, then, is to control the environment and the components of the system—whether they be people, materials, or machines—so that the natural variability remains within certain predictable limits. The next objective is to fine-tune the environment and the components of the system to shrink the variation.

To illustrate the nature of systems and of variation, Deming has devised two demonstrations that have become the highlights of his four-day seminars. In the first exercise, known as the red bead experiment, Deming illustrates a "typical" production scenario to show two things: first, that the performance of individual workers can be no better than the system (as defined by management) allows: second, that the performance of any system is by nature variable, and therefore differences between the performance of two different workers are a matter of chance and thus frequently utterly meaningless. In the second exercise, known as the funnel experiment, Deming demonstrates that only the most carefully reasoned changes in a stable system can hope to improve it; on the other hand, tampering with or changing a stable system without a soundly reasoned theory as to the source of the common causes of variation is likely only to make the system worse.

With the red bead exercise, which is generally conducted on the second afternoon of Deming's four-day seminars, Deming pokes fun at management's misguided assumptions about both production processes and the power of workers to control the quality of their output. To make his point, Deming transforms his dais into a production line, recruiting employees from his audience, and describes the process with the sarcasm and derision he feels befit most U.S. management processes. "This is a very complicated job," explains Deming. "It takes months to train a foreman, and we don't have that kind of time, so I'll act as foreman. I need six Willing Workers. I need two inspectors, experience not necessary, I need a chief inspector . . . women will be considered."

With his employees lined up on the podium, Deming is ready to describe the job and to explain the rules of the workplace. "Are you all willing to put forth your best efforts?" he thunders. "You understand you have jobs as long as your performance is satisfactory. You understand that your jobs are dependent on your own performance. Is that clear?

"The material comes in a vessel. The customer will take only white beads; the material that comes in will have some red beads in it. But your job is to make only white beads. You understand there are two vessels, are you clear? You understand they're rectangles. You understand what a rectangle is? You grasp the large vessel on the broad side and pour from the corner into the smaller vessel at a distance of ten centimeters. You'll keep the vessel in the same plane. You understand gravity? You all know about gravity? Gravity will take the beads and push them down into the lower vessel. You do not shake it, or turn it. Keep it in the same plane. Just tilt it. Gravity will do the work, gravity is cheap and dependable. You will then return the beads from the small vessel into the large one. Same procedure."

The vessels contain a total of 4,000 beads, 3,200 white ones and 800 red ones. Deming, in his new role as foreman, explains how the work is done, using a paddle with fifty depressions in it. "Why are there fifty holes in the paddle?" he asks.

"One for each bead," volunteers one of the Willing Workers.

"There's a better reason," says Deming sternly. "Why are there fifty holes in the paddle? Because there are five in one direction and ten in the other." (The audience laughs loudly.) "We understand our business here. We know what it is. Our procedures are absolutely fixed, no departures."

Deming returns to his instructions: "The next step after you pour the beads . . . you take the paddle, grasp it on the broad side, two fingers, dip it into the beads, gentle agitation, no shaking, raise it, axis horizontal, tilt forty-four degrees. There will be no excess beads, every hole is filled."

Deming demonstrates the procedure. When he pulls the paddle out of the bin, there are some red beads mixed in with the white. Says the guru, "I've purposely [drawn] some red beads so you'll know what they look like." (Again, loud laughter from the audience.) "You'll carry them over to inspector number one, who will make a count in silence and record it on paper. Next, inspector number two will count and put it on paper. The chief inspector is responsible for the count. If they differ, there may be a mistake. If they agree, there may be a mistake. The chief inspector is responsible." Twice during the exercise the "inspectors" fail to agree on the count, demonstrating the folly of relying on inspection as a means of quality control.

The Willing Workers, appropriately cowed by their stern foreman, are ready for a trial run. When production finally begins, a woman named Riester is up first. She follows Deming's instructions and presents her results to the inspectors. The chief inspector bellows, "Six. Dismissed!"

The foreman does not look pleased. "Do you understand that your job is to produce white beads?" asks Deming. "The management has decided to establish a quota here. Fifty beads per day, not more than three red ones per work load. Any questions about your job? Your job depends on your own performance. Our procedures are rigid. No departures. No questions."

Next it's Dan's turn. He draws out the beads and looks nervously at the foreman. "I have more than three."

"That's because you didn't agitate for five seconds, axis horizontal, forty-four degrees," says Deming. "Follow the procedures." He gives Dan another chance.

"I still have more than three red beads," says Dan, even more nervous this time.

"Carry it to inspector number one, no comments, no questions on this job," says the foreman. No more Mr. Nice Guy.

"Eleven. Dismissed," announces the chief inspector.

"Things are getting worse," laments the foreman. "Look at that. We started with six, that's bad enough, now it jumps to eleven. I sure hope Jo De will do better."

And Jo De does.

"Five. Dismissed," announces the chief inspector.

"If Jo De can make five, anyone can make five," exclaims the foreman. "Five should be the maximum."

No one does better. So Jo De gets a merit raise. "Pauline and Earl—nice boys and girls, what a shame we have to put them on probation. If Jo De can make five, no one should make more." Deming instructs the recorder to add up the day's production, and she announces a count of fifty-two red beads; fifty-two defectives were produced that day.

The foreman isn't pleased. The next day, however, things improve. This time the six Willing Workers draw a total of forty-five red beads. Dan, who had drawn eleven red beads on the first day, draws only five red ones the second day. That's good enough to win him a merit raise. Jo De, on the other hand, produces eight red beads the second day, as opposed to the five she had produced on day one, and the foreman concludes that success has "gone to her head." The procedure is repeated for two more days.

Management is very displeased. On none of the days do the Willing Workers meet their quota of no more than three red beads per day. Management demands that the workers do better, and to make the point the foreman lays off all but the three "best" Willing Workers, the ones who produced the smallest number of red beads over the hypothetical four-day run of the production line. Production begins on the fifth day of the production experiment with the remaining three Willing Workers working double shifts. Almost without exception their performance is worse than on any of the preceding days.

At the end of the production run, Deming plots the results of the process on the control chart. Lo and behold, the system is in control.

That is, the system is functioning in a stable manner, given the materials, tools, and procedures that define the process (see Chart 2). The reason for the defects is *inherent* to the process; they have nothing to do with external circumstances.

The moral of the story, of course, is that only management, not the workers, can govern the system. There are a number of ways the production of red beads could be minimized, but none of them is within the control of the Willing Workers. One way would be to make sure that there are fewer red beads (or defectives) coming from the supplier in the first place. Only management can change that by either switching suppliers or working with the existing supplier to improve the quality of its production. Another way would be to give each worker a pair of tweezers and let him or her systematically pick out only the white beads. Again, it's up to management to furnish the tweezers and the new work rules.

The funnel experiment is conducted on the third day of Deming's four-day seminar. It is designed to show the damage that can be done by tampering with, or overadjusting, a stable system. When Deming defines tampering, he says that in the process of "adjusting a stable process to try to compensate for a result that is undesirable, or *for a result that is extra good*, the output that follows will be worse than if [the tamperer] had left the process alone."[61]

The materials and equipment that go into the demonstration process consist of a funnel, a glass marble small enough to drop effortlessly through the funnel, a table with a flat surface, and a holder for the funnel. The action that defines the process consists of setting the funnel into the stationary holder and dropping the marble through the funnel fifty times. The object is to drop the marble as close to the same spot over and over again. The process is stable because there is no external influence interfering with any element of the process: The funnel is always in the same position and so is the surface of the table. The path of the marble doesn't change. The process is, however, subject to natural variation. Drop the marble through the stationary funnel fifty times and it is unlikely ever to drop in the same spot twice. It will always drop close to where the original marble dropped, but not precisely in the same spot.

A person unfamiliar with the nature of variation might try to devise a way of narrowing the dispersion. Deming explains that there

Deming's Red Bead Experiment; Indianapolis, January 25, 1989

Record of the number of defective items produced by Willing Workers each day

Willing Worker	Day 1	2	3	4	All 4	5
Riester	6	8	10	9	33	8 13
Dan	11	5	9	11	36	
Jo De	5	8	9	12	34	17 10
Joe	6	7	6	6	25	11 11
Pauline	12	8	10	13	44	
Earl	12	8	10	17	47	
All Six	52	45	54	68	219	70
Cum x	8.7	8.0	8.4	9.1	9.1	xxx

Wooden beads
Census count,
one by one

Red 800
White 3200
Total 40000

Inspectors: Chris, Phyllis
Chief Inspector: Phil
Recorder: Kathy

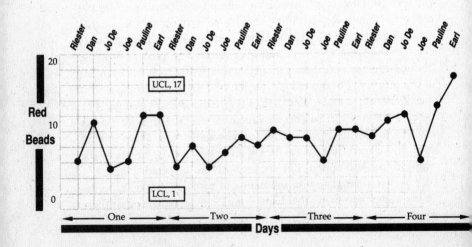

The process exhibits fairly good statistical control. This conclusion is based on intimate knowledge of the procedures followed by the six Willing Workers, as well as on study of the chart. There is no evidence that one Willing Worker will in the future be better than any other. Differences between Willing Workers and between the defect levels on different days are attributable to variation inherent in the system.

The Willing Workers have put into the job all that they have to offer.

One way to decrease the proportion of red in the product is to reduce the proportion red beads from the incoming material (management's responsibility).

The control limits are extended into the future to show that one can predict the amount of variation to expect in the near future from continuation of the same process.

Points added for Washington, August 24, 1988, use the same beads, same paddle, same procedures, different people, same foreman.

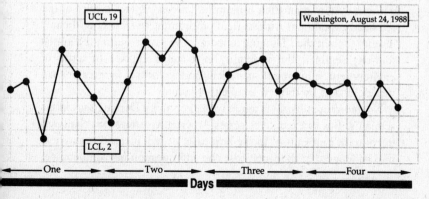

Diagram: Antonia Gabor

are a number of ways one might try to adjust the funnel so that the marble will fall exactly in the same spot over and over again. For example, if on the second drop the marble comes to rest one inch to the right of the original drop, then, to compensate, one could try to move it one inch to the left. Or you could keep moving the funnel over the spot where the marble last came to rest. Deming shows that in either case, the dispersion will be wider than if you had left the funnel in its original, stationary position.

Deming makes the analogy to the following real-life processes. A worker mixing colors in succeeding batches mixes the color from each batch based on the shade of the previous batch, not on the basis of the original swatch. Gradually the batches of color get further and further from the target color on the swatch. Or "a drunk man, trying to reach home, falls after each step and has no idea which way is north. He steps in any direction, with no memory. His efforts eventually send him by faltering steps further and further from the target."[62]

Deming demonstrates that, given the system, the best result comes from leaving it alone. Of course, it is possible to improve the system. But because the process is stable, improvement requires careful analysis, experimentation, and ultimately probably a dramatic change in the process itself. For example, if you trade in the glass marble for a steel ball and place a magnet directly under the funnel, then, when you drop the steel ball, it is likely to drop in the same spot every time.

Deming's audience has far less trouble accepting the funnel experiment than it does the message of the red beads. Many observers believe workers have more control over the product of their output within a system than what is permitted according to the rules of the red bead experiment with its rigid procedures. In fact, says Michael Tweity, one of the "Deming helpers" who assists during the guru's four-day seminar, the variability in a real workplace in terms of environment, equipment, materials, and so forth is far greater than that described by the red bead experiment.

No one is ever likely to agree with everything Deming says in his seminars. But as executives across America have learned, challenging him isn't much use. In the best case, he will pretend not to hear his challenger. In the worst case, he will question his competence.

In fact, Deming is occasionally swayed by compelling new arguments. For example, while he once advocated strict single sourcing, one of his graduate students, who did her thesis on managing suppliers, won Deming over to the view that it is important to work closely with just a *few* suppliers. To keep his audience entertained and to emphasize various points, Deming issues a steady stream of diatribes and bons mots with the conviction of a man who is certain he is absolutely right:

- On one CEO of a Fortune 500 company: "We'd be better off if some people didn't put forth their best efforts."[63]
- On other quality experts: "Managers go to the School of Hot Air. And two years later they find that all they've got is hot air."[64]
- On what the business books teach about competition: "Just choke off the competition. Never mind about the customer, he doesn't enter into this at all."[65]
- On management by objective: "I call it retroactive management, running a business by looking in the rearview mirror. You wouldn't drive a car that way."[66]
- On executives who don't understand variation: "Executives meeting to discuss policy without benefit of profound knowledge . . . off to the Milky Way."[67]
- On American management: "Most management today is reactive behavior. You put your hand on a hot stove and yank it off. A cat would know to do as much."[68]
- More on American management: "I gave some lectures to the State Department and I told them do not export North American management to a friendly country."[69]

Variation is the scientific theory on which Deming has based his view of management. But like some of the great physicists of the nineteenth and early twentieth century who persisted in believing the universe is static despite abundant evidence to the contrary, Deming is driven by less-than-scientific convictions, in particular a religious, puritanical belief system. Variation explains the logic of his philosophy of management. Religion accounts for the evangelical passion with which he pursues it.

Deming's view of the world can be seen by the following confluence of scientific and humanistic conviction: The nature of variation means that management controls the vast majority of the factors that affect processes and the quality of their outcomes. Similarly, the enterprise and the livelihood of individual workers are at the mercy of the quality of the decisions made by management. Thus, scientific theory places the onus of quality squarely on the shoulders of management.

Deming's definition of management's responsibility is buttressed, he believes, by no lesser authority than God. "Joy in work is . . . anybody's birthright. Joy in work means not joy for one's self, but joy in cooperation with other people that also take joy in their work,"[70] says Deming, who also quotes frequently from the book of Ecclesiastes: "Wherefore I perceive that there be nothing better than that a man should rejoice in his own work."[71]

Deming's religious conviction has shaped his belief that business has a social responsibility to survive, to grow, and to "provide jobs and more jobs." He also believes that "stiffening global competition has made it increasingly difficult for firms to meet this responsibility."[72] Learning to understand and manage variation, process optimization, and continuous improvement are the crucial requirements for achieving the long-term health and survival of a business enterprise.

FROM AMERICAN
PIONEER TO
JAPANESE *SENSEI*

Deming stands at the window of his hotel room in the monolithic Keio Plaza hotel, looking out on Shinjuku, Tokyo's answer to Times Square, on a brisk October afternoon in 1988. The forty-five-story building, one of the tallest in the city, is also one of the best spots from which to see the extraordinary expanse of modern-day Tokyo. Deming is mesmerized by the view, particularly the regiments of cranes that surround the hotel, filling up once-empty lots with imposing new structures and transforming the city before his very eyes. No sooner had Deming caught sight of the view than he went to the lobby to buy a camera for the express purpose of recording the scene outside his window; back in his room, he asked one of his American visitors to take several pictures of the cityscape. From Deming's window, Tokyo snakes out as far as the eye can see, disappearing into the smog on the horizon. Shinjuku itself has blossomed since Deming first began visiting the city in the 1940s. The district boasts Tokyo's busiest train station, three major department stores, a half-dozen international hotels, dozens of the Japanese-style game arcades known as pachinko parlors, video game stores, and thousands of restaurants and nightclubs that range from the sleazy and bizarre to the elegant and homey. The Keio Plaza itself is the city's first high-rise hotel. Undistinguished architecturally, it was at the time of its construction a triumph of state-of-the-art earthquake-resistant construction.

The view from the Keio Plaza provides a reminder of the transformation that Tokyo, indeed, all of Japan, has undergone since World War II. It also is an appropriate backdrop for the tea party Deming is giving for former colleagues and friends on the last day of his visit in 1988.

The tea, held in a small banquet room at the top of the hotel, brings together once again, in what has become virtually an annual ritual, some twenty elderly men whom Deming has known since the 1940s and 1950s, many of whom played important roles in Japan's postwar renewal. Eizaburo Nishibori, a former Toshiba executive and one of the oldest and most loyal of Deming's Japanese colleagues, sits in the place of honor at Deming's right, speaking animatedly so that the American, who is hard of hearing, will understand him. The other guests, former executives, professors, and management experts whom Deming has known for more than thirty-five years, sit silently listening to Deming and Nishibori or speaking quietly with one another in Japanese. Several of the visitors, including Rokuro Hattori, the former senior managing director of Bridgestone Corporation, who has brought Dr. Deming a newly published book on quality control (in Japanese) barely speaks any English. Another fellow with little English is Shuhei Ogawa, president of Fujikin International; just about the only thing Ogawa is able to communicate is that he has just purchased an apartment in New York City's Trump Tower. No one is sure what Ogawa and his wife are doing here—the couple appear to have defied Japan's strictures of politeness by crashing the party. They cling to Deming's side as though to a long-lost relation, jockeying for position in the photographs of the guru that several of the guests take during the course of the party.

Midway through the afternoon, the atmosphere livens up with the arrival of Sumi Moriguti and Miti Iwatsubo, the wife and daughter of Sigeiti Moriguti, a retired professor from Tokyo University, and one of the men responsible for inviting Deming to return to Japan in 1950. Next to Nishibori (who died a few months after Deming's 1988 visit), Moriguti is one of Deming's oldest Japanese friends. The two Moriguti women are both stylishly dressed and very talkative. Deming, his daughter Diana Deming Cahill, and

Nida Backaitis, Deming's traveling companion and a business professor at the University of Southern California, had been invited by the Morigutis for a lavish Chinese meal the previous evening. Still, Deming welcomes them as though he is seeing them for the first time in years. The Morigutis, who knew Lola Deming well and seem genuinely saddened by her death, spend much of the afternoon reminiscing about how much both Lola and Dr. Deming meant to them, especially in the early years after the war.

The Morigutis were among the first Japanese who got to know Deming after the Allied occupation, in the days when even food and clothing were luxuries. Deming and Lola always came bearing gifts. And Miti, Moriguti's daughter, says she still remembers the taste of candies Deming brought from Washington when she was three years old—they were the first sweets she had ever eaten. Her mother also reminds her of the two dotted-swiss dresses, one in pink and the other in blue, that the Demings gave her. But for Mrs. Moriguti and other Japanese wives, there was something even more meaningful about the Demings' visits. Lola Deming, sensitive to the daily drudgery and hardship faced by Japanese wives, especially in the immediate postwar years, always insisted that they accompany their husbands for the elaborate dinners that were held whenever the Demings were in Japan. For many of these women, it was their only chance for an evening out. And Diana, a soft-spoken, pretty blonde in her mid-forties who bares a strong resemblance to her father, fights back the tears as she hears the Morigutis talk about her parents. She is as touched by the fond memories of her mother as she is by the esteem in which they hold her father.

On Deming's itinerary, the tea party is billed as "a get-together with old friends." But of all the men who have come to see Deming, the one to whom Deming seems the most attached is Nishibori, a jovial, rail-thin man in his mid-eighties. Nishibori, who led Japan's first expedition to Antarctica in 1957, speaks better English and is more westernized than any of his colleagues at the gathering. He is solicitous of his American friend and shows an affection that far surpasses professional courtesy. Deming presses Nishibori to recall the circumstances of his visits to Japan in the 1940s and 1950s. And the Japanese obliges with flattering memories of the reception Deming received during his early travels to Japan. "I took [Deming] around to major plants in Tokyo, Nagoya, and Osaka," recalls Nishibori. "He was a very keen observer. He listened very carefully to ordinary workers as well as to managers. That quality impressed us very much."

But when one of the few American guests asks Nishibori why, of all the U.S. advisers who had come to Japan with the occupation forces, it was Deming whom they asked to return, Deming doesn't give Nishibori a chance to answer the question. "I was famous!" snaps the guru. "Even then I was famous."

Just as Tokyo's first great skyscrapers are becoming hard to distinguish amid the exploding skyline and whirring construction in neighborhoods like Shinjuku, Deming seems afraid that Japan's rapid progress will eventually obscure his own contributions to the country's revival. Deming is like a gifted father who is at once proud and fearful that his accomplishments are being eclipsed by those of a precocious son. And as he leans his large frame toward Nishibori, cocking his ear forward so he won't miss a word, Deming is listening only for the stories that will preserve the legacy of Demingism in Japan.[1]

Deming needn't worry. Demingism has helped reshape both the art of management in Japan and the standards of international competition. The Japanese undoubtedly deserve the bulk of the credit for recognizing the potential of the process-oriented approach to management advocated by Deming, for mustering the national dedication that was needed to implement the philosophy, and for continuing to improve on it. However, Deming's vision was a powerful influence in helping to transform what was, after World War II, still a relatively arcane scientific concept into a popular management movement. Also, the Japanese were particularly receptive to his message because of the unusual level of interest and respect he showed them at a time when their national self-esteem was at its lowest point in modern history.

With the possible exception of General Douglas MacArthur, Deming has been hailed as "the most famous and revered American in Japan in the postwar years."[2] There are several reasons for the exalted position that, over the years, Deming has come to command in Japan's postwar recovery. In sharp contrast to the somewhat condescending approach of many of the American advisers who went to Japan in the 1940s and 1950s, Deming shared with MacArthur a deep respect for the abilities of the Japanese, a dogged determination to help rebuild the country, and a keen curiosity about Japanese culture. For the vanquished Japanese, Deming's early lectures offered an optimistic vision of the role an economically strong Japan could play in world affairs. And Deming's openness and the sense of humility he was known for at the time—though no longer—were deeply appreciated by the Japanese and enabled Deming to make Japanese friends relatively easily.

Equally important, his work and the relationships he developed in the country during the late 1940s would help Deming win two unique honors that would serve to immortalize his name in Japan. In 1951 the engineers and industrialists who had formed the Union of Japanese Scientists and Engineers (JUSE) created a quality award they dubbed the Deming Prize. Deming had been to Japan twice before, first before the award was created, to work on a national census, and later, at JUSE's invitation, to give a series of lectures on quality improvement. The award was created when Deming returned to Japan for a second time at JUSE's invitation but refused to accept royalties on a book the organization had compiled from his lecture notes of a year earlier. To show their appreciation for both his work and his generosity, the leaders of JUSE used the money to establish the quality award.[3] With a canny talent for promotion, JUSE helped parlay the Deming competition into a national event that has played a crucial role in shaping Japan's management agenda and in developing what has come to be known as total quality control (TQC). The TQC movement institutionalized the use of statistical analysis to control variation and to bring about improvement throughout virtually every sector of Japanese industry, and in every management discipline. It also made "continuous improvement" the rallying cry throughout Japan. Sought after by Japan's leading companies, the award for corporate excellence has come to be as prestigious in Japan as the Nobel Prize is in the West. And in 1960, in final recognition of the enormous impact that both Deming and the prize had had on Japanese industry, Deming received the honor of being one of the first Americans to receive the Second Class Sacred Treasure, a medal bestowed on Deming by Emperor Hirohito.[4]*

* * *

* It is noteworthy that Dr. Joseph Juran, who also visited Japan in the 1950s and also is given extensive credit for helping to shape the country's approach to quality management, did not receive that award until 1981.[5]

Deming was first summoned to Japan in 1947, just two years after the Japanese surrender, by the administration of General Douglas MacArthur, the Supreme Commander of the Allied Powers (SCAP), the occupying government of the country. Deming was asked to join a statistical mission that had been organized by MacArthur's administration. He was one of several U.S experts assigned to work with Japanese statisticians to develop the national census of 1951, which was intended, among other things, to help assess the level of devastation in the country after the war.[6] The survey would be used to measure such things as the amount of new housing that would need to be built in order to accommodate the vast population that had been left homeless as a result of World War II.

His first job in Japan was a natural extension of the work Deming had been doing throughout the 1930s and 1940s, when he had worked for the U.S. Census Bureau and organized statistical seminars to introduce the Washington community to the ideas of pioneering statisticians such as Shewhart. By the end of the war, Deming also had toured India and Egypt as part of a U.N. statistical mission, and had cemented his international reputation as a leading statistician.[7]

The nature of Deming's work on the Japanese census gave him a unique opportunity to travel around the country and to get to know Japan. While many of his American colleagues looked with disdain on their former enemies and kept to their American enclaves, Deming went wherever he could. He toured both the cities and the countryside and even sneaked off to the Kabuki theater, which at the time was off limits to Allied personnel.

In the late 1940s, there was little but wreckage left in the most populous parts of Japan. Yet Americans working with the occupying government could easily have overlooked it. "This is a pretty soft life and not at all what I expected in General MacArthur's chairborne army," wrote Deming in his first diary notations. "A good room and meals in a good hotel, a telephone in the room; good office; plenty of heat, snack bars at Army centres where I can get malted milks, ice cream etc." Deming was particularly relieved to find a six-story PX where he could buy cigarettes, chocolates, shoestring potatoes, ice cream, and Ritz crackers, and other rare delicacies he often bought in huge quantities for his Japanese friends.[8] A man who always had

an eye for pretty women, Deming found no lack of female compan-
ionship. Virginia Eyre, one of the Americans working with the occupation forces, became his regular dinner and Kabuki theater
companion. And in one diary notation he recalls a Miss Doris Carlton
who "belong[s] to a club which is holding a dance tonight and she
must snag a man, and in desperation invited me." Deming also was
fascinated by the war crimes trials and frequently went there during
his spare afternoon hours.[9]

Deming, however, was just as interested in life far removed from
the American enclaves. His travels around Japan offered him an
introduction to people trying to survive inside abandoned ware-
houses and under bridges; they left a lasting impression. He traveled
frequently through some of the most desolate parts of Japan. He first
learned just how desperate the lives of many Japanese were on a visit
to Nagoya, an industrial city between Tokyo and Osaka that had
been almost entirely demolished during the war. Over drinks at a
hotel bar one evening, he and Margaret Stone, a colleague from
SCAP with whom he was traveling, met a Captain Aldon, one of the
U.S. officials stationed in Nagoya. Aldon offered Deming and Stone
a unique glimpse of the city, a midnight tour of the railroad yards,
where dozens of homeless people regularly bedded down after dark,
stretched out on rice mats on the floor. Near the train station, the
Americans stopped at a warehouse where, on this occasion, five
people had sought shelter. Among them were an old man and a little
boy "both in rags, huddled around a charcoal burner, scarcely a
spark left. . . . The captain decided to take [the boy] along to a
screening centre not far away. . . . The captain gave the little boy
some gum, and I would have given a dollar for a chocolate bar for
him," Deming recalled.[10]

Deming was confronted with the same destitution on his return to
Tokyo. "Crossing a bridge over one of the numerous canals, I spied
a man, little boy and girl, all in tatters. The little boy was sobbing on
his daddy's knees. The little girl just sitting; looked at me with her
big Japanese eyes. . . . Homeless, no doubt, and hungry: probably
much else wrong also, but not much else counts. What could I do?
They were not begging: I had seen only two beggars in Japan—most
remarkable testimony to these people. I went back and gave him a
package of cigarettes: He could barter them for food. But would he?

I went to my office. A thought came to me: I'll go to the Ernie Pyle snack bar and purchase some doughnuts to take to them. So I did—two dozen. It was nearly dark now and blowing chilly. I gave them the doughnuts."

Deming, who as a small child had endured what was often a hand-to-mouth existence, respected both the pride with which the Japanese bore their misfortunes and their dogged determination to overcome harsh circumstances. "Practically all of the area of heavy industry between Tokyo and Yokohama and in every big city is a complete blank, some concrete and twisted steel left, [yet] new wooden homes are springing up like mushrooms everywhere over the seared areas," he wrote in his diary. "The debris is practically all cleared away; what isn't being built on is in winter wheat or garden." In 1988, a few months before his annual trip to Japan, Deming recalled, "The [Japanese] people were hopeful, happy, clean, they looked forward to another day, though they were hungry. Nothing impressed me so much as the striking contrast between the happiness of the Japanese and their devastation."[11]

Their progress and dedication would lead Deming, during a subsequent trip in 1950, to predict that "Japanese [manufacturing] quality would capture markets the world over by 1955." At that time, Deming also wrote Kenichi Koyanagi, who was managing director of JUSE, "Let us hope and pray that 1950 may mark the rebirth of Japanese industry, and much wealth and happiness for Japan! Be assured that I shall always be ready to do anything possible for you."[12] And the Japanese, with their battered national psyche, would soon have an opportunity to show their appreciation for his respect and faith.

While individual Japanese were trying to reconstruct their homes and lives out of rubble, Japanese engineers and businessmen, with the encouragement of MacArthur's administration, were determined to revive their country's industry. Quality improvement would come to be viewed by the Japanese as nothing less than a matter of survival. In losing World War II, Japan had lost its colonies in Manchuria, Taiwan, and Korea and thus the natural resources on which its economy had come to rely. What's more, while Japan had focused on building a strong defense industry ever since the Meiji Restoration, the country was lacking the sort of consumer products expertise it would need in order to launch an export drive. Experts point out that while most budding capitalist economies start out with the production of consumer goods, Japan focused instead on developing a strong defense industry.[13] As a result, the production of Japanese consumer products was "compelled to remain at a primitive stage technically."[14]

Luckily for Japan, both the personal mission of MacArthur and the political interests of the U.S. government converged to foster the creation of a prosperous Japan. Although the U.S. allies were clamoring for reparations, MacArthur fought from the beginning to save the island nation from having to make onerous payments. Moreover, by 1947 the threat of communism in Asia would mark a turning point in conflicting American perceptions of the occupation. While many in the United States still hungered for retribution, such urges were overcome by the single-minded Yankee determination to make Japan a bulwark of free enterprise against the threat of socialism.[15]

Soon the United States was actively engaged in making Japan safe for capitalism. Japanese industry was enlisted by MacArthur to build materiel for the U.S. Army fighting in Korea. And while MacArthur favored the dissolution of the monopolies, known as *zaibatsu*, they were never fully dismantled, in part because the United States needed a strong Japanese industrial base to help supply the Korean war effort. Japan was also saved from its radical labor movement— while MacArthur had at one time encouraged the formation of unions, during the struggle against communism in the 1950s, organized labor was purged of its radical elements and coopted by management.[16]

MacArthur set out to endow Japan's civilian industries with some of the same capabilities the U.S. armed forces had come to expect of the country's military production. During the war, the general himself had noted the quality of such weapons as the Arisaka rifle and the Nambu light machine gun, a modified version of France's deadly Hotchkiss weapon. And former U.S. General Robert Eichelberger once remarked that "the Japanese Zero [fighter planes] were superior in maneuverability [to U.S. fighter planes] and that the Japanese pilots of that time were well trained and highly skilled."[17] Before the war Japanese industry had even begun to experiment with statistical techniques. But these early quality control efforts derailed with the start of the war. "The prevailing policy was one [vacuum] tube today rather than ten tubes tomorrow," says Koji Kobayashi, who would become chief executive officer of NEC Corporation.[18]

After the war, the communications industry once again became the focus of major improvement efforts. Even before MacArthur landed in Japan, he issued a directive that during the occupation, a radio receiver was to be placed in every second household to enable communication within Japan; he soon found out that the country lacked the facilities to build even a fraction of the radios that would be needed for such a project. MacArthur, however, couldn't have anticipated that by the late 1950s, radio talk shows would be one of the principal ways Japan's burgeoning quality movement would communicate the new methods of statistical quality improvement to factory foremen around the country.

In the late 1940s, the Civil Communication Section (CCS) of SCAP sponsored a series of management lectures for members of the Japanese communications industry. Part of the lecture series included a segment on quality control, delivered by American experts including Homer Sarasohn, Charles Protzman, and Frank Polking-horn, most of whom had previously worked at Western Electric or Bell Laboratories.[19]

The CCS lectures were probably Japanese industry's first formal introduction to the principles of statistical quality control. The thirty-six-page lesson on quality, which was authored by Sarasohn, discussed many of the principles that are today accepted by leading practitioners as the key elements of quality management.* However, while the CCS lectures touched on many of the important principles of quality management, including the importance of receiving high-quality materials and the idea that high quality leads to lower costs, they had a few shortcomings.

---

* The course emphasized the importance of controlling variation as well as the correlation between improving production processes and building high-quality products. Sarasohn explained that the purpose of quality control was to "prevent rejects before they occur," rather than to weed out defective items by relying on inspection. He introduced the concept that improving the quality of products and processes ultimately reduces costs. He also pointed out the importance of getting high-quality materials from suppliers. In his concluding pages, Sarasohn even mentioned that the ultimate purpose of quality management is to bring manufacturing "closer and ever closer to an ideal state of quality control."[20]

Most significantly, Sarasohn's approach, in sharp contrast to what would become accepted practice at leading Japanese companies, emphasized the importance of inspection and cast inspectors as the gatekeepers of quality. "The selection of personnel for inspector's jobs is . . . an important one. The quality of the product and hence the reputation of the company rests very decidedly on the skill, judgement and honesty of these people."[21] Sarasohn's view of quality, with its emphasis on the establishment of a quality constabulary in the form of inspectors, became standard practice at leading U.S. companies—that is, before they embraced Deming's quality model in the early 1980s.

While the Japanese eagerly adopted many of the teachings of the CCS lectures, there was a widespread feeling that what was being taught by some of the visiting experts was far too technical for nonstatisticians to understand. NEC's Kobayashi, who at the time was the general manager of the Tamagawa plant, would say of his early exposure to U.S. theories of quality control, "I came to have some doubts about [quality control's] implementation . . . a few experts were discussing the theory of distribution and the theory of errors, which made quality control seem complicated. . . ." Kobayashi says he was later won over by Deming: "In 1950, I had the opportunity of meeting W. E. Deming. I frankly discussed my misgivings with Deming. . . . I could understand his explanation very well and I thought that we could easily implement it."[22]

With the approval of Sarasohn's department at CCS, JUSE invited Deming to Japan in 1950, in large part to help demystify the statistical concepts of quality management.* Among the early members of JUSE were Moriguti and Nishibori, who were already familiar with Deming's reputation as a statistician and probably had read Shewhart's *Statistical Method from the Viewpoint of Quality Control*, which had been edited by Deming. Although American science and management books were not widely available in Japanese, the

* JUSE was formed after the war. To ensure MacArthur's approval, the group's founders, knowing the general's fondness for labor unions, included the word "union" in JUSE's English title; however, in deference to several of its leading Japanese members, who objected to the labor movement, they left it out of the Japanese moniker.

knowledge-hungry Japanese made bootleg translations of many such works.

Deming's lectures promised a much-needed remedy for the country's pressing economic woes and became an overnight sensation. "There had been in Japan some sort of confusion and disorder in the application to industry of statistical quality control methods, which we hoped might be brought to a settlement by Dr. Deming's enlightenment," wrote Kenichi Koyanagi, managing director of JUSE, in an introduction to Deming's presentations in 1952. "With simple explanations and adequate demonstrations, Dr. Deming's lectures were so effective and persuasive that they left an unforgettable impression upon our minds."[23]

For the American's first series of addresses, JUSE scheduled over a dozen lectures from Tokyo to Kyushu. At his first engagement at Tokyo University, Deming was overwhelmed both by his reception and by the level of knowledge exhibited by those who came to hear him speak. More than five hundred people attended, including government officials, professors, and students. So many came, in fact, that the lecture had to be transferred to a larger auditorium. "There were six good questions. Probably 80 percent of the students understood me in English," recalls Deming. His subsequent lectures each attracted as many as six hundred people. Deming was gripped with a growing sense of elation: "Life continues to be interesting, and more so day after day. I never felt so important day after day."[24]

Deming's message, combined with his self-deprecating charm, made him the focus of widespread attention and admiration. In his diary entries, he gives some indication of the sense of the humility with which he received the honors that were being heaped on him. Describing one of the ceremonies in which he was given an honorary life membership in the Japan Statistical Association, Deming writes, "Dr. Ouchi explained that they were not worthy of so great an honor [as Deming afforded by his visit], that they were only children compared with the attainments of so great and distinguished a guest, but that they knew of the kindness of my heart. . . . I thereupon accepted, reversing the honors, and assuring them of my unworthiness, but desiring to work with them."[25] In a country where appearances are of paramount importance, Deming's manner and his generosity would win him a special place in the hearts of the Japanese, long after other Westerners began pouring into Japan to help with the country's postwar recovery.

In 1965 *The Mainichi Daily News*, a Tokyo newspaper devoted to commerce and industry, would print this ebullient report of Deming's contribution to the industrial resurgence of Japan: "Behind this success are the fatherly guidance and devotion of a leading American statistician, Dr. W. Edwards Deming, now professor of New York University. In the early postwar years, he opened the eyes of the Japanese manufacturers to the modern approach to the quality problem and taught them how to make their products attractive among world customers. . . . Dr. Deming has been an unequalled teacher and consultant to Japanese industry. He has worked together with thousands of Japanese corporate executives, engineers and scholars for the past 15 years. He set the guideline to bring prosperity to this island country burdened with scarce natural resources. What the U.S. scholar showed his Japanese students was the scientific way to turn out more products that have greater uniformity, dependability and marketability all over the world."[26]

Deming was embraced, however, for much more than his knack for making accessible what had heretofore seemed like engineering alchemy. He stressed the importance of viewing quality concepts as part of a holistic new management philosophy in which every member of the organization must play a part. Deming began his lectures with an all-encompassing vision of the role quality management would play in Japan's revival and with a sort of Calvinistic message of redemption. "We are in a new industrial age," said Deming. "International trade is an essential component of peace and prosperity . . . statistical techniques have brought new meaning into all these requirements of international trade."[27]

In contrast to Sarasohn, Deming downplayed the role of inspectors, shifting the burden of quality improvement to the men on the factory floor. Referring to the quality control chart, a sort of industrial EKG that helps both to determine whether a process is in a state of control and to pinpoint process improvements that might be made to improve it, Deming said, "The quality control chart is a very simple device. . . . It is so simple that a shop foreman can learn to use it in a few hours or days, he can and will immediately start to improve the quality and uniformity of his product."[28] Deming used golfing analogies, for example, instead of arcane statistical theory to make his points about variation, improvement, and control.

THE DEMING CYCLE: FOCUSING ON THE CUSTOMER

Most important, Deming recognized quality control as management's principal responsibility and as the organization's best means of identifying and anticipating the needs of customers. As he told the Japanese in his lectures during the early 1950s: "For the reliable and economical communication with the consumers and non-consumers of a product, it is necessary to carry out statistical tests and surveys. I shall now speak to you about this particular aspect of quality control, and I shall remind you that its main purpose is *re-design* of the quality of your product, and *adjustment* of the plant . . . *to meet rationally predicted changes in demand.*

"Consumer research is an integral part of production. As I said earlier, the terms 'good quality' and 'quality control' have no meaning except with reference to the consumer's needs. . . ."[29]

To link consumer research and product manufacturing, Deming introduced what has come to be known as the Deming cycle.[30] This cycle of continuous testing and improvement, Deming taught in his earliest Japanese lectures, inevitably leads to the redesign of the product on the basis of additional consumer research. "The main use of the consumer research is to feed consumer reactions back into the design of the product so that management can anticipate changing demands and requirements, and set economical production levels. Consumer research takes the pulse of the consumer's reactions and demands, and seeks explanations for the finding."[31] The analysis inherent in this "plan, do, check, act" continuum has been adapted by the Japanese to help monitor almost every process within a corporation.

In fact, it has become the basis for the Japanese strategic planning system known as policy deployment, which today forms the basis of TQC and is the way management goals at leading companies, such as Toyota, Kansai Electric Power Company, and Fuji-Xerox, are disseminated, executed, analyzed, and improved. "We developed our organizational system to practice the Deming Cycle," asserts

Zenzaburo Katayama, general manager of Toyota's TQC Promotion Division. "The cycle is operated in each functional area and each division of the company" as the basis for establishing corporate policies and strategies. "Japanese management philosophy was transformed by Dr. Deming's ideas," he adds.[32]

Florida Power & Light, which adopted both the Deming cycle and policy deployment from Kansai Electric, a Japanese utility, offers the clearest U.S. example of how the concept works to set strategic priorities, and to create a feedback mechanism to make sure everyone in the company stays on track:

Plan

At the corporate level, FP&L started out by conducting a series of market surveys and reformulating its definition of customer satisfaction; instead of being satisfied with what for decades had been a fairly good record of interruption-free electricity service, the company started to hone in on the needless inconveniences to which its customers were subjected when power outages did occur. Even infrequent interruptions, FP&L recognized, could infuriate customers if they lasted for hours. So the company began scrutinizing both the frequency and the duration of outages when they did happen and the reasons behind them.

At the division level, each unit was analyzed according to its performance vis-à-vis the new customer satisfaction criteria. As divisions pinpointed the principal reasons for their power outages, such as lightning storms and trees that got tangled in the electrical lines, they also began formulating plans for reducing those problems. Based on these plans and estimates of how long the improvements would take, the company established a five-year plan with annual targets for reducing the length and frequency of electricity outages.

Do

As the divisions identified improvement projects, such as making transmission lines less vulnerable to lightning, they assigned managers to come up with creative solutions.

Meanwhile, the rank and file were organized in work teams to identify how they could work on the power outage problem. Some solutions took the form of entirely new procedures for hooking up new homes to transformers.

Check

FP&L standardized a procedure to which all improvement projects are subjected. For instance, to make certain the work teams tackle fundamental problems rather than merely their symptoms, the teams have to present an analysis that identifies a root cause before they can set to work on a solution. They have to write up a cost-benefit analysis. They have to devise a procedure for making sure the problem doesn't recur in the future. And they lay out a timetable for completing the project.

At the work group level, improvement projects are assessed periodically throughout the year to see how well they are adhering to the standardized procedure described above. And once a year, management reviews the results of the work group projects to see which ones have come up with ideas that should be applied elsewhere in the company. For example, an experiment conducted by a team near Palm Beach served as a blueprint for connecting new houses to transformers without causing interruptions to neighboring homes (see Chapter 6).

At the division level, managers were subjected to monthly and bimonthly reviews to make sure they were on target in reaching their goals for reducing power outage levels.

At the corporate level, top executives were subjected to annual reviews conducted by outside experts from Japan, in which the progress of all divisions was assessed both individually and together to see how they were doing in achieving the overall corporate customer satisfaction targets.

Act

Based on the results of the monthly and annual reviews, middle managers and top executives revise the company's strategic plans and their targets to reflect unanticipated problems or unusually good performance.

But before strategic plans are changed, middle managers are given a chance to make suggestions and changes. When agreement is reached, the new plans are disseminated to the divisions, which in turn revise their own targets and strategies.

The rank and file forms new teams to tackle new improvement projects.

The cycle begins again.

JAPANESE-STYLE STRATEGIC PLANNING: POLICY DEPLOYMENT AND TOTAL QUALITY CONTROL

Driven by Deming's early teachings, TQC has become the raison d'être of Japanese corporations, and policy deployment provides the management structure for consistently bettering it. While in the early 1950s TQC referred primarily to the application of the Deming cycle to production problems on the plant floor, by the late 1970s it had come to mean the application of the cycle to virtually all the disciplines in a company.

This universal approach to integrating quality management into every facet of a company's operations began to develop in the 1960s. The term "total quality control" was originally coined by Armand V. Feigenbaum, a quality consultant and former manager of manufacturing operations and quality control at General Electric, who wrote a book by the same title in the 1950s.[33] But while Feigenbaum advocated the establishment of a special bureaucracy of quality engineers whose job it was to ensure quality control throughout a company, the Japanese insisted on maintaining a cooperative approach in which everybody was responsible for monitoring the processes with which they worked.[34] By adhering to this more collaborative approach to TQC, the philosophy and the techniques have become as rudimentary for Japanese employees—at every level of a corporation—as knowing a company's product line. It also leads to an active approach to quality that goes far beyond the common U.S. pursuit of "defect-free" products to a definition of quality that is ever-changing and an effort to constantly adapt designs, production, and marketing to the needs of customers.

Policy deployment is based on three elements: top management's philosophical commitment to the concept of continuous improvement, middle management's ability to standardize improvements throughout the organization once they have been arrived at, and the ability of the entire organization to innovate on the basis of those standards and improvements.[35] In other words, policy deployment is a way of coordinating numerous continuous improvement projects throughout a company to culminate in a major innovation that will take the organization and its products to new plateaus of excellence.[36] And the entire system is structured around the sort of rigorous management reviews that are part of the process of evaluating Deming Prize applicants. The reviews provide the checks and balances to ensure that a company keeps its eye firmly focused on process improvement long after it has won the Deming Prize.

Thus, in a typical year-end review at Fuji Xerox, a joint venture between Xerox and Fuji Film that has been practicing policy deployment since it won the Deming Prize in 1981, top management's focus isn't on earnings or revenues. Instead, President Yōtaro Kobayashi analyzes both his latest blockbuster color copier and the system that created it. The meeting focuses on information that has percolated up through the corporation throughout the year as teams of workers and managers analyze their products and processes, work on incremental improvements, and document the results in monthly reviews at the divisional and team level. For example, throughout the year, the sales staff transmits detailed computerized records of customer complaints and comments to the marketing department, and these are then compiled and analyzed to plan improvements for future product lines. (See Chapter 7. It is telling that not even U.S. Xerox has developed nearly so systematic an approach to incorporating customer feedback in its marketing and strategic planning process.) During the annual review, a final assessment is made of the company's products, positioning, and weaknesses. And it is in the annual review, and the preparation for it, that the company positions itself to make well-reasoned strategic leaps in the future. The president rallies various departments throughout the company, such as the heads of marketing, manufacturing, and R & D, to agree on both a new set of product improvements for the next generation of copiers and ways of improving the product development process (see Chapter 7).[37] Unlike the wishful thinking inherent in many such U.S. decisions, in a TQC company they are based on a detailed, documented assessment of the organization's capabilities and weaknesses. There is much less effort made to tell the boss what he wants to hear, because the boss views constant problem solving as everyone's job, including his own.

HOW JUSE INSTITUTIONALIZED TOTAL QUALITY CONTROL AND THE DEMING CYCLE

Over the years Deming's influence was cemented with the help of JUSE, frequent visits to Japan, the influence of the Deming Prize, and Deming's own relationship with Japanese CEOs. JUSE was instrumental, for example, in arranging a meeting between Deming and a group of top executives who would become the greatest champions of quality management. During Deming's visit in 1950, Ichiro Ishikawa, the first president of JUSE and the then chairman of Keidanren (the Japanese Federation of Economic Organizations), Japan's most powerful business group, threw a dinner for Deming and the twenty-one chiefs of Japan's leading industries at Tokyo's Industry Club.[38] Indeed, by taking on the presidency of JUSE, Ishikawa almost ensured the lasting importance of JUSE and, by association, of Deming. Ishikawa's presidency would establish a tradition whereby the head of JUSE was always the sitting or former chairman of Keidanren.[39]

With that meeting, Deming crossed Japan's Rubicon. "I talked to them for an hour. I think they were impressed because before the evening was over they asked me to meet with them again, and they talked about having a conference in the mountains around Hakone," Deming wrote afterwards in his diary. According to Ishikawa's son, Kaoru, the subsequent one-day conference that was held at a mountain retreat in Hakone was a key event in getting the presidents and top managers who attended to "realize the importance of quality control for their companies." Says Nishibori, "He told them that quality should be their top priority. That quality came before profit, because it was quality that creates profit. And he told them that only through long-range planning could they hope to build truly successful businesses."[40]*

---

* Today many Japanese give Joseph Juran much of the credit for elevating quality control to a management tool. In fact, the Hakone conference and the content of Deming's lectures indicate that Deming well appreciated the importance of management's role.

It is unlikely that Deming would have left such a lasting mark in Japan without this support from the executive suite. The Hakone meeting added a crucial spark to the movement, spreading it throughout the ranks of both management and workers and giving it a momentum that would last for decades. Forty-seven executives from such major companies as Kawasaki Steel and Hitachi attended the meeting.[41] And both the rapport Deming found with the executives at Hakone and the relationship he had developed with much lower-ranking Japanese were undoubtedly behind many of the honors he received. The emperor's medal and the creation of the Deming Prize, in particular, were instrumental in making Deming the principal icon of Japanese quality management.

To promote TQC, JUSE offered an entire curriculum of training programs in statistical theory, organized quality conferences for engineers and managers, issued several publications and journals, and acted as a conduit to leading experts in quality control. To reach workers and foremen who were scattered around the country, JUSE even produced radio programs. Kaoru Ishikawa, in his book *What Is Total Quality Control?*, writes about how JUSE overcame the logistical difficulties of educating factory employees in far-flung parts of Japan, who had inadequate means of transportation: "We solved that problem by utilizing the mass media, and began a QC correspondence course for foremen . . . through the Japan Shortwave Broadcasting Corp. In 1957 the Japan Broadcasting Corporation (NHK) agreed to broadcast our programs as part of its educational programming. The program was well received by the public, and the text sold 110,000 copies."[42]

Although there was some recognition of the role management would have to play in the improvement process as early as the 1950s, initially the efforts of both Deming and JUSE were focused on the factories. Bringing about improvement, they recognized, would require that workers and foremen themselves be able to use statistical methods to analyze production problems and to come up with ways of improving manufacturing processes. To help foster the study and understanding of statistical methods, JUSE took up the cause of worker participation in the form of study groups called quality circles.

Sponsored in part by JUSE, these informal, spontaneous sessions, which initially involved factory foremen, got started in the late 1950s and would develop as an important corollary to Japan's quality movement. They would succeed in "harnessing the energy, ingenuity, and enthusiasm of employees to solve company problems."[43] And while quality circles started in factories, they soon spread throughout other companies, even in the service sector. By the 1980s, Tokyo's white-gloved cab drivers, who are known for keeping their cabs spotless down to the headrests covered in white cotton doilies, had formed their own quality circles. Even the city's Esquire Club, a Japanese version of the Playboy Club, has followed the trend. Buxom waitresses in candy-colored bunny suits with cotton tail and ears, disposable lighters clutched in their cleavages, all participate. They discuss everything from finding better ways to serve the customer to improving the way they do their hair and apply makeup.[44]

Although Deming was not directly involved in creating the quality circle movement, it is a natural outgrowth of the cooperative management process he advocated from the time of his very earliest lectures, and that found easy acceptance in this society influenced by Confucian and Buddhist values. By the early 1960s, JUSE had a thousand of these groups registered in Japan. That number ballooned to two hundred thousands by 1984, with roughly ten members per quality circle.[45] Some of the earliest quality circles were convened by foremen who, in turn, encouraged the participation of workers. Eventually there were quality circles for almost every participant in an organization, including managers. While U.S. supervisors often feared worker participation would dilute their authority, Japanese foremen found their role was enhanced with the adoption of quality circles: In Japan, "less formal planning is done by the engineers and the top managers. Rather, a good deal of the planning is left to the production supervisors. Production supervisors therefore develop much broader responsibilities than in the United States."[46]

This is in sharp contrast to U.S. efforts to adopt quality circles, which began as early as the 1970s. Basil Deming (no relation), manager of human resources in the communication division of Allied Signal Aerospace (formerly Bendix Corporation), remembers a typical American scenario about his company's halfhearted efforts to establish quality circles during the early and mid-1980s. "They were tied here and there in several divisions," he recalls. "But they just died on the vine because there was no strong leadership to support them and to create an environment that would encourage them to grow."[47]

While the formation of formalized work teams gradually began to catch on in the United States during the late 1980s, the early experiences with quality circles largely discredited the creation of the more informal groups. "These days executives are embarrassed to even talk about quality circles," says Tai Oh, a professor of management at California State University, who estimates that more than 70 percent of quality circles in the United States have failed.[48]

Deming would play an important role in redefining the relationship between labor and management in U.S. industry. Larry Sullivan, who headed Ford's supplier quality assurance groups and attended Deming's initial meetings with Ford executives in the early 1980s, remembers how Deming captured the imagination of American workers during a factory visit in 1983, while nearly alienating their managers. Sullivan was assigned to escort Deming on a tour of a Ford supplier plant that is owned by United Technologies Corporation and makes electromechanical parts. On the morning in question, a foggy day in November 1983, Sullivan and Deming met John Bruce, then president of UTC's automotive products division at the Detroit airport for the flight to Zanesville, Ohio, where the plant was located. Deming, who had spent the 1930s and 1940s globe-hopping in Constellation propeller planes, took one look at the "little bitty" twin-engine Cessna Citation that was to fly them to Zanesville and refused to board the plane. Sullivan and Bruce succeeded in coaxing the guru onto the Cessna, but by the time they got over Zanesville the visibility was so bad they couldn't land. The plane circled the area for a while and was finally forced to return to Detroit. "Deming got in a real bad mood," recalls Sullivan. "He lectured all the way back, a stinging lecture. He was asking the president some questions, and the answers he was getting weren't right. He began to bore in, and bore in. [Finally] he told Bruce he didn't understand what his job is, that he didn't understand quality. [Bruce] was so embarrassed he just stopped talking."

Despite that experience, both Bruce and Deming agreed to reschedule the trip a few weeks later. This time the flight went without a hitch. But as soon as they got to the plant, Sullivan was certain he was going to witness a repeat of the prickly exchange that had taken place on the earlier, aborted flight. "We went into the executive conference room where the plant had arranged to have all the [managers] meet," recalls Sullivan. "They thought they were going to listen to a seminar. But Deming started by saying, 'I don't want to talk to you, you don't understand quality, it's a waste of time. I want a meeting with your hourly workers.' "

The plant manager balked at first but finally agreed to shut down one of the lines. "Deming took the workers into the lunchroom," Sullivan recalls. He made the executives sit in a row in the back. Then he astutely questioned the workers about the process of building such things as switches for ignitions, headlights, windshields, and miniature relays. Deming asked about their jobs, their work, the production quotas they had to meet, whether they had had any training in statistics, how many defects they found on the line, how much help they got from management, and what management did to help improve process capability on the lines.

"It was one of the most constructive exchanges I've ever heard from Dr. Deming," recalls Sullivan, who notes the respect and consideration with which the guru treated the workers. "It was a wonderful experience. The reason he did that was as a learning experience for the executives. He identified some of the frailties in how the workers were trained and managed that all led right back to management."[49]

Thirty years earlier, the credo of cooperation that blossomed in Japan with the growth of voluntary work groups was invaluable in bridging the divide between management and labor and in getting the two groups to work together on improving Japanese production. Indeed, one of the most fascinating conundrums of the Japanese quality movement is how the country made the transition to relatively benevolent labor relations, given a rich history of autocracy and repression and a militant labor movement following World War II. Many management experts have plenty of problems with the modern Japanese workplace, including the long and intense working hours and discrimination against women. Yet today's Japanese company is a model of enlightenment compared with its prewar predecessors.

From the time of the Meiji Restoration in the nineteenth century, Japanese business culture was little more than an industrial feudal system. "Beneath Confucian homilies of harmony [lay] . . . a fundamental opposition of class interests."[50] Until the late nineteenth century, Japan was largely an agrarian, feudal society. At the turn of the century, only 1 percent of the population worked in factories. Workers were housed in hovels on factory grounds and were little more than serfs. Often these laborers weren't permitted to leave for months. And to make sure no one tried to escape, guards were employed to patrol the grounds. It was common for workers, a majority of whom were women, to work fifteen- to sixteen-hour days. In 1897 a survey by the Cotton Spinners Association showed that 87 percent of the women working in that industry were "sick or suffering from injuries."[51]

The extraordinary transformation from an oppressively autocratic industrial state to a more cooperative and meritorious corporate Japan came from both the catharsis of World War II and the management philosophy Japan adopted. "Simply staying in business required unending progress," writes Masaaki Imai in *Kaizen*, which means "continuous improvement" in Japanese.[52]

Japan's defeat was a great equalizer that leveled many of the country's personal fortunes and would help rewrite the rules of the workplace. It also created a bunker mentality that rallied all Japanese around a common commitment to industrial revival. Some Japanese argue that while the *zaibatsu* had not been entirely dismantled, the elite leaders of many of Japan's largest companies had been removed from their posts and replaced by lower-level, more middle-class executives, which helped prompt a change in culture.[53] And, writes Kenneth Hopper, an advocate of Japanese-style quality management since the 1950s, "The Americans probably made their greatest contribution to Japan's very effective new management, when following the purges of top executives who had associations with the war-time regime, *they chose replacements from the ranks of operating managers*."[54] After purging the labor movement of its radical elements, the country's quality crusade was instrumental in convincing Japanese managers to get their workers to join them in the improvement process.

The new management movement Deming helped create and the

new cadre of managers, as well as the way democracy in both government and the workplace was championed by MacArthur, were all instrumental in reinventing the Japanese corporation. It is worth noting that Japan's postwar transformation had a precedent in the revolution of the Meiji era, when "Japan had to create in a generation what other nations had spent centuries to develop."[55]

However, neither the culture of cooperation that rose out of the ashes of war nor the spread of statistical theory begins to explain the all-encompassing nature of Japan's quality renaissance. These ideas were given shape and momentum by the concrete requirements of TQC and the Deming Prize, which have become as much a rite of passage for businesses in Japan as is the pursuit of an M.B.A. for business students in the United States.

THE DEMING PRIZE

Winning the Deming Prize by mastering TQC has been an obsession, at one time or another, of the biggest names in Japanese quality and product innovation and, indeed, is an integral part of the country's intellectual life. There are five versions of the Deming Prize. The company prizes are awarded to a large corporation, a division, a factory, or a small company. Major corporations often demand that their suppliers pursue the prize as well. Toyota, for example, one of the most prolific winners of quality awards in Japan, saw to it that eleven of its major suppliers had won the award by the late 1980s. Junji Noguchi, the director of JUSE, who rates Toyota among the best of the TQC practitioners, says that almost every year a Toyota-affiliated supplier wins the Deming award.

In what reads like a *Who's Who* of Japanese companies that have dealt serious blows to U.S. industry, more than a hundred company prizes were awarded between 1951 and 1985. Winners include Toyota, construction equipment maker Komatsu, copier manufacturer Ricoh, the diversified Toshiba Corporation, tire manufacturer Bridgestone, and Matsushita Electric Industries Company. Not surprisingly, these same companies have beat out, bought out, or completely devastated a slew of U.S. competitors—including GM, Firestone, and General Electric's erstwhile consumer products business. For the truly ambitious, there is also the Japan Quality Control Medal, established in 1969 as a sequel to the Deming Prize, for which companies can compete five years after they have won the Deming Prize. As of the late 1980s fewer than a dozen companies had won this prize, including Toyota, Komatsu, and Nippon Steel Corporation. Executives and academics are also candidates for the individual Deming Prize, awarded for outstanding work in furthering statistical theory. And several of the individual prizewinners have included managers who are, or would go on to become, chief executives, including Shoichiro Toyoda, the president of Toyota, and NEC's Kobayashi.[56]

Indeed, Japanese companies have made the Deming Prize a moving target. It was Toyota and Bridgestone, which won the Deming Prize in the 1960s, that invented policy deployment, thereby raising the stakes of the award dramatically. While early contestants had been able to win the prize by showing their agility at improving the production process and preventing snafus on the factory floor, that was no longer enough. Now companies would have to demonstrate their mastery of the process across divisional lines and prove their agility and adaptability in meeting new customer demands and market conditions.

The emphasis on education, self-improvement, and cooperation, which are key to TQC, is buttressed by the corporate educational system at the larger Japanese companies. The typical Japanese employee who arrives on the job with a degree from a technical high school begins work with a year of full-time schooling, not on-the-job training. The new recruits, who often live in company dormitories during their induction, are given lessons in the company's history, its product lines, and—most important—statistical process control. If the employee does not have a technical degree, the education process can last three years![57]

With so much clout behind the prize, it's small wonder the ideas behind it have worked their way into everyday life. By the 1980s, statistical theory had become part of the basic curriculum in Japanese high schools. And most bookstores today feature a TQC section devoted exclusively to books on quality.

In a culture of group competition such as Japan's, much of the appeal of the Deming Prize lies in the challenge of the race itself.

Indeed, the prize is so difficult to win that one executive has likened the competition to "the trials of Abraham." Most corporate contestants spend three to five years honing their operations in preparation for the competition, which involves everyone in the corporation, from workers to top management. With that kind of effort, once a Japanese company declares itself a candidate for the competition, it can't afford to lose. Seiko, the watchmaker, is one of the few companies known to have lost during the early years of the prize, and the company never reapplied. Indeed, once an applicant has lost, experts say, it never dares try again.[58] Pride does not allow it. In addition, with each succeeding year the standards for winning have become more difficult.

To help companies win the prize, JUSE established a network of counselors or *sensei*, who review the operations of candidates and pass judgment on their performance. Men like Professor Tetsuichi Asaka, the *éminence grise* of the Deming Prize consultants, are able to strike fear in the hearts of the highest-level managers because of the influence and respect they command. The manager of a company aspiring to the Deming Prize is typically grilled for hours every few weeks by Asaka or one of his academic associates on the progress of his division and his understanding of its shortcomings. He may be cross-examined on everything from material quality to his dealings with suppliers to the specific quirks of particular types of machinery. But the standards of Asaka, a former major in the Japanese army who is today a professor emeritus at Tokyo University, are so tough that a passing grade from him is considered a guarantee for passing muster with the judges, who award the prize on the basis of a two-week-long quality audit.[59]

There is a variety of reasons for entering the competition. According to a 1980 report by Ishikawa, the competition for the prize makes a company able to compete in international markets and to weather economic downturns. Ricoh, the copier maker that won the prize in 1975, said it wanted to "make [the] company recession-proof." Echoing that approach, Takenaka Komuten, a construction company that won the prize in 1979, said its goal was to "improve the corporate health and character of [the] company, to upgrade [the] quality of [its] products, and to raise [the] profit picture."[60]

Competitiveness was certainly the reason why Texas Instruments

Japan, a wholly owned Japanese subsidiary of Texas Instruments, decided to go for the prize. Before TIJ entered the Deming competition, the company was riddled with production problems. Various company departments squabbled about their difficulties and tossed responsibility for them back and forth, like a hot potato. Sachiaki Nagae, who was manager of TIJ's Hiji plant in 1980 when the company began focusing on TQC as a way to cope with customer complaints, recalls, "We were the technology leader. But from the mid-1970s, we began to realize that we were not the quality leader. Quality problems were stopping us from penetrating the market further. We had a lot of visual defects in our chips, things like bent leads, cracks in some packages, and even some products that were improperly labeled."

The solution, TIJ discovered, involved improving both worker training and the level of consistency and accuracy in chip production procedures. "We noticed that different workers using the same equipment had different quality levels," says Nagae. "You might think that's a personnel problem, but it isn't. It's a job standards problem. In other words, we hadn't done a precise enough job describing the task to be performed. . . . The description of any job standard must be precise enough and understandable enough so that anyone, even a newcomer, can perform the task perfectly." Nagae and his colleagues rewrote the job standards and made adjustments to the machinery to make sure the speed and sequence of the operations matched the job standard description. In so doing, TIJ virtually eliminated the need for visual inspection, cutting production costs by close to 50 percent and boosting worker productivity by close to 30 percent between 1980 and 1984. The Hiji plant would go on to win the Deming Prize in 1985. And the company continued to nurture its TQC program, so that by 1986 there were two hundred quality circles at TIJ.[61]

By the late 1980s, the Deming Prize competition began to come under fire by some Japanese who viewed its do-or-die approach to both competition and TQC as a distortion, and sometimes even as a liability. Kenichi Ohmae, managing director of McKinsey & Company in Japan and a leading expert on U.S.-Japan business practices, is one of many management experts who liken the Deming Prize to a cult, and who contend that many companies who have won the prize "are suffering an overdose of the dogma."

The formalism of policy deployment and TQC can, in some extreme instances, foil innovation. By the late 1980s, a management heretic at Toyota, which has won more quality prizes than any other company in Japan, would say that conventional TQC is too inflexible to be applied effectively to the creative, often spontaneous business aspects of marketing, such as developing advertising campaigns and wooing clients. Ironically, these complaints were made just months before Toyota's introduction of the Lexus, its first major bid for a stake in the luxury segment of the U.S. auto market. Nor have such warnings prevented the marketing mavens at Procter & Gamble from encouraging the use of TQC not only within its own operations but also at its army of advertising agencies.[62]

Fuji Xerox managers also complained of the limitations of TQC. Some Fuji Xerox managers were hinting that the rigid way in which TQC requires that every management move be justified with data may have inhibited laboratory creativity and impeded basic research. Japanese quality control "has become too regimented and formalistic," says Yōtaro Kobayashi, who is experimenting with a number of changes, including augmenting the structured management reviews with less threatening informal ones.[63]

Some executives contend that even competing for the Deming Prize can sometimes be counterproductive. For example, Shimizu Construction, which won the Deming Prize in 1983, spent so much time and effort chasing the prize that that same year its financial results showed a clear drop from the year before. "The fervor shown by proponents of total quality control is exactly like that seen in adherents of some religious cult," says one company executive.[64]

The human toll also can be high. Some companies go so far as to gather their middle management at the foot of Mt. Fuji for a kind of hazing session, subjecting the group to seven days of marathon discussions that last from 5 A.M. to 10 P.M., during which each participant admits he has been neglecting his work. Sachiaki Nagae of TIJ says that for the last year before going for the Deming Prize he and his managers went without vacations and routinely worked seven days a week. Another TIJ "salaryman" says he started drinking more after the company decided to compete for the Deming Prize. "You have to in order to patch yourself up after the criticism of your coworkers," he says. At another company, a manager reportedly collapsed in front of a subway train after spending several all-nighters in his company's final push for the prize. Reports of suicide also abound. At one machinery maker, for example, three employees committed suicide during the first year after TQC was introduced.[65]

More than anything else, many Japanese have come to resent the way the Deming Prize serves as a constant reminder that the seeds of TQC were made in the USA, not in Japan. It doesn't help that Deming has come to bask conspicuously in his celebrity as the founder of Japanese TQC. Kaoru Ishikawa, for example, who was Japan's most respected authority on quality management until his death shortly after Deming's 1988 visit, kept what was said to be a deliberate distance from Deming. In an introduction to the Japanese edition of a book on Deming, Ishikawa noted that Deming had borrowed many of the ideas for his Fourteen Points from Japanese TQC and Joseph Juran. The qualification doesn't appear in the English translation. Not even Junji Noguchi can resist a little criticism, recalling that during a lecture trip to Hiroshima in the early 1980s, Deming referred in the title of his talk to the "twenty-three new principles" of quality control. "Everyone was disappointed because there was nothing new," remarks Noguchi.[66]

Over the years, the issues of national pride and the exacting requirements of the competition, as well as the intense publicity that goes with it, have sometimes dissuaded Japanese companies from competing for the Deming Prize at all. Canon, for example, is one company that decided against entering the competition because its founder, Takeshi Mitarai, feared that pursuing the prize would rob his organization of its flexibility. He pulled the camera and copier maker out of the 1962 competition and authored his own quality guidelines instead.[67]

While many companies relish the enormous publicity that goes with winning an award, Honda wasn't interested in that kind of attention. Because rivals Toyota and Nissan had captured the Deming Prize in the 1960s, some TQC experts believe that Honda feared it would look like a latecomer if it pursued the prize in the 1980s (Honda didn't even begin building automobiles until the 1960s). In fact, says Noguchi, "Everyone assumes Honda already has won the award." Japan's third largest automaker, known for such maverick management practices as modifying a seniority system considered virtually inviolable at most other Japanese companies, insists that its principal reason for avoiding the Deming Prize was that, like Canon, it wanted to avoid the regimentation required by the judges.[68]

Other potential contenders have balked at Deming Prize demands to bare their ledgers, and sometimes their trade secrets, to judges and coaches. The requirement reportedly was sufficient to scare off the Japanese subsidiary of IBM. Not having the prize, however, hasn't tarnished the reputation of IBM, which, among young Japanese, is still considered one of the most desirable places to work.[69]

Despite its excesses, the Deming Prize has been an unquestionable boon to Japanese industry. So much so that by the late 1980s, Western companies, including several in the United States, began testing the waters of the Deming Prize competition. In 1988 JUSE offered its first seminar in English, introducing foreign managers from companies such as Volvo, Rolls-Royce, Dow Chemical, and Xerox to the basics of TQC. The week-long seminar featured such Japanese quality veterans as Ishikawa and a slew of other professors and consultants, as well as a lecture by Deming. One of the lesser-known JUSE consultants was Ichiro Miyauchi, a former engineer with Ishikawajima-Harima Heavy Industries, a maker of ships and heavy machinery, whose excellent English and good humor made him one of JUSE's first consultants to specialize in counseling overseas companies. Miyauchi has begun working with several foreign firms, including Weyerhaeuser and a company in Colombia.[70]

In 1987 the U.S. Congress established the Malcolm Baldrige National Quality Awards, modeled after the Deming Prize but named after the first secretary of commerce in the Reagan administration. While Ernest Ambler, director of the National Institute of Standards and Technology (NIST), which runs the contest, contends, "The standards set for this award are the highest, on a par with Japan's Deming award," the facts speak otherwise.[71] For one thing, few leading quality experts in the United States have any real experience with policy deployment, which today provides the fundamental management structure for TQC. Moreover, the corporate consciousness that helped raise the standards of the Deming award in Japan simply doesn't yet exist in the United States. Although the NIST solicited applications from ten thousand companies, the request was answered by only sixty-six. However, by awarding only three out of a possible six awards, the committee began to establish its credibility as both a catalyst and critic of U.S. quality management.

Just as President Reagan was getting ready to bestow the Baldrige Awards on the first winners, another U.S. company was marking another milestone on the rocky road to U.S. quality management. Florida Power & Light, the sunshine state's largest utility, became the first U.S. company to announce its candidacy for the Deming Prize (see Chapter 6). For FP&L, the contest marked the culmination of a quality management effort that began in the early 1980s and that led the company to immerse itself in Japan's quality ethic more than perhaps any other U.S. company. Regiments of U.S. managers, including everyone from the Coors brewing family and the top guns at Xerox to the leaders of Procter & Gamble and Alcoa, have been flocking to FP&L's Miami offices. And the utility's efforts are seen as a crucial test of whether quality management ideas that had their roots in the United States, and came to full bloom in Japan, can be repatriated.

NASHUA CORPORATION: THE MOUSE THAT ROARED

For the Ford Motor Company, no event was more "significant" in its adoption of Deming's philosophy of quality management than a trip several executives made to Nashua, New Hampshire, on May 15, 1981. Three months after Deming's first major presentation to the auto company, a dozen Ford men, including Bill Scollard, who would soon become the head of manufacturing, took a corporate jet to this former mill town at the foot of the White Mountains. They came in search of a real lathe-and-wrench example of the guru's philosophy at work. They did not go home disappointed.[1]

The Ford men spent that spring day at the Nashua Corporation, which in the 1980s was making office and computer products and had become the first U.S. company to adopt Deming's quality management principles. Nashua's quality strategy had become a near obsession for William E. Conway, at the time the company's chief executive officer. Just two years after Deming first came to Nashua, Conway would be able to boast an organization in which workers and managers understood the implications of variation, in which employees at all levels of the company were trained to improve their own processes, and in which continuous improvement had become the principal goal of the organization. Moreover, during the same period, the company, which had started out making bread wrappers and playing cards at the turn of the century, would win market share wars in several of its product lines, including mail order photofinishing and computer memory disks.

In the words of Larry Sullivan, who was part of the visiting Ford team, "the bomb dropped" almost as soon as Conway began talking about his own transformation.[2] The CEO began his story by explaining the competitive circumstances that had led Nashua to turn to Deming, and then focused on the main themes of Deming's philosophy. He hammered away at the idea that management, not workers, controls business processes and that it must therefore take the initiative in improving quality and productivity. And he insisted that working better with the statistician's arsenal of tools that chart the variation in processes was the *only* way to improve business systems on a constant basis. Conversely, he insisted that the behavioral approaches to improving worker productivity, which had become the rage in the 1970s, would be of little use at all in solving systemic problems.[3]

Nashua had been making carbonless paper for the U.S. market for years, Conway explained. But when the company began exporting to Europe, it discovered that what was perfectly satisfactory in the United States wasn't good enough overseas. Quickly the Japanese began moving in on Nashua's European market. What was most galling to Conway about this encroachment were the obstacles the Japanese had had to overcome in order to produce a competitive product at all. For one thing, the Japanese had to purchase their paper pulp in the United States and ship it back to Japan for processing. Then, for shipments going to Europe, the Samurai paper mills shipped their stock across the Sea of Japan to Vladivostok, where it was loaded onto railcars for the 10,000-mile journey on the Trans-Siberian railroad to Leningrad, from whence it was distributed to Europe. "In three or four years they took twenty-five percent of the premium market," said Conway. "And here we are a hundred and fifty miles from the trees in Maine, and by the time we'd taken the paper and coated it, we couldn't be competitive in either cost or quality."[4]

As the CEO was trying to resolve his problems on the Continent, Conway told his visitors, he recalled a peculiar experience that several Nashua executives had had during a trip to Japan to visit the headquarters of Ricoh Corporation, which was just getting ready to market copiers in the United States and which had agreed to let Nashua distribute its machines outside the United States. "Our vice president of research and development, Austin Davis, came back in August or September of 1974," Conway told his visitors from Ford. "I said 'How'd the meeting go?' "

" 'Well, it was a funny meeting, Bill,' he told me. 'We got there on Wednesday, but no one would talk to us. Thursday morning we got a phone call. The Ricoh executives couldn't meet on Thursday either because they were working on the Deming award.' " Finally, on Friday night, another call informed the men from Nashua that they could meet for several hours starting at 10:00 P.M. There would be no meeting on Saturday. But another one would be scheduled on Sunday afternoon for five or six hours. Each time the excuse was the same: "It's the Deming award."

"We didn't know anything about this Deming, and I didn't know one statistic from another," Conway recalled. In fact, he forgot about both until Ricoh's photocopy machines began to arrive. "In about 'seventy-five we started to get the machines, and they turned out to be the greatest copy machines, they were a tremendous success story, [came to be] known as the most reliable copy machines in the world." They were, in fact, the first reliable low-cost desktop copiers built at the time.[5]

"Meantime, I went to Japan in 'seventy-eight and went through the Ricoh plant, [and saw that] everything just worked right all the time. I didn't know enough about making copy machines, other than I was seeing something significant. [Then I] went through their plant out in California and saw how few people they had there [in the plant], just turning out a couple thousand machines each month on one shift like it was nothing. . . . I got an appreciation of the level at which they were operating."

So in February 1979, Conway held a meeting with his staff to talk about the company's quality and marketing problems; they talked about the Japanese and the Deming award. And they agreed to call Deming. "The call went out on a Tuesday and Deming came on Friday, March 10, 1979," Conway says, pausing for emphasis. "Deming and I spent about four or five hours in my office. He basically told us about the technical tools we'd need and about statistics. We told him about our needs.

"And then he made a very strong point. And I can't make this strong enough to you fellows," Conway said to the Ford executives. "The only way it would work [Deming told me] is if I supported it personally, if I used statistics myself, if I met with the people, got into the program, pushed and sold it every way possible. I agreed to do that, and he agreed to work with us. It won't fly if someone wants to do it down below, without the strong support of top management, it wouldn't happen. That's what Deming told us. At the time I didn't realize how important it was. Soon I saw that it was absolutely crucial.

"At the time, of course, I hadn't had statistics in school. I'd seen a few bell-shaped curves in my life, but that was the extent of it. I took it on faith. It just made sense, what he said. And I've acted accordingly ever since."

Conway impressed upon his guests the importance of distinguishing between what he called "feel good" behavioral approaches to improving worker productivity and a no-nonsense determination to enlist the entire organization in a campaign of variation control. The latter, he pointed out, was infinitely more useful and rewarding for everyone concerned. "See, you can break the whole world down into two groups. You take all these things called attitude and psychology, on the one hand. And then there's statistics. Attitude and psychology cover all the things you hear about General Motors' quality of work life, incentive programs, treat the people nice, make 'em feel good, have the foreman be interested in the people. All the other things you read about, you take 'em and drop 'em in a great big pile. If you want to get where you want to get, separate that pile entirely from the technical tools of statistics.

"Get in your mind, right from the first, that the whole program is based on one simple theory, that is, you're going to help people.

"No more bats and sticks, you're not just going to beat them over the head when they do something you don't like. You're not going to just get them to achieve things through cooperation and by getting people to feel good about things. Certainly I'm not trying to downgrade at all the whole thought of improving relations with the people who work for you. These are all things you want. But don't get that confused with the technical things you need to do with the job."

To drive home the point, he used a simple allegory to show how management controls the system and with it the limits of productivity and quality: "Let's say we're running a contest. Bill [Scollard] will be in the contest, and Charlie. I take Bill in my office and we talk about the contest we're going to run and there's going to be a big prize. So he won't have to worry about making cars anymore, he'll get a big trip around the world, and a big pension, and it'll all be indexed to inflation, so he'll be all set. He's really enthused. All he has to do is win the award. So he's all psyched up, just like the Celtics last night for the basketball game. He wants to win.

"So then I take Charlie into my office and give him the same story. And Charlie gets all psyched up. I give him the whole box we call attitudes and psychology. . . . Everyone loves everybody.

"Then I take 'em into this room with two pine boards made of soft pine wood, and I reach into my pocket. The contest is to put wood screws into the pine board. I give five to Bill and five to Charlie. Then I say here Charlie, I'll give you a screwdriver. Bill, tough luck, use your fingernails. Charlie goes bing, bing, bing, bing. Bill goes and breaks his thumbnail, swears a few times, and the contest is over. Charlie has the pension plan and Bill's without.

"Now they both had the right attitude, everything was wonderful."

The point, explained Conway, is that "All the things people are trying to tell you at productivity conferences all over the world . . . most of that is attitude and psychology. And with it, I'm sure you'll make some improvements. You will improve some quality.

"But if you get confused and think at *all* that that is what makes the Japanese so successful or that that's what's going to get you fellows out of the hell of the problems you're in, then you're nuts. You're just plain nuts, someone's kidding you. Ninety-nine percent of the world that is talking about productivity and quality are nuts, they miss the whole point of the subject.

"The only way you're going to do it is to use the technical tools of statistics. No other way. You've got to train all your people from A to Z, people have to understand the power of [controlling variation]. We keep telling people, the main secret behind any social or economic advance is relentless daily pursuit of increased productivity and quality.

"At first I had a hard time believing that unions would regard this sort of thing as help. But they do. No problem with the workers. None. All the problems are with the managers, all of them. The resistance is tremendous. I guess people are worried about their jobs, they get into bad habits, find it hard to change as much as they'd like to change. . . . You're going to have a hell of a time convincing people they can change.

"I do know one thing, the whole damn thing won't fly at all until the top people are one hundred percent behind it, pushing and shoving every single day.

"See, you're not talking about occasionally using statistical thinking or statistical methods to do some particularly great big problem. You're not talking about that at all. You're talking about a *totally* new way to manage your business, from the minute you start to think about it in the morning until you go to bed at night. You're talking about thinking statistically about every problem, every day. . . . This is total change for everybody in the organization. After two years and two months we're probably twenty-five percent effective and we're getting ten percent results. Doing all the things I've described—we're in a period of tremendous upsweep. My guess is, by the end of the year we'll be fifty percent effective. Now everyone wants to get into the act, because we've got enough success stories. People are now convinced that it won't go away. Even [with our plants] in Australia, we're on the phone every day, I'm telling them to send me a chart on this, or a chart on that. Once you see it starting to happen, it's the most satisfying thing in the world."[6]

To show them what he meant, Conway gave the Ford managers a guided tour of the Mamaroneck plant, where the company was making fourteen-inch computer memory disks at the time. Nashua's disks, which are built into disk drives, are the "grey matter" of computers, and the quality of those disks has to meet the exacting requirements of the drive and computer manufacturers, such as IBM, Seagate, and Miniscribe. Not unlike the nineteenth-century cobbler or tailor, makers of hard disks must keep up with the specialized needs of their most influential customers, a task that became ever more difficult as the pace of technological change in the computer industry picked up rapidly throughout the 1980s.

In groups of three and four, the Ford executives began their tour of the disk factory, starting at the place where the incoming raw aluminum disks are received from Nashua's suppliers, then move on mandrels through nearly a dozen stages in the production process to where they ultimately are packaged and shipped out the door. They watched as the raw aluminum disks were unpacked and bathed in an alodine solution to rid them of any impurities and as they were moved to their first drying station. The disks were then etched in preparation for the iron oxide and resin coating that makes the disks magnetically responsive; the etching helps the coating adhere properly to the disks. The coated disks were then moved into an oven, where they were baked and cured. The freshly baked disks were then ground with an abrasive tape to rid them of any surface irregularities that might interfere with the computer head when it flies over the disk. Finally, the disks were electrically tested for magnetic defects, or "holes," that won't hold data.

A straightforward manufacturing process, to be sure, but the Ford executives walked through the plant as though they were on an alien planet. The factory seemed to be missing one vital component—except for the final electrical certification process, there was no formal inspection procedure, or what, at Ford, was known as a "buy-off" operation. For years U.S. companies like Ford had relied on these "buy-offs" as part of their quality control process; at each stage of manufacturing, right until the finished products were shipped out the door, inspectors would monitor the materials, the work in progress, and the finished product. They would separate the good from the bad, sometimes inspecting every last item.[7]

While Nashua had also practiced quality by inspection at one time, Deming led the company to abandon that system. "Routine 100 percent inspection to improve quality is equivalent to planning for defects, acknowledgment that the process has not the capability required for the specifications," says Deming.[8] Deming also points out that inspection is an expense that can be reduced, and in some cases even eliminated, if a process is kept under control with a minimal level of variation. Instead of inspecting incoming materials, for example, Nashua began to work with its suppliers to establish precise quality standards that they were expected to meet. Thereafter, shipments of parts or materials by a vendor were accompanied by a control chart that verified the integrity of the supplies and their conformance to Nashua's process requirements.

Establishing high process requirements within Nashua's own operations was also important. Before Deming arrived, Nashua was still struggling with the job of applying the correct quantity of iron oxide and resin coating to its disks. The company employed two inspectors on each shift whose job it was to monitor each coating machine every two hours. The coaters were constantly adjusted to compensate for minor changes in the process; consequently too much coating often ended up on the disks. As a result, the final polishing process was actually used to grind off the excess coating, rather than to give the finished disks a final buff.[9]

Deming insists that overadjusting a process, as Nashua attempted, is a cardinal sin. In his book, predictability is the most important virtue of any process, while overadjustment increases variability and unpredictability, and generally causes more problems than it solves. This phenomenon, which he refers to as "tampering," was studied at some length by his friend Lloyd Nelson, a statistician and twenty-nine-year veteran of General Electric who was hired by Nashua at Deming's behest. He once remarked that "a process under control with sixty percent yield is better than one not under control, and producing ninety percent yield." Nelson's point is that it is better to have a process that is working at only partial capacity but producing a consistent level of quality than a process going at full bore but producing defectives. Not only do the defective items have to be inspected out at added expense to the manufacturer, and ultimately to the customer, there is always a risk that some will slip through to the customer.[10]

Nashua's coating problem proves the point. The technicians began to let the coating process run unadjusted for a while. They discovered that, left alone, the process was fairly predictable, consistently spreading about three thousandths of an inch of coating onto each disk. Moreover, with that level of consistency, Nashua's customers were fairly well satisfied. Almost immediately, the company was able to cut down to just one checker per shift and cut back on the time needed to polish the disks, since polishing was all that was needed once the process was no longer depositing excess material.

Having learned that little lesson, Nashua set out to improve its yields. In 1980 Nashua knew it was wasting both time and money during disk production. Yields on some types of disks were a mere 55 percent. One of the problems that accounted for the high percentage of rejects was the appearance of magnetic holes on the disks. The holes, also known as missing pulse errors, are the result of a flaw in the disk's coating that makes it impossible to store data there.

In the past Nashua had tinkered randomly with its processes to fix this problem, and of course the attempt hadn't reduced the number of holes. Again the technicians let the process run uninterrupted, and this time they found "special causes." To identify the source of the problem, they developed a sampling plan that tested small quantities of disks, which were taken off the line at random at various stages. The sampling plan was designed to produce two types of information—the location on the disks at which the problems occurred most often and the point during the production process in which the spots appeared in greatest numbers. In so doing, they discovered that 15 percent of the disks developed spots during the alodine wash. By adjusting the solution used in the wash, Nashua was able to reduce the number of rejects from this stage of the process to just 5 percent, at a saving of $150,000 a month.

Once that problem was solved, Nashua continued sampling the disks and found that the system was now in control, although it was still producing a large number of defectives. And because it was in control, Nashua's variation patrol knew that only a fundamental change in the production process would produce further yield improvements. By continuing to study the process, Nashua discovered that a large number of defectives was being produced during the drying stage. A new dryer solved that problem. Nashua's new process-mindedness improved yields on rigid disks by thirty percentage points in just three years, to 85 percent by the end of 1982. By 1988 the company was realizing yields of 92 percent at a saving of $300,000 per month.

As the process was improved and refined, workers were taught how to use control charts to monitor the processes and make sure they remained stable. The monitoring also gave workers an understanding of the variations that occurred around them and made them feel more at ease with their work. There was virtually no need for inspection in the plant because Nashua had thoroughly stabilized its process. If the process was stable, the company could accurately predict the level of product quality the process would produce. In one fell swoop, Nashua had saved itself the expense of dozens of inspectors and millions of dollars in defective products, while at the same time succeeding in improving the quality of both its products and its processes.

The Ford executives weren't able to see the incremental progress that had taken place over the course of more than a year. Yet for men like Bill Scollard, what they *could* see in Nashua's disk operation, the dearth of inspectors, spoke volumes. "Bill Scollard grew up in a manufacturing assembly environment in which you insisted on having a buy-off operation," explains Sullivan, who represented Ford's supplier quality assurance groups at the time. What Nashua was doing "represented a fundamental change. Scollard must have asked about four times where the buy-off operations were. They couldn't comprehend a system without inspection. The systems at Ford were based on very elaborate inspections—you'd inspect the paint luster, the door fit, et cetera. I don't think any of us fully understood what Conway was talking about, because we were so product oriented" (as opposed to process oriented).[11]

But if there had been any doubts about Deming's message, the Nashua visit dispelled them. "This was the single greatest event that ever impacted Ford Motor Company" in its quality drive, says Sullivan, recalling the animated discussion that occupied the executives all the way home on the corporate jet and that continued for some time into the night at Ford's airport hanger in Detroit. "They started questioning how they were doing things. They were awed by a manufacturing process where the quality effort was focused on the capability of the process, rather than on controlling the product. That change in thinking is very well entrenched now. But the beginning was at Nashua."[12]

In time, Ford would gradually surpass Nashua's progress in the level of sophistication with which it applied Deming's quality management principles to both operations and corporate decision making. But at a time when Japan's very success was beginning to make it difficult for a proud Yankee company to turn to the upstart samurai for guidance, Nashua offered a comforting domestic model for change. The New Hampshire company's management fostered upstream process improvement instead of downstream damage control as the principal tenet of its corporate culture. And it pushed the use of statistics down through the ranks, rigorously educating both managers and the rank and file to achieve incremental improvements in process after process.

Nashua stands out from other U.S. companies in that it turned to Deming *before* the company faced a major crisis, in a conscious effort to prepare the company for a future of intensifying foreign competition. By the late 1970s, Japanese copier manufacturers had battered their U.S. rivals, and Conway figured it was just a matter of time before Ricoh revoked Nashua's lucrative marketing agreement. In addition, Nashua was beginning to discover that copiers and paper supplies weren't the only businesses in which the Japanese were proving to be able competitors. The New Hampshire company found that by the end of the decade fully 70 percent of its product line was up against a new crop of high-quality products bearing names such as Hitachi, Fujitsu, and Fuji.[13]

The specter of a whole new cadre of international competitors was a rude awakening for the New Hampshire company. Nashua still occupies two old mill buildings on Franklin Street, just off Main Street in downtown Nashua. And although its copier and computer disk businesses hint at the high-technology renaissance that is blossoming along New England's Route 128 and in the area immediately surrounding Nashua, the company still has the look of an outdated factory in the midst of a New England village past its prime. The visitors' entrance to Nashua Corporation is smaller than a regional rent-a-car office and less prepossessing. The second-floor conference room, down the hall from the chief executive's office, is a modest affair, furnished with a Levitt interpretation of Queen Anne furnishings. And the glass brick that lines the hallways isn't the trendy 1980s variety, but vintage 1950s.

But Nashua's modest trappings belie the company's importance to this aspiring high-tech hamlet, which once thrived on now-defunct textile mills and iron and steel foundries;[14] it employs 6,700 people, making it one of the largest employers in the region. Nestled in rolling hills that become the Green Mountains, the town, which has retained little of its pioneering charm, is the sort of place where Main Street is renamed the United Way during the charity fund drives and where you can't get a cup of coffee after five o'clock—except, of course, at the Dunkin' Donuts, where the locals gather after work. There is a gourmet food store sandwiched between the fast food joints and gas stations, but it too closes in the afternoon. So when George Bush came campaigning here during the New Hampshire primaries in the spring of 1988, the narrow pavement in front of Nashua Corporation was just about the only place for him to take a stand.

Today Nashua's management credits the methods introduced by Deming not just for making the company a key player in the computer memory disk business, but for making it possible for the company to stay in that business at all. The advent of the personal computer, which replaced large computer mainframes, and the maturation of the industry prompted a major shakeout among suppliers of computer storage units. Companies such as Xerox and 3M were forced out of the business altogether. To maintain its disk operations, Nashua would have to lower prices by 15 to 20 percent. The company's incremental improvements made it possible for Nashua both to meet those competitive prices and to achieve efficiencies that increased its profit margins from about 10 percent to close to 17 percent. Nashua's performance prompted *Business Week* magazine to call it "one of the industry's most efficient producers." Indeed, by the early 1980s, only two players remained: IBM and Nashua, which at the time had total gross revenues of less than $700 million and controlled 20 percent of the market.[15]

Computer memory disks weren't the only industry in which Nashua faced a do-or-die quality challenge. The mail order segment of the photofinishing market, in which Nashua had long been a major player, contracted from about 35 percent to about 15 percent in the late 1970s. Nashua was hit hard by the decline and had trouble breaking even, so the company moved to improve its service and lower costs, again using variation control. Within a few years it had lowered the prices of its mail order photofinishing by as much as 20 percent, but had cut its costs by fully 30 percent. And Nashua emerged as a leader in that industry as well.[16] Nashua would also make some improvements in its carbonless paper products, which originally had ignited Conway's concern.

*　　*　　*

Changes in international trade far beyond the borders of rural New Hampshire and its pioneering efforts in quality management would turn Nashua into a national celebrity. In 1980 the NBC documentary *If Japan Can, Why Can't We?*, which introduced Deming to the occidental world, featured Nashua as the sole counterweight to the Japanese quality juggernaut. The film nudged Nashua into the national spotlight and helped launch the auto industry's quality drive.

Nashua's adoption of Demingism wasn't seamless, however. Some pockets at the company remained stubbornly resistant to change for many years. And in 1982 the company suffered a serious strategic setback that nearly forced a restructuring and placed many of Nashua's improvement efforts on hold. The story of how Nashua has taken to the Deming philosophy is, indeed, a lesson in both the do's and don'ts of quality management. What Nashua didn't do, at least not within its first decade of Demingism, was to develop the sort of formalized, all-encompassing total quality control system that has become commonplace at large Japanese companies and that now is being emulated by a handful of U.S. firms. Perhaps because of its relatively small size, Nashua may never have an urgent need to develop the TQC approach, which is designed to speed the dissemination of information through a corporation and to expedite decision making by applying to the setting and execution of strategic plans the same problem-solving mechanisms that govern production.

Nashua has emerged as a textbook example of how a company grasped the early phases of quality management, particularly a commitment to continuous, incremental improvement. Conway launched the effort with his own unflinching commitment to "helping the people" who work throughout the corporation as the principal means of achieving constant improvement. With that in mind, Conway undertook a dual course of action: He initiated a dialogue with the rank and file in an effort to mend the damage that had been done by decades of acrimonious labor relations. He also instituted training programs in Deming's philosophy and in statistical methods, and required both managers and workers to attend them.

Initially, much of Nashua's reeducation during the early 1980s was conducted by Deming himself, who held lectures, including his red bead experiment, and advised managers on specific production problems. The guru began to hold a series of four-day seminars, which were attended by everyone in the corporation from the lowliest clerical worker to Conway himself, as well as by customers and suppliers.[17] Hour after hour, for four straight days, Deming delivered his fire-and-brimstone message of corporate redemption. The significance and role of variation form the leitmotif of every seminar. Management, as Nashua was to learn, is the principal target and the whipping boy of the sessions. And the importance of anticipating the needs of customers is the pervasive message. Quality products, quality processes, and quality management are all stepping-stones toward customer satisfaction.

The Nashua seminars, which started in 1979, were prototypes of the ones that would come to be sponsored by a variety of organizations during the 1980s and that Deming would give at the rate of thirty to forty per year by the end of the decade. Although Deming had not yet articulated his Fourteen Points as a total doctrine at the time of the first seminars held for the company, the major themes were already evident in Nashua's curriculum and have remained fairly constant over the years.[18] Deming exhorted Nashua to:

- Work closely with just a few suppliers
- Foster interdepartmental cooperation
- Work toward eliminating inspection
- Build a relationship of trust with workers
- Strive for continuous improvement throughout operations
- Work closely with customers (indeed, customers were invited to the seminars given by Deming at Nashua)

Charles Clough, who would succeed Conway as Nashua's CEO in 1983, believes that Deming's focus on management is crucial. "There has to be training at several levels, especially for managers," he says. "See, the workers pick this up very fast, they understand what's going on. The managers are very difficult, because a lot of them are scared, they see that their jobs are going to change."[19]

Just as Nashua was launching the first of its Deming seminars, Nashua's top management realized that little could be done without mending the fences with labor and tearing down what Deming calls "the barriers of distrust" that had crept up over the years. This became abundantly clear in February 1980, when the bargaining committee of the United Paperworkers International Union (UPIU) faced off against Ed Johnson, then vice president of personnel, for the round of labor negotiations the company held every two years. The negotiations should have been effortless—the company was offering a 15 percent pay increase to its paper workers. However, in exchange for the pay rise, management wanted work rule changes that would violate the sacred rules of union seniority. So great was the perceived threat to the union that under the traditional rules of the game its bargaining committee exercised its right to take the workers out on strike without first presenting management's plan to them. For the next twenty-three days, Nashua workers were locked out of the company's Mamaroneck factory while management hired replacements and put both foremen and salaried managers on the production line. Four times a day the company brought food into the factory, where strikebreakers were working twelve-hour shifts. The union was finally forced to surrender. While the workers got their 15 percent raise, the corporation won the right to transfer any worker to any job without regard to tenure.[20]

As life at Mamaroneck gradually returned to normal, Conway was determined to change more than work rules. At Deming's urging, the CEO, together with Johnson, initiated a dialogue with workers and union leaders at the dinner table, instead of the bargaining table. At least twice a year, Conway and the heads of the executive committees of each union represented at Nashua would meet for dinner in a private room at the Nashua Country Club. The dinner conversation would focus on the problems and goals the company faced and the way management and strategic changes were related to business conditions. Workers were also asked to become more actively involved in the management of the production process. "Dr. Deming had a lot to do with it," says Robert Amberg, who runs a coating machine in Nashua's Mamaroneck carbonless paper facility in addition to having headed the UPIU local on and off for years. "He got [management and the union] working together to pinpoint the problems in the company. He got us sitting down and honestly resolving the problems."[21]

Even the explosive issue that resulted in the strike of February

1980 at the Mamaroneck plant was eventually worked out in the spirit of reconciliation. Nashua was interested in making two changes that were designed to make the plant more flexible. First, the company wanted to split up the finishing department, the place where paper is pressed and cut into sheets, into two groups—a move the union would surely resist. The reason for splitting up the department into separate slitting and sheeting units was to get around a cumbersome personnel system that was designed to give the highest-seniority workers first crack at any new job opening. "If you get a department that big it's hard to control. There's a bidding procedure. If someone has a job and he leaves, it goes up for bid. It goes on the board for five days. Say I bid on that job, now my job is open, and it keeps mushrooming. It can take three or four months to get all those jobs filled. Cut the department in half, and you'd cut the confusion in half. We liked the big department because if jobs are eliminated then the high-seniority guys would have [more] options of taking the [jobs that are] still open," says Amberg.

The company also wanted to simplify the rigid job classification system that prevented workers from performing a variety of jobs. At the time, building flexibility into job descriptions was practically heresy in union circles. It wasn't that the union didn't realize change was necessary. "They knew things had to be changed," says Amberg about the rank and file. "Everyone had a little free time; I think they knew sooner or later it would catch up to them. People weren't fully employed. Everyone realized that if the company didn't make those changes, there was no way we could be competitive."[22]

But getting the union to give up the protection of numbers in the large departments and to tinker with job descriptions for the sake of efficiency required more than a corporate directive. It called for the building of a whole new management-labor relationship based on mutual trust and patient negotiating. And the initiative would have to come from management. "How much is the company doing to make it possible for people to work together without fear?" Deming would ask management.[23]

In the spirit of fostering cooperation and trust, Johnson first worked with Amberg and the executive board of the local to agree on a proposal. Instead of following standard practice and letting Amberg present the changes to the rank and file, Johnson delivered a presentation himself, meeting individually with three separate shifts of workers. Minutes were taken methodically so that no disputes would arise about the conclusions that had been reached during the course of the meetings. If certain points couldn't be agreed upon, Johnson would go back to the negotiating table with the union leaders. Finally, after three months of horse trading, Johnson and the union worked out the details of the split. "They realized it was being done in an honest way," says Amberg.[24]

Nashua's new labor ethic would do a lot more than just improve quality and efficiency. When Conway, intoxicated with his initial successes in quality improvement, made a major strategic blunder, the rank and file helped the company avert bankruptcy. Afraid of losing his Ricoh copiers, Conway had decided to manufacture his own brand. (The decision may have been influenced by Conway's memories of his visit to the Ricoh plant in California and the deceptive ease with which the Japanese company was turning out copiers.) The experiment was a disaster. In 1982 Nashua lost $42 million and had to write off $28.5 million. It also owed its creditors $140 million.[25]

To keep the banks at bay, Nashua had to find a quick way to save $2 million; but it was also under contract to give the union a 6 percent wage increase. Ed Johnson, from personnel, again braced himself for a meeting with union leaders, including his old adversary Amberg, to ask them to forgo the raise *indefinitely*. At 8 A.M., two days before Christmas, Amberg and the heads of Nashua's other unions met with the company's beleaguered chairman to tell him that they had voted, by a six-to-one ratio, to give up all pay increases for the foreseeable future. Just two years after the strike of 1980, the union had delivered to Nashua the breathing room it needed to negotiate with the banks.[26]

Conway insists that had the company been further along in absorbing the Deming philosophy, it would have had a shot at making it in the cutthroat copier market. "First there was this euphoria when we could see how well [Deming's methods] were working," explains Conway. "But the Japanese had been working at it for twenty or thirty years. We needed either a total breakthrough in technology or one in quality and cost. We didn't have the [technological] breakthrough. And we weren't far enough along on the learning curve in [quality]."[27] Conway would never get a chance to find out whether or not he was right; he was forced to resign in 1983.

Charlie Clough, who had been with Nashua throughout Deming's initiation at the company, had become—despite serious differences with Conway—a champion of many of Deming's ideas. A soft-spoken man from Concord, New Hampshire, Clough had married the daughter of James R. Carter II, a descendant of one of the early investors in Nashua and the man who had been the company's CEO until 1971. When Clough took over the job in the early 1980s, Nashua was already a widely held public company subject to the short-term profit demands of the marketplace. While he was forced to abandon some businesses, Clough insisted on keeping others, including the mail order photofinishing business. And while he replaced key Conway loyalists, including the vice presidents of each of Nashua's three major business segments, Clough held on to both Nelson and Deming, and with them to the principles of quality and continuous improvement. Deming continued to visit Nashua two days every other month, becoming a regular fixture at the Nashua Country Club, where the staff had become well schooled in his special requirements for service and comfort. And Conway's relationship with Deming was close enough so that at least once after the death of Lola Deming, Clough and his wife visited Deming at his home in Washington, D.C., dining with him on a Saturday and attending church services with him on Sunday.[28]

Clough recognized that one of his biggest challenges during this difficult period was to maintain the trust of Nashua's employees and the momentum of Deming's philosophy. At the time, the company laid off five hundred to six hundred workers out of a total of about 3,500 employees. However, unlike companies such as GM, which acquired a reputation for cavalier cutbacks (see Chapter 8), layoffs at Nashua were a matter of immediate survival. And Nashua spread the pain throughout the organization. The biggest cuts came in the executive ranks, where more than 20 percent of the white-collar work force was eliminated. Nashua's top management also took a pay cut of 10 percent and did not approve a pay raise for management for another year and a half. Deming's visits also provided a strand of consistency that helped get Nashua through the trying days of 1982—the guru would meet with, and advise, five or six groups of managers or engineers on each of his trips to the company.[29]

TEAMING UP WITH A SUPPLIER TO IMPROVE COMPUTER DISK QUALITY

Gradually, as the short-term financial pressures abated, Nashua resumed its efforts at continuous improvement. The brush with bankruptcy would virtually derail the company's quality progress in some businesses, but Nashua was determined to remain a major player in the disk business. And for that the organization would have to strengthen its quality improvement efforts; the increasingly competitive nature of the computer memory disk market demanded it.

A rapid change in disk technology that called for ever more finely tuned production processes meant that Nashua had to be as concerned about the improvement efforts of its suppliers as it was about its own operations. Throughout the 1980s, the disk business was driven by the growing sophistication of the computer manufacturers. As computer makers sought to endow their machines with more processing muscle and more sophisticated software, the capacity of disk drives had to grow in tandem. "Our salespeople have had to become more technically oriented," says Walter J. Powers, manager of marketing. "We must be there early in the drive development phase. We must establish good relations with the account and get to know the people who are designing the new drives."[30]

The quality and technical demands of the computer disk business are so rigorous that they have called for a virtual marriage between Nashua and its suppliers—even more so than for less changeable businesses. Nashua estimates that its product life cycles can be as short as two years, and product and tooling changes can occur as frequently as every six months.[31] Companies such as Nashua, which produce finished, coated disks, depend on vendors both to deliver aluminum substrates that are high in quality and to maintain those levels of quality throughout endless product changes.

When Nashua emerged in the early 1980s as one of the few players in the disk business, one of its biggest challenges was to find suppliers who could keep up with the industry's swift product development pace, as well as with the quality requirements of finicky customers such as IBM. Those demands prompted Nashua to acquire Disk Tec, an Illinois processor of raw substrates, on the theory that ownership would be the best way to retain complete control over the quality of its principal raw material. However, Nashua found it would have to continue relying on outside suppliers for quite some time before it would be able to bring Disk-Tec up to speed. Enter KSI Disk Products of Chino, California.

In 1987 Nashua began purchasing uncoated disks from KSI in what would be a single-source relationship until the problems at Disk-Tec had been worked out. Although KSI was working its way through Chapter 11, a predicament it had gotten itself into by diversifying prematurely in the early 1980s, the company had a reputation for producing high-quality media. And because of consolidations throughout the industry that made it difficult to find reliable suppliers, within a year KSI came to command 100 percent of Nashua's business.[32] (Nashua had lost its chief media supplier, prior to the Disk-Tec acquisition, when the company was bought out by a competitor.) Thus, forced largely by exigencies of the marketplace, Nashua developed a sole-source relationship with KSI.

Indeed, the alliance between Nashua and KSI has come to resemble that of parent and subsidiary, rather than that of client and supplier. As Nashua has access to everything at KSI from its plant floor to its books, "There's a very high level of trust involved," says Bill Masuda, the company's president. "Nashua insists on three things from its suppliers," he says. "That they use statistical quality control techniques; that they make money—they know it won't do them any good in the long term if their suppliers lose money; and that you have an open, honest, two-way relationship." Nashua executives visit KSI at least twice a year. To make sure its processes are able to meet quality levels and the demand for rapid product changes, KSI was asked to hire a resident statistician, a friend of Lloyd Nelson. Nashua's goal is to eliminate the time-consuming and wasteful process of inspecting incoming materials. And to make sure the materials are up to par, the company has instructed KSI to send periodic reports on the quality of their product.[33]

To further foster KSI's own improvement efforts, Nashua began sending weekly reports to KSI to let the company know how its products functioned during the assembly process in New Hampshire. Soon Nashua began issuing daily reports so that KSI would have the information it needed to improve its production processes on a day-by-day basis.

The relationship began to pay off for both Nashua and KSI almost immediately. As part of Nashua's ongoing effort to reduce the number of magnetic holes in its disks, it called on KSI to deliver aluminum substrates that would be less apt to develop the pesky spots. KSI set to work on the problem and within seven months came up with a new type of substrate that would help prevent the creation of holes when the disks are coated at Nashua's plants. "The technology is extremely sensitive and difficult to control," says Masuda. "The chances of success are enhanced if you're closer to your customer. You have to have a supplier and customer basically working out problems together because very few companies understand the whole technology."[34]

For KSI, producing a near-perfect product has become a matter of survival. "A drop in yields of two or three percent can be catastrophic," explains Masuda, whose processes boasted 92 percent yields in 1988. "Because our profit margins are so slim, a one percent change in product yields below our target will reduce our gross profit. If we took a five percent yield hit below our target for one month, we would make no money." While Masuda claims that as a small company KSI naturally followed many of Deming's precepts of cooperation and worker empowerment, Nashua's demands for a more rigorous approach to quality control and documentation drove those principles farther down the line. While supervisors had once been responsible for monitoring quality control, workers were now put in charge of that function.[35]

Ironically, it is such rapid-fire product change that has virtually locked the Japanese out of the disk market. "The Japanese just can't keep up," says Masuda, who is a Japanese-American. "The chances of success are so much enhanced if you're physically close to your customer."[36]

Such a hand-in-glove approach became particularly important in the late 1980s, as the disk business took a quantum leap in capability with a new technology known as thin films. While traditional disks were covered with relatively thick magnetic iron oxide coatings, the new technique coats the disks with a microscopic metal film. Because of the thinness of the films, the drive heads can get closer than ever to the disks, making it possible to pack at least fifteen times more information on a thin-film disk than on their bulkier brethren. However, the delicate coating also makes thin-film disks more vulnerable to production snafus, and makes a highly controlled, high-quality production process more vital than ever. Moreover, because product life cycles are notoriously short, thin-film disk manufacturers don't have the luxury of a leisurely learning curve. Thus, the more sophisticated the technologies Nashua used, the more important it was for the company to get control over its process quickly.

Today few operations connected to Nashua remain untouched by the Deming philosophy. Nashua's performance in the past several years has won praise from analysts such as Harry E. Wells of Adams Harkness & Hill, a brokerage firm in Boston, who calls Nashua "the quintessential modern management company."[37]

STRUGGLING TO FOSTER COOPERATION BETWEEN MANUFACTURING AND ENGINEERING

Yet even in a business that considers continuous improvement the norm, Nashua has important changes to make. After its initial improvements in the 1980s, progress in the carbonless paper business, which had prompted Conway's original quality concerns in the 1970s, were stalled so much that the business has become a revolving door for division managers.[38]

In addition, Lloyd Nelson contends that manufacturing and engineering still don't coordinate their improvement efforts well enough. As Nashua is an engineering-driven company, its manufacturing operations often fall victim to the "tampering" of engineers. "Engineers tend to see things in terms of black and white," says Clough. "Nobody has ever questioned them before. A lot of times they just keep modifying a machine or process without stepping back to take a look at the total operation. That can be extremely dangerous." Adds John Montesi, former head of engineering and now head of research and development, "Engineers have a propensity to want to change everything. This is counter to the principle of continuous improvement, which relies on gradual, incremental change."[39]

For many years, Nelson had been frustrated by the meddling of well-intentioned engineers in stable manufacturing processes. A scientist at heart, Nelson once shocked a group of visiting managers with one of his "statistical" experiments during his days at General Electric's research labs. The labs were a routine stop on GE's public relations tours. And Nelson, who often used a deck of bridge cards to work out the sequence in which to conduct quality improvement experiments, was so engrossed in a card sequence one day that he failed to notice the visitors standing in his lab. From their incredulous faces, Nelson realized that they thought one of GE's renowned researchers was spending his afternoon playing a game of solitaire.

Nelson—a statistical path breaker in his own right and one of the few men Deming regards as both a friend and professional equal—began to work with Clough on devising an organizational plan that would put more power back into the hands of manufacturing.[40] Says Frank Faticanti, process engineering manager for rigid disks, about the company's experience in the rigid disk business, "At one time the engineering groups had a lot of responsibility regarding what went on in manufacturing, so conflicts would arise. [It was unclear] who had the responsibility to do what when a product was being made. Manufacturing was never really given the authority or the responsibility to run the process."[41]

The company had found that delineating the responsibilities of manufacturing and engineering had been a crucial factor in upgrading both the quality of disk production and the final product. To free manufacturing of the engineers' sporadic tampering, Nashua gave the manufacturing department the opportunity to train its work force in the rudiments of variation control. And instead of giving engineers carte blanche to fiddle with production processes, manufacturing is now in charge both of determining when improvement projects need to be undertaken by the engineers and of monitoring those projects once they are under way.

Like other quality pioneers, Nashua has discovered that the more progress you make in the pursuit of quality, the harder it is to wring successive increments of improvement out of the system. In the long run, both Nelson and Clough recognize that future milestones in quality and cost efficiency will require developing closer relationships among engineering, research and development, and manufacturing. The challenge is to foster cooperation while preventing engineering from poaching on manufacturing's prerogatives. To that end, Nelson enlisted the help of his friend John Montesi, who is running the company's latest acquisition, Lin Data, which makes Nashua's state-of-the-art thin-film computer disks. With its sensitive high-tech processes, Lin Data (which was renamed Nashua Computer Products Corporation) is a prime candidate for improvement. And Montesi is experimenting with a more team-oriented approach to managing engineering, manufacturing, and R & D. "In high-tech areas, especially, engineering takes over, and manufacturing abdicates," says Montesi. "What you get is engineering people saying that production workers aren't capable of running sophisticated tests on their processes. The answer is to get them working together—if the tests are too sophisticated, then you need another test. Manufacturing has to be given the tools to run their operations."

Even after the "easy" improvements have been made, the effort continuously to improve product and manufacturing quality is well worth it. Because of shortening product life cycles, "overinvestment" in quality management is almost impossible. Indeed, the expertise developed by Nashua in making incremental improvements in disk production technologies will be crucial to the company's ability to make a successful leap to next-generation memory products.[42]

For Nashua, thin films represents the new frontier in both technology and quality improvement. Montesi's goal is to improve manufacturing to the point where it can break the industry's 70 percent yield barrier. That, he figures, should help Lin Data, a company with $50 million in revenues, improve on its current market share of 15 to 20 percent. Montesi is only just mapping out the unit's improvement strategy. But as a first step, he began his stewardship of Lin Data by launching a reeducation campaign in the teaching of Deming's principles.[43]

FORD'S BETTER

IDEA . . .

4

Deming's most lauded corporate pupil in the United States is the Ford Motor Company. Deming's philosophy helped fashion a new corporate culture at the company, one that shifted management's attention from a myopic focus on the bottom line to a broader vision that included the customer. His ideas were also behind numerous management innovations, including a bold new strategy for working with suppliers that was designed to secure the highest-quality components. The new supplier strategy and a revived commitment to the customer would become the hallmarks of a whole line of Ford successes that rolled off the assembly lines in the mid- and late 1980s, including the much-lauded Taurus Sable cars and recent editions of the Thunderbird and Lincoln Continental.

However, the alliance between Ford and the proud quality pioneer wasn't an easy one. Neither Deming's philosophical bent nor his pointed questioning went over well with many of Ford's managers. That he made the inroads he did was largely due to three factors: Dealing with Deming was more palatable to Ford managers than having to learn from the Japanese; in 1980 the company's desperate straits demanded a drastic change; and chairman Donald E. Petersen was determined to work with Deming. "In casting about for . . . good ideas, one of the finest and most thought-provoking resources we found was Dr. Deming," insists Petersen. "I'm proud to call myself a disciple of Dr. Deming."[1]

Several months after the airing of NBC's 1980 documentary *If Japan Can, Why Can't We?*, which introduced Deming to Detroit executives, Ford dispatched a small group of middle managers to Deming's home in Washington, D.C. While Ford was one of the first major U.S. corporations to solicit Deming's expertise in quality management (although he had conducted statistical surveys for numerous U.S. corporations since the 1950s), he did not receive the delegation with open arms. The first meeting with the Ford representatives lasted a mere thirty minutes.[2] That Christmas, Bill Scollard, vice president of manufacturing for Ford, took a copy of the documentary home to review over the holidays. Seeing the video helped convince Scollard and his colleagues that Deming should be invited to Detroit.[3]

It would, however, take several entreaties by Ford managers to convince Deming to visit the company. He was finally persuaded to make the trip in February 1981 by the prospect of lecturing to thirty of the company's top executives, including Petersen. Among those who attended that first meeting were Scollard, Harold ("Red") Poling, who was then head of North American Automotive Operations (NAAO) and would soon be named president, Louis R. Ross, who would succeed Poling as head of NAAO, and Lewis C. Veraldi, who became the father of the Taurus.[4] The February meeting, just a few months after Deming turned eighty, marked the most influential group of U.S. executives that had ever gathered to hear what the quality expert had to say.

The initial contacts were unsettling ones for Ford. Instead of delivering a slick presentation on how the automaker could solve its quality problems—the sort of thing that became the stock in trade of U.S. quality "experts" during the 1980s, Deming questioned, rambled, and seemed to take pleasure in making a laughingstock of his listeners. During the first meeting, wearing one of his signature timeworn three-piece suits, Deming glowered at the car executives with steely blue eyes. Fingering the emblem in his lapel, a tiny metal chrysanthemum* awarded to him by the Emperor of Japan

---

* Deming believes the little emblem to be a chrysanthemum, although it is shaped like a wheel and could represent the Deming cycle, which also is occasionally referred to as the Deming wheel.

that is his most prized possession, Deming asked the executives in the room what their jobs were. One of the first men to answer was John Manoogian, who got up, told Deming he was the director of product assurance, and sat back down. "But what is your job?" Deming inquired again.

"To manage the improvement of our reliability systems," answered Manoogian, this time a little less casually.

"But what is your job?" Deming asked again.

"That led to a fairly embarrassing exchange," recalls Larry Sullivan, who then represented Ford's supplier quality assurance groups, and who also attended the meeting. "Manoogian was talking about his role *administering* quality, but Deming was looking for his role in *facilitating* quality *improvement*. I don't think the question was well put or well understood. But Manoogian's answer was along procedural lines, whereas Deming [was making a point about] the involvement of top management." Adds Lou Ross (who is now executive vice president for international automotive operations), "He made me mad. He was right about what he was saying, but he said it in a very abrasive manner. He was a prosecutor. He said, 'The hourly employees aren't responsible. Management is responsible for eighty-five percent of the quality problems in this country.' "

"Why can't America compete?" Deming would ask, sputtering with rage. "The aaanswer iiis—MANAGEMENT!"

And finally, "What is quaaaality?" he would thunder, in a voice that said he was sure no one in the room knew the answer.[5]

The apparent contempt in which Deming held Ford managers did not go over well. Nor did the fact that Deming "refused to deal directly with automotive quality and insisted on talking instead about Ford's management philosophy and corporate culture."[6] Initially the alliance between Deming and Ford was much more like an arranged marriage than a love match. The partners would eventually develop respect, trust, and compatibility; romance had little to do with it. And although the association strengthened over time, the fact that it survived the first tense encounters was due almost solely to the commitment of Petersen, who is a member of the Mensa society, an organization of individuals with high IQs, and who seemed to actually enjoy the sometimes confrontational, and often theoretical, debates with Deming. On February 28, 1990, his last day before retiring the chairmanship at Ford, Petersen penned a short letter to Deming; the final lines testify to the respect and affection he felt for the guru: "You have had a major impact on my life and my thinking. Your friend, Don."[7]

On the other hand, Petersen's lieutenants, who had responsibility for the day-to-day business of turning out automobiles, weren't interested in theory and found Deming's academic approach enormously frustrating. "My interest was in applications," admits Scollard. "How do you translate the philosophy to applications? It was clear we couldn't do [business] the way we had previously done. But it also was clear that Dr. Deming didn't have the patience to answer questions."[8]

After ruminating on the problem for some months, Scollard thought he had found the answer in Japan. Ford's efforts to turn around its supplier base brought the company into contact with the Union of Japanese Scientists and Engineers (JUSE), Japan's leading quality organization, which had invited Deming to Japan in the 1950s and that dispenses the Deming Prize. In 1983 Scollard asked JUSE to put on a seminar for Ford executives. JUSE sent none other than Kaoru Ishikawa, one of the country's leading quality theorists. "What we saw in JUSE was that they had taken Deming and fine-tuned [his ideas] in a very practical way over twenty years," says Scollard.[9]

But the Ishikawa seminar completely backfired. Scollard held the seminar in Chicago and invited a broad cross section of Ford management. In addition to manufacturing executives, who had already had some exposure to quality management ideas, Scollard invited executives from sales and finance. Much of the material covered by Ishikawa, however, was technical and difficult for the uninitiated Ford managers to understand. There was even a backlash against the nontechnical material, which focused on bringing all business disciplines into the improvement process. Scollard recalls, for example, that the sales executives took offense at Ishikawa's suggestion that quality improvement in marketing is just as important as quality improvement in manufacturing. "The manufacturing guys were nodding, but everyone else wasn't sure anyone *but* manufacturing should do this," recalls Scollard. "Most of the executives had had no exposure to Deming, no exposure to Japanese manufacturing, and, in many cases, not much exposure to *our own* manufacturing. Our executives weren't ready for this." To make matters worse, by this time many at Ford were "sick of hearing about Japan."[10]

Deming might be ornery, but at least he was an American.

Scollard was forced to abandon his notion of supplementing (or perhaps supplanting) Deming's place at Ford with the more pragmatic influence of JUSE. With the Japanese out of the picture, Deming's role strengthened. By 1983 Petersen and Deming had settled into a cosy routine of monthly breakfast meetings where they discussed everything from the company's reward systems to how the company defines quality. Those conversations would shape several broad policy decisions at Ford. They prompted the formulation of a new corporate vision that was defined in Ford's statement of Mission, Values, and Guiding Principles, and placed quality and customers ahead of profits. And they led the company, which had always defined quality in terms of such negative measures as warranty costs, to shift to a more positive measure of customer desires. Said Petersen of his conversations with Deming, "[An] interesting thing that came out of our introspection and thinking was a realization that a great deal of what we were using as our measures of quality were [ones] that were convenient for us, because in engineering [there] would be certain ways we could measure things . . . whereas what it should be is an approach where the entire focus of your definition of quality is driven by the customer, and the customer's wants and needs. And it wasn't until [then] we made that transition and got ourselves all thinking in terms of the customer, and what it takes to provide to our customers the best possible products and services that meet fully the customer's wants and needs over the lifetime of those products and services at a cost that represents real value. Then at that point you have achieved quality, true quality."[11]

Deming also convinced Petersen to hire a statistician well versed in his philosophy.[12] Initially Deming had wanted the master statistician to report directly to the president; Ford had wanted Deming to select an expert from its own ranks. The curmudgeon and the corporation compromised: Deming, who had summarily rejected a list of sixty-four Ford candidates for the job, was permitted to choose his own man, Bill Scherkenbach, who had been one of Deming's students at New York University.[13] But instead of reporting directly to Poling, Scherkenbach would work for James K. Bakken, the vice president for corporate quality.

With Scherkenbach at Ford, Deming had a surrogate in place. Scherkenbach headed the statistical methods group, which served as a sort of quality command post for Deming's philosophy. The statistical methods group would certify the quality consultants that could be used throughout Ford. A statistical methods council to make quality policy recommendations was formed of Ford representatives from all over the world. The group also offered consulting services in statistical improvement techniques, as well as some training, to operations throughout the company. And until he moved to GM in 1988, Scherkenbach was a vocal proponent of Deming's more controversial ideas, such as overhauling Ford's performance appraisal and merit pay system[14] (see Chapter 8).

When Scherkenbach switched to GM, not everyone was sorry to see him go. As Deming's surrogate at Ford, Scherkenbach never became a Ford man, instead cultivating a unique position in Deming's inner circle. Among the group of young statisticians who surround the guru, and who fall in and out of favor according to his whims, Scherkenbach is clearly a favorite son, and is believed to view himself as the natural heir to Deming's mantle. A youthful-looking man who radiates quiet self-confidence, Scherkenbach acquired a reputation at Ford as a persistent and somewhat arrogant corporate gadfly who never shied from pressing Deming's concerns no matter how controversial. Ford executives, who had found Deming's outspoken contempt difficult to stomach, found the more genteel version of it in the younger man even more unpalatable. Animosities between Scherkenbach and key Ford executives probably limited his usefulness toward the end of the 1980s; it was then that Deming let GM know Scherkenbach was available.[15]

Scherkenbach, however, played his role well. By the late 1980s, there wasn't a single Ford executive who hadn't been exposed to Deming's ideas.[16] No self-respecting Deming manager would be caught without a copy of the company's Mission, Values, and Guiding Principles, which had been printed up on wallet-sized cards. Indeed, according to Larry Sullivan of the American Supplier Institute (ASI), Deming's ideas would come to have "more impact on the thinking of executives at Ford than anybody could have before, because of his stature and his abrasive approach, and because he was sponsored by Petersen, who continued to meet with Deming."[17]

Building on the philosophical base of Demingism over the course of nearly a decade, Ford gradually pieced together a strategy that would bring the company ever closer to the Japanese concept of total quality control (TQC). Top executives who represented a wide variety of disciplines and who in the go-go 1960s might well have thought twice before sharing a meal together began meeting regularly to set quality priorities and to establish standard corporate practices for making sure the needs of customers were met. And Ford operations throughout the company began to work closely with suppliers.

The rise of Demingism at Ford marked a sharp diminution in the power of the beancounters with their individual fiefdoms and fixation on the bottom line. The supremacy of the numbers men, personified by Robert McNamara, who had come to Ford as one of the Whiz Kids after World War II, would be replaced by a new spirit of cooperation. By the time McNamara was named president of Ford, a position in which he served for only two months before being named secretary of defense by President John F. Kennedy, the role of manufacturing had been completely eroded. Cutting costs, not improving automobiles, was the mission of the day. "To the finance people, innovation not only was expensive but seemed unnecessary. . . . Change, in the latter part of that era, was contrived not to improve but in the most subtle way to weaken each car model, year by year. The company, in its drive for greater profit, would take the essential auto structure of the year before and figure out ways to increase the profits by reducing the cost of some of the parts."[18]

In sharp contrast to the 1960s and 1970s, when manufacturing was a ghetto at Ford, a close alliance developed between Scollard and men like Max Jurosek, head of car development, and R. L. Rewey, head of sales for North America. Under the leadership of Louis R. Ross, who succeeded Poling as the head of NAAO, and stayed in that position until 1989, the three men who most influenced the ultimate look and quality of automobiles gradually institutionalized the key elements of a quality management strategy. "We work as a team," asserts Scollard. "We know better now than any [of our predecessors] in the history of the organization what each other's jobs are."[19] This new alliance between traditionally rival departments was born of a realization that quality cannot be measured in terms of individual components nor even in terms of a car's styling, but comes from viewing the car as a totality.[20]

One of the most fundamental changes at Ford had to do with how the company perceives its relationship with customers. In the past "their products and their methods of doing business all sprang from the same family of ideas," wrote F. Alton Doody and Ronald Bingaman in *Reinventing the Wheels*, a book about Ford's comeback. "More importantly, Detroit carmakers were locked into a static, rote, reactive procedure for creating supposedly new products. . . . They worked within the constraints of the often ethereal and sometimes ephemeral vision of a car that top management felt the public ought to have."[21] Ford would have to rid itself of this narrow viewpoint. It would also have to change standard operating procedures that dated back to the days of the Whiz Kids and that had stood in the way of building quality cars.

One vivid example of how far the company had drifted from its customers was evident in the rust problem that plagued Detroit cars for years. The company knew of the rust problem, and knew how to fix the problem. In 1958 Ford had developed a rust-resistant paint process known as E-coat that solved the pesky problem of getting paint into the nooks and crannies of automobiles. The process was so good that GM licensed it. And it was installed at Ford's plant in Wixom, Michigan, which produced the pricey Lincoln Continentals.[22] But the manufacturing men in Ford's domestic operations couldn't convince the finance department that the process, which cost $4 million per plant, was worth standardizing at all the company's plants. There were two reasons they were unable to make their case: First, Ford's beancounters hadn't figured out a way to calculate the cost of a happy customer. Second, rust problems often occurred outside the period covered by the company's warranties, so the company figured it wouldn't have to pay for the problem! As of 1973, only a fraction of Ford car plants were equipped with the E-coat system.[23]

By far the starkest example of Ford's primitive system of cost-benefit analysis could be seen in the decision-making process that led to the disaster of the Pinto, an inexpensive subcompact that was introduced in the 1970s and had a nasty habit of blowing up in rear-end collisions. Exploding Pintos caused at least fifty-nine deaths and, as a result, gave Ford the dubious distinction of becoming the first U.S. carmaker ever to be charged with reckless homicide. Although the company would be acquitted of that criminal charge, civil suits continued through the end of the 1970s, making Ford's quality debacle a staple of tabloids and the TV news.[24]

The Pinto's problem was due to the placement and configuration of the gas tank, a design that technically could have been solved without much trouble, but that financially couldn't be justified under Ford's cost-accounting system. The Whiz Kids had brought to Ford the system of cost-benefit analysis that had been developed by the military during World War II. The system had been used by the National Highway Traffic Safety Administration (NHTSA) to calculate the price for a human life—$200,725, based on such factors as the loss of productivity, hospital costs, pain and suffering, and funeral costs. A similar system was used by Ford to calculate whether the Pinto's design should be modified to solve its safety problems. Ford had identified a number of techniques, including such options as sheathing the inside of the gas tank with a rubber lining, which would help avoid burn deaths, at a cost of $137 million. At the same time, Ford estimated the total cost of burn-related injuries, deaths (at $200,725 per life), and damage to the cars themselves at $49.5 million. Thus, since the cost of avoiding burn accidents would be nearly triple the benefit of doing so, the company could not justify the change.[25]

Another obstacle that led to the Pinto disaster was the marketing objectives management clung to despite evidence that they might not be feasible. Ford engineers simply were not permitted to raise objections to the design plan if they interfered with management's timetable for the project or its catchy, but ultimately catastrophic, marketing goal, which was to build a two-thousand-pound vehicle that would sell for two thousand dollars. Said one Ford engineer to *Mother Jones* magazine, "Whenever a problem was raised that meant a delay on the Pinto, Lee [Iacocca] would chomp on his cigar, look out the window and say, 'Read the project objectives and get back to work.' "[26]

Ford gradually came to realize it would have to reexamine the assumptions on which it had heretofore based its product development decisions. For one thing, market research would have to take on a new role. As Petersen would put it, "Maybe we'd better do it right for a change and do the research before making the decisions."[27] Market research had traditionally been a corporate staff function that operated out of the company's World Headquarters' "Glass House," an arrangement that isolated research from the operating units that actually designed and built the cars. Not only did this separation sometimes prevent research from addressing the most germane issues facing the operating staff, they "sometimes took advantage of their corporate level, big-shot mystique to embarrass members of other operating groups."[28]

In November 1979 Lou Ross was put in charge of car product development with an express mandate to do something about Ford's product problems. If the Pinto hadn't been enough to convince him of the need for institutional change, Ross had personal reasons for wanting to do something about the quality of the company's cars. In 1975 he had returned from an assignment in Brazil and had gone shopping for a company car for his personal use; he had been dismayed to find that in Ford's entire product line, there was none that really interested him. When he took up his new job as the head of product development, Ross decided to hold a novel car "clinic" in Chicago, in which customers were asked to comment on Ford cars already in production. While Ford had traditionally held clinics for vehicles in the prototype stage, the company had never attempted to measure customer reaction to cars already on the road.[29]

The Chicago experiment was an education for Ross. It would spark the beginning of a quality management strategy that would cut across departmental lines and link all design and engineering decisions, including ones concerning every exterior line, paint shade, and dashboard configuration, to what customers might want. Although the Ford buyers who participated in the study often couldn't identify exactly what they *didn't* like about their cars, their dissatisfaction with what Ross would come to refer to as "tremendous trifles" was abundantly clear: "They said the shininess, the gloss level of the plastic in the interior is too high, it's too plasticky, so the car comes off looking cheap; I had never thought of it that way before. They said we need to provide more storage space for maps, we need to consider what a woman is to do with her purse. They told us the cars weren't as nice as the GM or Japanese products. I thought they were overstating the GM position, but I came to recognize the advantage of dealing with what people like, rather than what they dislike."[30]

Ford learned that just because customers didn't have concrete problems with a car didn't mean that they liked it. For example, in a test of the Ford Granada, satisfaction among customers who reported *no* problems with their cars was only 75 percent, while customer satisfaction among those who registered *some* problems was 55 percent. "We wanted to get to ninety-five percent customer satisfaction," says Ross. "So we said, there's something missing; that 'something' was what customers *like* about a car." Throughout the 1970s, Ford's principal customer satisfaction index had been based on warranty costs, which tended to identify only things that broke. In 1980 the company had begun to measure "things gone wrong," which identified some, but not all, of the subjective measures of quality. While it might pick up on such things as insufficient storage space or an inconvenient placement of the radio dials, it wasn't good at identifying that *je ne sais quoi* that distinguishes a car people love to drive from one that is merely acceptable. Ford would soon develop a new customer satisfaction measure that focused on a car buyer's ideal wish list.[31]

Realizing that the company knew very little about what its customers specifically wanted in a vehicle, Ross decided to convene a quality strategy committee in January 1981. A group of about fifty of the top executives at NAAO first met for an eight-hour meeting, then broke into groups that focused on three crucial strategic issues: The first group set about coming to grips with what the Ford customer wanted; the second group focused on how to change the way product development operated based on what group one had learned about the customer's desires; and the third group set about finding ways to change the culture and reward system to support the efforts of groups one and two (see Chapter 9). For months the executives met in their teams for fifteen to twenty hours a week in addition to their normal forty-hour work schedules. Typically, weekday meetings started late in the day and lasted through a supper of sandwiches and into the late evening. The groups also met all day Saturday.[32]

Initially everything hinged on the information produced by group one, which launched the first of Ford's in-depth focus groups, in which customers were asked to critique every Ford vehicle then on the road. In Chicago and Los Angeles customers were offered a dinner for two if they would bring their cars in to one of the clinics on a Saturday. Ford corralled 150 to 300 managers from the design, engineering, and product planning departments, as well as hourly workers from manufacturing, for the clinics to listen to what customers had to say about such things as wind noise, paint quality, and steering. In addition, Ford surveyed buyers of imported cars in cities like Atlanta to find out what they liked about foreign cars.[33]

The clinics were intended to get everyone to set the priorities of their own jobs according to what was important to the customer. For example, the typical paint inspection system in the assembly plants was designed to look for every conceivable problem, from areas where the paint had gone on too thinly and the level of glossiness to runs and chips, without discriminating according to any hierarchy of need. The clinics, however, revealed that customers cared most about chips and scratches and least about runs on the insides of doors, enabling manufacturing to prioritize its inspection priorities.[34]

But to make the system work, Ford had to change or discard myriad corporate rules and practices. Some procedures, such as the company's procurement requirements, which at one time had required special approval for the purchasing department to use *less than two* suppliers for a product, would be changed to require approval for *more than one* supplier. Similarly, a company directive that required purchasing agents to get special approval for supplier contracts lasting *more than one year* in duration were replaced by a directive requiring special permission for *less than a multiyear contract.*[35] Multiyear contracts were recognized by Ford as an important way to begin mending relations with suppliers and to turn them into partners. It was a sharp reversal of the traditional company policy, in which "suppliers were treated much as production workers: as marginal assets to be utilized at times of peak demand but jettisoned during troughs."[36]

Changes also had to be made in other less official, yet equally insidious unwritten policies that had eroded quality throughout the company. For years some units at Ford had made engineering improvements subject to a minimum two-to-one quality improvement payback ratio. Thus, a plant manager who had an idea for improving door fits that would cost one dollar per car and would save only one dollar in warranty costs would not be permitted by the beancounters to make the improvement. An innovation that cost one dollar would have to generate at least two dollars in savings. The biggest problem with this way of measuring costs was that the company "focused only on savings that the company could identify through its cost control system," says Sullivan. "It didn't look at savings in terms of owner loyalty and repurchase intentions, which can't be factored into the cost control system."[37]

Developing new operating procedures and processes that would be consistent with Ford's new customer-driven agenda was the responsibility of the strategic policy committee's group two. It formalized entirely new approaches to market research so that initial planning began as much as two years before actual product development got under way. Ford also began to conduct consumer clinics throughout the design phase and tinkered continuously with new car designs so that they would reflect the "voice of the customer" right up through completion. To build the '89 Thunderbird, for example, Ford got together thirty-two "design optimization teams" (DOTs) at the beginning of the project. The teams, which consisted of five to ten people each, specialized in a variety of components, such as door handles or air-conditioning systems. The DOTs pored over the consumer research, struggling to make their initial designs fit customer specifications as closely as possible.[38]

Group two also initiated the development of analytical technologies. For example, Ford spent nearly four years developing a computer system designed to detect design features that create what it refers to as "body boom," which includes steering wheel shake and the vibrations that can occur when a car idles. The system was standardized throughout North American product development. Group two also ironed out the details of a program management system in which one manager had responsibility for the development and marketing of a single model, assembling a team of designers and engineers who worked only on that one car. Under the old system, responsibilities were diffused. An interior designer, say, might work on several cars, and the buck wouldn't stop until it hit the desk of the executive in charge of, for example, the entire intermediate car segment, which includes the Tempo, Topaz, Thunderbird, Cougar, and Taurus. Group two also formalized a procedure for launching new vehicles that called for a lengthy report that would specify everything from how and where hourly workers are to be trained to specifically what top management needs to do to make the launch a success.[39]

Ford also developed a benchmarking procedure that had its origins with the Taurus and that has since become standard practice throughout Ford. For the '89 Thunderbird, for example, Ford chose 357 so-called "best in class" features, which range from power door locks to engine performance. The development team was to aim to develop these performance characteristics in such a way that they either matched or exceeded the performance of comparable features found on more expensive cars, including the Mercedes-Benz 190 series and BMW 500/600 series. At the same time, they were to be unique to the T-bird in both appearance and price. The T-bird design team would eventually meet or beat 270 of the targeted standards and fall short of "best in class" on seventy-eight. The characteristics the team couldn't match are to be set aside for future study and—ideally—improvement of subsequent models.[40]

Other parts of the corporation gradually got sucked into the process. At the urging of Ross and Red Poling, before he was named vice chairman, Petersen permanently reassigned most of the market research staff to the operating units. The Alpha project, which had been established to develop new processes and technologies for future automobiles, was also drawn into the improvement game. Alpha, for example, worked on developing a standardized system for the scheduling and delivery of products from suppliers.[41] And throughout Ford, the purchasing groups established the most stringent supplier qualifications in the history of the company. As will be seen in Chapter 5, more than any other of Ford's quality initiatives, the supplier policies reflected Deming's vision. In addition, the supplier standards established by Ford would come to have a major impact on the practices of component manufacturers throughout the country, making them more sensitive than ever to the needs of their client companies.

5

. . . AND HOW THE
AUTOMAKER
SPREAD THE WORD

N o enterprise in American business has ever matched the size and complexity of the auto industry. As far back as 1915, when Henry Ford began planning his revolutionary manufacturing complex on the banks of the Rouge River, his dreams encompassed far more than just a car factory. His empire would include coal and iron mines, forests and rubber plantations, In short, he envisioned a vast production behemoth that would receive raw materials at one end and spit out finished cars at the other end.[1] Ford did, in fact, come to create a totally self-contained, full-menu automotive complex. And for several decades, auto companies followed Ford's model, integrating vertically and controlling every facet of production. However, that vision ended with the era of foreign competition.[2]

The huge capital, labor, and administrative costs of such a multifaceted auto enterprise came to be seen as too unwieldy. By the 1980s competition from inexpensive foreign cars, compounded by Ford's own outdated, bureaucratic management practices, threatened to crush the company under its own weight. For the first time since the 1940s, Ford was hemorrhaging red ink; the automaker's losses totaled $3.26 billion during the three years beginning in 1980. The empire Henry Ford had built found it could no longer afford to feed the capital needs of all of its component-manufacturing offspring. At the same time, many experts were contending that managing such a "vertically integrated" empire was a thing of the past, and that in the new age of foreign rivalry and growing quality requirements the only way to ensure the production of top-of-the-line componentry would be to spin off those businesses to dedicated suppliers. "In an integrated company, the wheel division doesn't get close attention from upper management," explains David Cole, director of the Office for the Study of Automotive Transportation and the son of former GM president Ed Cole. "But a manufacturer who lives and dies to build wheels will give them his undivided attention."[3]

Beginning in the early 1980s, all three major auto companies began in earnest to shed their parts production units. By the end of the 1980s, Ford and Chrysler made only 50 percent and 30 percent of their parts, respectively, down from about 60 percent in 1980. Only GM settled on the opposite strategy. GM would retain close to 70 percent of its parts production by the end of the 1980s, down from a high of about 90 percent.[4]

Of course, holding on to its suppliers would not be easy for GM, and would require the ultimate in management prowess. GM's strategy was born of a confluence of circumstances. The company was unable to sell all of its nonperforming supplier operations. It was under pressure from the United Auto Workers, which saw its power slip with each new plant closing and every layoff announcement. And GM hoped that it could still take advantage of potentially huge economies of scale. At the same time, GM recognized that success in honing its internal supplier operations would be the acid test of GM's quality management strategy and an important key to the company's ability to win back ground both from the Japanese and from Ford.

Today, whether a company has chosen to keep its vendors under one roof or to work with independents, suppliers are recognized as the most important variable in the quality equation. Similarly, the materials and supplies automakers purchase for their cars, as opposed to what they spend on administrative expenses and labor, offer the greatest opportunity for savings and improvements in productivity. The price of materials and supplies accounts for no less than 50 percent of the cost of the content of a car. For some parts, such as engines, the percentage reaches as high as 80 percent. Now U.S. auto companies, led by Ford and guided by Deming, have set out to change their relationships with suppliers dramatically. "We can no longer leave quality [and] service to the forces of competition for price alone—not [with] today's requirements for uniformity and reliability," said James Bakken, who served as vice president for corporate quality at Ford during most of the decade, in January 1981.[5]

As far back as the early 1950s, Deming insisted that the only prudent way to buy parts and reduce the variation of incoming components was to select a supplier with the know-how to produce a high-quality product over and over again. Deming has since become known for exhorting management to winnow its supplier base and to forge close alliances with the companies that remain principal vendors. To managers who want to retain multiple suppliers as an insurance policy against routine production delays or even the freak catastrophes such as a fire, Deming insists that two suppliers are twice the trouble. "You'll have two fires instead of just one," says Deming, who goes so far as to assert that if companies were to foster cooperation with their competitors, it would be far more efficient and profitable to share certain key resources in the event of an emergency, instead of building in redundancy.

This new single-supplier approach, however, flies in the face of a variety of American industrial truisms. It conflicts fundamentally with the competitive bidding process that governs the purchase of most parts and subassemblies in the United States. And while Deming's vendor philosophy began to catch on during the 1980s, many of the problems that continue to plague both industry and the Pentagon's procurement activities stem from the lingering practice of awarding contracts to the lowest bidder.

In Japan, on the other hand, a close relationship between customers and vendors was an idea that quickly caught on during the 1950s. It was to an audience of eager Japanese engineers and scientists that Deming first began to outline his thoughts on the subject. "Price has no meaning except in terms of the quality of the product," Deming told his Japanese students as early as 1950. "Your raw materials may indeed be raw, or they may be sub-assemblies, or pieceparts from another manufacturer. . . . Anyway, there will be a chain of produc-

tion, and . . . statistical techniques are essential in all these stages."
Deming saw the delivery of goods to the customer as a continuum
that required quality control in every stage of production "from raw
material to the consumer."[6]

At many major Japanese companies, suppliers have become virtual extensions of the companies themselves. Toyota, for example,
controls close to three hundred suppliers—many of them located in
or around Toyota City—through direct or indirect equity ownership
of their stock. For example, Toyota controls about 50 percent of
Aisin Seiki, which makes both auto parts and household appliances
and is one of the automaker's largest suppliers. Of that ownership
stake 22.5 percent is held by Toyota directly. The rest is indirectly
held by the company through affiliates, such as Toyoda Automatic
Loom Works, which owns 4.6 percent of Aisin Seiki, and Tokai
Bank, which owns 4.1 percent of Aisin Seiki and is one of Toyota's
principal banks.[7] Similarly, Toyota holds 19 percent of Koito Manufacturing, another auto parts supplier in which T. Boone Pickens,
the Texas takeover artist, recently bought a stake, sending tremors
from Tokyo to Toyota City.

Moreover, a vast network of Toyota executives—both ones who
are climbing the ladder and ones who have recently retired—occupy
top posts at supplier companies. So when it comes to a supplier's
books and operations, nothing is kept secret from the automaker.
"Toyota knows their costs, technology and tells them what their
prices will be," says analyst Maryann Keller. Toyota will even make
adjustments in the prices they pay their suppliers based on a vendor's capital spending needs.[8] Even without an ownership stake, the
long-term relationships between the company and its suppliers
makes for more cooperation than has traditionally existed between
U.S. companies and their vendors.

This arrangement made it relatively easy for large Japanese companies and their suppliers to work on everything from product and
part design to quality control, enhancing both the efficiency and quality of the products that their customers built. (While this system has
created hardships for some small suppliers, who have little bargaining
power with their large customers, they are probably no worse off than
their U.S. counterparts, who can be summarily cut off at the first sign
of a market downturn or the arrival of a lower-priced competitor.)

Such close supplier relationships would also be crucial to the country's experiments with two new, interlinked production concepts—TQC and just-in-time (JIT, or the *kanban* system in Japanese) inventory control procedures,[9] each of which is dependent on the other. TQC called for absolute control over every facet of the production process, without which it would have been impossible to institute an orderly *kanban* system. "When JIT is managed as an outcome rather than a process, it usually leads to grief," notes Professor John Whitney of Columbia University. "But when JIT leads to a richer understanding of the procurement, manufacturing, distribution and other administrative processes, it is a catalyst for important change—not just reduction of raw materials, work in process or finished goods."[10]

Some thirty years later these ideas began to take root in Detroit and would gradually inch their way through the rest of the country. In 1980 auto companies became the first major U.S. industry to recognize the significance of Deming's work, especially the idea that meaningful, long-term improvement could be achieved only through a complete redefinition of supplier relationships. The singular importance of the auto industry within the national economy has helped popularize Deming's principles. And no U.S. company has played a greater role than Ford in legitimizing, if not strict single sourcing then certainly closer alliances between a customer company and a smaller coterie of vendors.

Ford's new vendor policy would lead to a drastic cut in the number of component makers with whom the number-two automaker would do business and, at the same time, a much closer relationship with its remaining base of preferred suppliers. This chapter explores the genesis of Ford's supplier strategy and describes how this supplier initiative has sparked wide-ranging changes throughout the auto industry. It also tells the tale of two companies—a Ford operation that makes engines for the Taurus and one of its principal engine parts suppliers—and shows the struggles and achievements involved in meeting the company's new supplier standards.

Ford's supplier strategy made huge strides because it evolved as part of a broad quality management strategy that demanded the same quality vigilance of the automaker's own divisions that it came to expect from vendors. In the course of forming its strategy, Ford, more than any of its U.S. competitors, would take its cues from

Deming himself; in so doing, it would shape the quality strategies of its vast network of suppliers, from small, family-run mill and drill shops to major steel and chemical corporations.

From the very beginning of its commitment to adopting Deming's management philosophy, Ford made the reevaluation of its supplier relationships a top priority. One of the first Ford executives to meet with Deming, in January 1981, was Larry Sullivan, who was then still serving as quality warden for Ford's supplier organization. Over breakfast one morning preceding a four-day seminar held by Deming in Miami, before Deming had even met with Ford's senior leadership, Sullivan outlined his idea for a series of Deming seminars for the company's suppliers. "He seemed immediately interested," recalls Sullivan. "He said that he had never worked with a large group of suppliers."[11]

Sullivan would launch a monthly training and education program on Deming's ideas and the virtues of statistical thinking that would, in turn, spark a dramatic change in the relationships between automakers and their suppliers throughout the Midwest. In February 1981, after his first meeting with Ford's top executives, Deming helped Sullivan outline a program for all Ford suppliers. The first session, taught by Deming and David Chambers, a retired professor of statistics from the University of Tennessee, was held at Ford in May and was attended by thirty managers representing ten supplier companies. Thereafter, Ford held one seminar every month throughout 1981. Demand was so great that beginning in 1982, the company scheduled the seminars for twice a month.[12]

Soon the clamor for the seminars spread far beyond Ford, and the company decided to spin off its training activities into a separate organization, the American Supplier Institute (ASI). According to Bill Scollard, ASI would be more likely to attract higher-caliber personnel as an independent training organization than as a direct affiliate of Ford. Antitrust considerations may also have played a role, as ASI offers training services to all three automakers and their suppliers.[13] While ASI is not affiliated with Deming, the organization developed as a result of, and as a corollary to, Ford's Deming-driven quality management strategy. It has emerged as one of the best resources for large and small suppliers to the auto industry, in that ASI helps keep them abreast of their customers' requirements and provides a fairly comprehensive curriculum of the latest quality management methods.

Even while ASI was being created in 1982, Ford was taking related steps to translate its quality commitment into a management policy that would embrace both outside suppliers and internal divisions. It was then, for example, that Ford instituted a compelling incentive plan designed to improve the quality of materials delivered by its vendors. The plan was known as the Q-1 Preferred Quality Supplier Program, a series of supplier requirements and examinations that could make winning the Indianapolis 500 seem like child's play. In short, Q-1 was the most rigorous set of supplier standards the company had ever authored; what's more, both internal Ford divisions and outside vendors would both be subjected to its requirements. While Ford had always spelled out the standards it expected suppliers to meet, codifying them in a document for suppliers, Q-1 was designed to spot the very best companies among its vast vendor base and create long-term partnerships with them.

Suppliers who qualified for Q-1 status would become the elite corps of Ford's supplier base, exempt from many of the inspections conducted by the company's quality cops; eventually they would become Ford's only suppliers. In the 1990s Ford's Q-1 suppliers will inherit the business of hundreds of former Ford vendors who did not live up to the new standard. Indeed, Q-1 represented a radical commitment by Ford to reduce the total number of its suppliers over the coming decade, and to establish stronger links with those who achieve Q-1 status. By the mid-1980s, the company had already begun to close low-quality internal divisions and to cast off hundreds of outside vendors. So tough were the new requirements, however, that although Ford had gotten over a thousand supplier plants onto its Q-1 roster by 1989, it was forced to delay cutting off some of the laggards until the early 1990s.[14]

To qualify as a Q-1 supplier, vendors had to answer Deming's call for a holistic, management-driven quality strategy. The Q-1 document called for "the commitment and active support of the supplier's management to pursuing never-ending improvement in quality." Topping the list of specific qualifications is a supplier's ability to control product quality through the use of "Statistical Process Control [SPC] on selected product characteristics or [processes]

that are significant to part function, fit, durability or appearance."
Other qualifications include the ability to deliver high-quality products and services over an extended period of time, the absence of
significant problems in the field, and the ability to pass muster in
initial product samples and deliveries without any start-up glitches.
Finally, before a supplier gets a Q-1 rating, several Ford departments—including product engineering, purchasing, and Supplier
Quality Assurance (SQA), as well as the division(s) that ultimately
use the supplier's parts—must unanimously agree that the supplier
has met the requirements.[15]

TAURUS: HOW DEMINGISM HELPED REDEFINE FORD'S FAMILY CAR OF THE 1980s

If the Pinto was emblematic of the 1970s nadir of Ford quality, the
Taurus would come to symbolize the company's 1980s determination to achieve high quality. Several historical events helped shape
the car: Following the second oil price shock, Ford was in desperate
financial straits. Henry Ford II, who in his later years had made
several important product planning mistakes, was no longer in
charge.[16] And the industry was on the threshold of a new quality
awakening that in the case of Ford had taken on added impetus as
a result of the Pinto disaster. Taurus was a chance for the company
to do something different.

In what might have been Ford's eleventh hour, the company's
leadership seized the moment and vested the Taurus with all the
quality know-how the company then possessed. "The Taurus was
successful because a lot of these new [quality] ideas matured in the
Taurus," says Sullivan. The car marked the first time market research was conducted *before* product development began.[17] The
project pioneered a new approach to teamwork and planted the
seeds for Ford's benchmarking system. The car was to be assembled
at a former Thunderbird plant in Chicago, which for two years had
been one of a handful of factories selected as pilot projects in process
improvement. For the first time a Ford assembly plant would be
brought into the product development process from the earliest design phase.[18]

But behind this oft-cited product development morality tale is a story of gradual change and profound breakthrough at two component factories, one belonging to Ford and the other to one of its suppliers, which together would help build a new engine for the Taurus. Ford's Essex engine plant in Windsor, Ontario, staked its future on winning a piece of the Taurus business; and J. L. French, a small, family-run engine parts supplier in Sheboygan, Wisconsin, bet the family store on becoming a Q-1 supplier to Ford.

Jim French, the founder of the small die-casting operation in Sheboygan, can attest to the hopes, the rigors, and the ultimate payoff that can accrue to a supplier dedicated to managing for quality. By the end of the 1980s, French would become the sole-source supplier of aluminum die-cast cylinder block front covers to the Essex plant, which today builds engines for the Taurus, Thunderbird, Cougar, and Lincoln Continental cars. The company would also parlay the expertise it had acquired working for Ford into a coveted supplier contract for a groundbreaking new GM engine. However, J. L. French's struggle to meet the quality standards of the automakers would also demonstrate the frustration that can come when a supplier tries to master quality management in tandem with its customer.

It was in 1980 that French encountered the new quality zealotry at Ford and first heard the name of W. Edwards Deming. That encounter sparked the beginning of the reeducation of Jim French. The soft-spoken Wisconsinite didn't know what awaited him when, in 1981, he was summoned to Detroit along with the representatives of some six hundred other suppliers to Ford's engine division. At the meeting in a large auditorium in the building that in headier days had been named World Headquarters, Ford managers outlined Deming's principles and their own quality goals, then announced that henceforth the same principles and goals would have to guide Ford suppliers as well. As an added incentive, Ford announced that its base of six hundred engine parts suppliers, which had already been winnowed down from about nine hundred a few years earlier, would be slashed even further, to no more than two hundred in all. Among the vendors represented at the meeting were those from Ford's own captive supplier base—they too would have to live up to the automaker's ultimatum or risk being shut down or sold.

French realized he was faced with the most important business decision of his career: He could either overhaul his business and remain a Ford supplier, or he could keep doing business as usual and seek his fortune elsewhere. "We knew that if they were going to dump their own sister divisions because of quality, they wouldn't hesitate to close us out," recalls French. "They were serious about what they were saying. They were talking about single sourcing."[19]

In the next few years, Ford delivered on its threat. The auto company slashed suppliers ruthlessly, going so far as to close its own die-casting operations in Sheffield, Alabama, the largest such operation in the world, and its iron plant in Flat Rock, Michigan.[20]

One of the Ford plants that watched this determined downsizing campaign with some trepidation was one of French's most important customers, the Essex engine plant. A brand-new factory just across the Detroit River from Motown, Essex had opened its doors in 1981 to produce V-6 engines for the LTD, Marquis, and Mustang cars.[21] In 1986 Essex stopped building the LTD and Marquis engines. And although the plant would continue production for Thunderbirds and Cougars, the 1982 recession reduced demand for midsized vehicles, and capacity at Essex was cut in half. Although Essex made a 3.8-liter V-6 rear-wheel-drive engine and Taurus was to be a front-wheel-drive car that would house a smaller three-liter engine, Essex had hopes that management would retool part of the factory to make engines for the new cars. That hope was dashed when Ford decided, instead, to relocate engine production for the Taurus to the company's Lima, Ohio, plant; it would be too costly to convert the Essex equipment that built the 3.8-liter engine to the smaller, all-new three-liter version.[22]

Being a new plant, Essex had none of the endemic quality problems of the older Ford plants. Yet economic conditions being what they were in the early 1980s, the plant's management realized that just staying open, let alone convincing management to give it new product lines, would require a major overhaul of the factory's standards. Leo Brown, the manager of three Ford plants in Ontario including Essex, was determined to make Essex the highest-quality plant at the company. In February 1981 the Ford veteran, who had started his career as an hourly worker after World War II, paid a visit to the Mazda plant in Hiroshima. "I won't forget that experience as long as I live," says Brown. "I was awestruck. I could see equipment running, producing good quality, with virtually no people, no inspectors, no rejects, no repairs . . . and they were doing it by understanding their process."[23]

Brown returned to Ontario determined to try some of the ideas he had seen in Japan. He first tested them on the operation that manufactured 5.8-liter cylinder blocks for light truck engines at one of the Windsor plants and quickly established an umbrella strategy for all three factories. Says Brown, "We started talking to our operators and told them to stop as soon as they see anything wrong. I took six months to make believers out of them, to get them to trust management. We tried to gather process data and realized we didn't know much about how to do that."[24]

One of the most important challenges would be to educate and train the plant's employees both in the new quality philosophy of the company and in Deming's approach to process improvement. Deming gave a four-day seminar in Windsor, and the Essex plant began working closely with David Chambers, who was also advising Ford. "Ford always had been heavily involved with statistical methods, but we used it to measure output. There was too much measuring results, rather than process conditions," said Mel Rowe, a veteran Ford man who was a quality control expert at the company for twenty-three years before becoming the production manager at Essex in the mid-1980s. "Deming said that's not where you should use statistics, you should use it upstream. Deming influenced the whole corporation in this."[25]

Essex launched a plantwide training program to get its workers to use statistical tools to control and analyze the manufacturing systems they operated. The training was developed with the help of Deming, David Chambers, and Byron Doss, a student of Chambers, and was eventually even picked up by the Canadian government. Everyone from the hourly workers to Brown himself was trained in statistical methods and in the new quality philosophy. All Essex employees received twenty-five to forty hours of statistical schooling during a four-month period. The exact amount of instruction depended on the rank and position of each individual and whether he would be simply monitoring a process to make sure it was in control or conducting experiments to improve it. In the beginning, Mel

Rowe and Jim Fullerton, the quality control manager at Essex, discovered that not everyone was learning the material properly. The plant's quality strategy depended on the statistical competence of its workers, so Rowe and Fullerton also instituted an examination in statistical methods for all trainees.[26]

Essex began to reap the results of its improvement strategy almost immediately. In 1986 it became the first Ford plant to receive Ford's coveted Q-1 award. Based on the company's older measures of quality, the things-gone-wrong statistics, Essex realized an 87 percent improvement between 1981 and 1986. As process control improved, the need for inspection diminished. Eventually, Brown planned to install computer workstations to tie together control chart data throughout the plant, and to give management quick snapshots of its quality performance.[27]

In about 1987, Essex would get the ultimate reward for its quality efforts. Taurus was proving to be such an unexpected success that customers were ordering cars faster than the Lima plant could roll out engines. In addition, consumer research had shown that there was demand for a more powerful engine, and Ford decided to make the 3.8-liter engine optional in both the Taurus and the Sable. When headquarters went searching for ways to add new capacity, they gave the job to Essex. The effort would require converting the rear-wheel-drive motor to a front-wheel-drive version of the 3.8-liter engine, as well as modifying the Taurus itself. And Ford would invest tens of millions of dollars to retool the Essex plant. "If we hadn't made the kind of progress [in quality] that we did, we wouldn't have gotten the [Taurus] model for 1988," says Rowe. "And if we hadn't gotten the engine, our future would have been uncertain."[28]

But the Essex story isn't about the accomplishments of just one plant. The improvements Essex realized couldn't have been accomplished without parallel efforts being made by its suppliers. When Ford rewrote its purchasing policies, Essex began scrutinizing its vendors carefully, analyzing the quality of both its incoming components and the systems that created the parts. Of course, old manufacturing hands like Brown, Rowe, and Fullerton had always known that having several suppliers build the same part can be a quality control nightmare. And they were overjoyed when Deming started talking about single sourcing and the company started listening. "We'd been saying that since the 1960s, but no one would listen," insists Fullerton, the current quality manager.[29]

One look at its four suppliers of front covers, and Essex realized it had a problem on its hands. Although plant officials worked for a few months with all its suppliers and made sure they understood its new requirements, Essex wound up eliminating three of the vendors—all except French. None proved as reliable as French, which by this time was deeply committed to winning Q-1 status. In 1985 French would become the sole-source supplier for cylinder block front covers for Essex, which cover the valve and oil pump. It would be another four years, however, before French won Q-1 status.[30]

French is a textbook case of how a small supplier came to alter its business, absorbing the latest in quality and engineering know-how and working closely with its customers to continuously improve its products and processes to meet the escalating demands of the marketplace. Since Jim French's awakening in 1980, the company had committed itself to a companywide quality improvement effort. To achieve the quality standards demanded by Ford, French tackled design and processes that had once produced leaky parts and reject rates that on some components occasionally ran as high as 60 percent.[31]

French, whose employees are not afraid to correct or contradict him in front of outsiders, had more than the usual incentive to keep his business growing. He is a devoted family man, all four of his children—two daughters and two sons—work for the company, and he was determined to leave them a thriving legacy. French moved quickly to overhaul his business and to meet Essex's new guidelines. As 1980 drew to a close, French hired seven engineers in the midst of a recession. For a company with fewer than two hundred employees, in which French himself was the only degreed mechanical engineer, the increase was monumental. French hoped that with the help of his new engineers and improved quality management, his company would eventually recoup its costs both by retaining Ford as a customer and by expanding his customer base even further. The company also hired a number of consultants, including one from ASI. Most important, the company began to change the arm's-length relationship that always had characterized its contacts with Ford.

Traditionally, a "Chinese Wall" philosophy had prevented customers and suppliers from collaborating on projects. In the compartmentalized world of Detroit, where warring departments spent as much time building ramparts against each other as in building cars, engineers worked on component designs in high-security design studios that even fellow Ford employees found difficult to penetrate. Moreover, because suppliers were treated as commodities, to be discarded when they had outlived their usefulness, companies like Ford lived in fear that suppliers might learn something about a design that could be taken to a competitor. Once completed, designs were handed over to Ford's suppliers as faits accomplis, with little opportunity for revision. It never occurred to anyone at Ford, nor for that matter at most U.S. manufacturers, to draw on the expertise of their vendors.[32] Consequently, while a design plan might be an auto engineer's ideal, from a functional point of view it often was designed with little regard for the part's manufacturability. As a result, the designs for engines—as for most other auto components—were often difficult to build, prone to quality problems, and susceptible to cost overruns.

In contrast to this segmented approach, the new goal would be "simultaneous engineering"—Ford and French engineers would struggle for months together over blueprints. The Ford engineers would strive for an efficient, compact engine; the French engineers would struggle to make the design one that would be easy to build without defects. These two sets of requirements might often conflict. But if the system worked right, the two groups, working together, would come up with a plan that would meet customer desires in ways that no blueprint devised by either one alone could achieve.

The pursuit of a high-quality front cover led both French and Ford to make fundamental changes in both the 3.8-liter model and the process that manufactured it. These changes began with an effort to overcome the obstacles of the old-style Chinese Wall. When Jim French was first handed the blueprints for the front cover in 1979, he was dismayed. From a manufacturer's standpoint the front cover was a nightmare. French predicted porosity and a resulting high oil leak rate that could cause messy oil drips and could, in extreme cases, affect the performance of the engine.[33]

Part of the problem was that the front cover was a combination of very thin and very thick sections that was difficult to manufacture. While thickness gradations aren't a problem for designers, they can be a quality disaster for manufacturers because of the way different metal thicknesses respond to the huge temperature swings in the die-casting process. The aluminum is heated to 1,400 degrees Fahrenheit and cast at 1,200 degrees; as the part cools to room temperature, it can lose as much as 10 percent of its volume. Thicker sections will cool and shrink unevenly, causing porosity and occasional leaks. The worst leak problem was found in the oil pump pocket, which serves as a reservoir for pumping oil through the engine. In the original blueprint, the pump pocket was designed to be part of the front cover, sticking to one side as incongruously as oversized tailfins. And because the blueprints were already completed, it took years to bring about changes in the original design. Says Charlie Walden, French's vice president of manufacturing, "Ford was locked in, the suppliers were locked in to making the front cover as it was originally designed."[34]

Over the course of the next three years, French and Ford worked together to improve the design and reliability of the 3.8-liter V-6 front cover. By the early 1980s, French was embarked on a quality improvement mission that would shift management's focus from merely building components from customer blueprints to actually designing and improving them. The new cadre of engineers—most of them refugees from the Big Three—soaked up the latest in quality management literature. They attended seminars by Deming and a host of other quality experts. Dennis Shimmel, the head of manufacturing, dusted off the old SPC texts that he had studied as a graduate student at the General Motors academy (GMI) but had rarely been called on to use before—either at his previous job at GM or at French. And the engineers began teaching the simplified techniques Deming had popularized to French personnel.[35] With each new increment of knowledge came insights and tools for making further improvements in the front cover.

French's results were impressive. By 1985, working on a variety of process improvements, French had slashed its reject level to 4.36 percent, and its scrap level was down to 1.71 percent.[36]

Yet although the existing design and machinery wouldn't allow French to make any further significant improvements, the company's accomplishments weren't enough to meet Ford's demands fully. While French believed it was close to achieving its long-sought-after goal of becoming a Ford Q-1 supplier and many at Ford agreed, Essex still wasn't satisfied. According to Ford rules, to receive Q-1 status, a supplier must pass muster not just with Ford's corporate purchasing department, but also with each department within the auto company that uses the parts supplied by the applicant. During a 1985 review French was passed for Q-1 status by every Ford department except the Essex engine plant.[37]

Ironically, what stood in the way of Essex's final vote of approval were problems that stemmed at least in part from the original, outdated design and production procedures that had so dismayed Jim French when Essex had first presented them in 1979. French's predicament in 1985 underscores the irony of Ford's new vendor criteria—Ford would have to change its *own* methods in order for vendors to be able to meet the new standards. Only with a major overhaul of Ford's own engine designs could French carry out the additional manufacturing improvements needed to make the front covers good enough to meet Ford's Q-1 standards.

In 1985 Ford management approved the additional capital that was needed to retool and redesign the 3.8-liter V-6 engine, and French was faced with the challenge of improving its product and process still further. One of the first projects tackled by French was the pump pocket. French convinced Ford that the pump pocket should be broken out of the design, manufactured separately, and later attached to the front cover. Of course, the reason the pump pocket had been designed as an integral part of the front cover in the first place was because Ford believed the one-step manufacturing process would save money. French, however, convinced Ford that breaking the part in two would not only improve quality, but by reducing the scrap and rework rate, which at its peak was about 38 percent, would also ultimately reduce costs.[38]

To make further improvements in its processes, Essex encouraged French to call on ASI and explore the Taguchi methods. Genichi Taguchi, a Japanese statistician whose ideas are being vigorously promoted by ASI, won a Deming Prize in 1960 for advancing new ideas in practical statistical theory; he sought to improve on traditional SPC by identifying an optimum level of quality for both products and processes.[39] And it was to the Taguchi methods that French turned in order to minimize still further the occasional porosity and leakage problems of its front covers. First, a team of French engineers held a brainstorming session on the problems with the front cover and came up with thirty-one process variables they thought would have an impact on the product's quality. Then they narrowed down the list to eleven key characteristics that would require careful evaluation and experimentation to determine their impact on the product's quality.[40] Throughout the improvement process, French engineers and plant workers teamed up with their counterparts at Ford to optimize the front cover design. At one point, French engineers took a die-casting machine out of service for an entire month to run tests and adjustments on it so the company would meet the required quality standard—an unheard-of event prior to 1980.[41]

By 1987 French was registering a new round of record-breaking improvements. The company had again slashed its reject rate on the front cover—this time fourfold—to 1.13 percent and brought its scrap rate down to just .76 percent.[42]

French would finally achieve Q-1 status in March 1989.[43] And the rewards for its engineering and manufacturing discipline extend far beyond the professional and financial satisfaction of having helped lick the problems of the V-6 front cover. Since 1980 French's sales have grown eightfold, according to Jim French, and by 1988 Ford came to account for some 63 percent of French's business. These days French insists he doesn't know how he ever functioned without modern quality management tools, including SPC.[44]

French also credits his Ford experience with helping him break away from mere die casting and making it possible for his company to begin producing more sophisticated and more lucrative subassemblies. In fact, for French the improvements made for Ford were just the beginning of a whole new series of business opportunities. The Sheboygan company would go on to get one of its first—and most profitable—subassembly jobs, the Quad 4 front cover for Buick-Oldsmobile-Cadillac (BOC), GM's big-car division, which had also tailored its supplier strategy to Deming's specifications. French is just one example of the growing number of companies that have joined an exclusive industrial club that requires its members to demonstrate an understanding of the quality management principles espoused by Deming. Increasingly, it is the one club they *must* join.

It was in order to create a subcontractor elite that ASI was established by Ford. While ASI is not affiliated with Deming, it grew out of Ford's Deming-driven quality management strategy. ASI sought to fill the vacuum of a market that has been largely devoid of a central resource that would provide suppliers with the quality management know-how they need to meet the growing demands of their customers.

To distinguish itself from other quality organizations, ASI's core curriculum was based on the methods of Genichi Taguchi. Unlike traditional SPC, which focuses exclusively on honing production processes, Taguchi's approach was aimed at improving the process of product development as well as that of manufacturing. Since it was spun off from Ford, ASI has expanded beyond Taguchi to teach the proliferating number of techniques developed in Japan.

Some critics, including Deming, worry that many companies new to quality management ideas plunge into a flavor-of-the-month approach to these techniques without first learning the theories on which they are based and without pursuing them in the context of a broad quality strategy. While this is all too often true, a number of firms have successfully used the methods taught by ASI to enhance their quality endeavors. And since both ASI and its curriculum have become all the rage at companies such as GM and Xerox, the rest of this chapter will offer a taste of how Taguchi methods and similar tools are intended to improve conventional product development.

The unique contribution of Taguchi to the quality management movement is that he seeks to ascribe a dollar value to the *loss* incurred by each increment of diminished quality of a product or process. According to Taguchi's "quality loss function," any deviation from an optimum level of performance results in a quantifiable loss to the company, the customer, or both. A loss to the company encompasses such conventional measures as the costs of warranty, inventory, or scrap, as well as the less obvious, long-term costs of downtime and lost market share. The latter is generally the result of losses suffered by the customer in terms of the time and inconvenience involved in getting a product repaired, or simply the annoyance of having to live with an inferior product, such as a television with a static-riddled image. Taguchi calculated that the level of loss increases quadratically the further the performance of a product diverges from its optimum target.[45]

The precision demanded by Taguchi's theory is in sharp contrast to the conventional U.S. approach to product engineering. The traditional view holds that a product is equally "good" as long as its performance falls within certain specified limits, and equally "bad" the minute it falls outside those limits. One problem with this notion is that it doesn't take into account the potential long-term effects of variation, which exist even within relatively narrow specification boundaries. Another problem is that engineers pick specification limits more or less at random, based on their professional experience. Engineers have no meaningful way of pinning tolerance limits to real-world requirements.[46]

To illustrate the shortcomings of performing to specifications, Lance Ealy, in his book *Quality by Design*, compares the performance of two football players competing for the quarterback position on a football team: "Both quarterbacks are usually able to place the ball within the receiver's catching range . . . both quarterbacks are conforming to specification. In examining the charts, the coach notices that the quarterback named Burt places the ball within the receiver's reach each and every time, but tends to vary widely in how close he gets the ball to the receiver's hands. The quarterback named Bubba, on the other hand, throws a few passes outside the receiver's reach, but otherwise all his passes drop right in the receiver's hands.

"Based on experience, the coach realizes that there's another factor to take into account—the receiver's balance after he catches the ball. If the ball lands toward the outer limits of his reach, he'll be more off-balance and likely to fall, fumble the ball, or be intercepted. Which quarterback do you think should get the job? The coach chose Bubba. His delivery was much more consistent and uniform than Burt's, even though his passes occasionally fell outside the receiver's reach limits. The receiver stayed in balance much more often when Bubba was throwing, so his chances of falling, fumbling, or having the ball intercepted were reduced."[47]

If consistency is useful in football, imagine how important it is when it comes to producing complex products that may be made up of dozens or even hundreds of parts. The more parts, the greater the risk that "tolerance stackup" will occur. "Tolerance stackup is the reason one car's transmission shifts so smoothly, while that of the next works like a stick twirling in a bucket of bolts."[48] In a complex product, small deviations will add up to the sort of major problems that result in companies employing legions of employees in repair or so-called "finesse operations." To get car doors to fit correctly during assembly, for example, auto companies used to hire battalions of door fitters whose job it was to bend door frames into shape, adjust hinges, and shim weather strips.[49]

In Taguchi's world of "optimum targets," an engineer's job is to develop "robust" products capable of resisting the outside forces that can degrade quality, like the old AT&T telephones that seemed to withstand endless banging, dropping, and coffee spills and still kept on ringing. Taguchi has developed procedures for conducting a series of engineering experiments aimed at identifying the ideal combination of product characteristics that will meet customer requirements and, at the same time, minimize the product's susceptibility to variation. Put simply, the search for this ideal quality target in the development of a car door, for example, might work like this:

- First, engineers use the results of market research to determine what characteristics customers want in a door. These include watertightness and ease of closing.
- Second, the engineer identifies the noncontrollable environmental characteristics that are likely to erode performance of the door. Rain, which causes leaks and rust, is likely to head the list. Other factors might include adverse road conditions that could, over time, throw the door fit out of whack.
- Third, the engineer conducts a series of experiments to determine what combination of design features will make the door easy to close and leakproof, will make it "robust" against environmental impediments over time, and will do so in the most efficient way possible. Some of the design possibilities will include using rustproof paints, special materials for weatherstripping, or new lock and hinge designs.

During the long and complex process of designing and building an automobile, staying on target demands continuous process improvement and detailed analysis. For example, it took Ford four years to develop the computer system that is used to ferret out the design features that result in "body boom." The company spent that time developing the computer system and mathematical models that can predict, as a new vehicle moves through the product development process, which design changes might result in body boom.[50]

But while the Taguchi methods are gradually being embraced by hundreds of U.S. companies, they have never fully caught on in Japan. Proponents of Taguchi point out that conflicting Japanese attitudes toward statisticians are a function of class and clique rivalries. Japan's incubator for quality management ideas and the dispenser of the Deming Prize is JUSE, which has been led from its inception in the 1950s by such Brahmins as Kaoru Ishikawa, whose father, Ichiro, was once head of Keidanren (the Japanese Federation of Economic Organizations), the country's most prestigious business group. In Japan's class-conscious society, Taguchi could hardly run in the same crowd; his family ran a small kimono factory and was of modest means, he came from the wrong side of the mountain, and he had received an entirely unsuitable education (he attended Kiryu Technical College for a year, but never earned a degree).[51] Nevertheless, in addition to winning the Deming Prize, in 1989 he would receive an award from the emperor for his work in statistical theory.[52]

There may, however, be theoretical reasons for Taguchi's less than universal acceptance in Japan. By suggesting that there is an "optimum" quality level products can achieve, the Taguchi method challenges, at least hypothetically, the fundamental tenet of quality management theory, as defined by Deming and the Japanese, which calls for continuous, *never-ending* quality improvement. In the United States, there is a real danger that companies that until recently were all too willing to fall back on the bottom line as an excuse for avoiding needed process improvements may seize on this loophole of the Taguchi method and misuse it. It is interesting to note, for example, that even Toyota, whose famed production system is capable of a level of quality so high that it rarely produces a reject, is never sanguine about its processes. As an extra safeguard against even the remote possibility that a single defective product or part will reach its customers, Toyota has installed a system of automatic inspection of several key car components.[53] For example, a propeller shaft is attached using four bolts. If, for any reason, one of the four bolts is insufficiently torqued, a sensor on the torquing equipment will identify the problem, set off an alarm to notify an operator, and automatically stop the assembly process.

ASI, however, has popularized another quality engineering technique that has gained wide acceptance in Japan and is beginning to catch on in the United States. Quality function deployment (QFD), as it is known, is a system designed to match product designs as closely as possible to customer desires by capturing, in the most efficient way possible, the diverse know-how of experts in such fields as marketing, engineering, and manufacturing. In the United States, it was probably introduced first at Xerox by Don Clausing, a former company executive who now teaches at MIT and who learned about the technique from Xerox's Japanese affiliate, Fuji Xerox, a Deming Prize winner (see Chapter 7).[54]

The approach also is known as the House of Quality because of the matrix that is used by QFD practitioners. The participants on a QFD team list customer requirements along the vertical axis of a chart and product characteristics that might fulfill those desires along the horizontal axis. The roof of the house pinpoints contradictory customer desires. For example, a customer's desire to have a car door that closes easily is in conflict with the desire for a leakproof door. The chart is a way of prioritizing various alternative solutions.[55]

The House of Quality has several advantages. It creates a mechanism for studying every option and including representatives from every discipline in the product development process. It slashes the time and cost of developing products. For example, Toyota says that in the early 1980s it significantly reduced the cost of a new minivan by 60 percent by using QFD. Equally important, the system creates a powerful institutional memory by capturing and documenting knowledge that usually is lost when experts retire, get promoted, or leave their jobs. The need for such a storehouse of expertise was driven home to Bill Scollard when he recently realized that some of his subordinates were trying to work through manufacturing problems he thought he had solved twenty years earlier.[56]

ASI was born out of the quality fervor Deming sparked at Ford, and by bringing techniques such as QFD and the Taguchi methods to American management, the organization has succeeded in greatly expanding the quality lexicon of U.S. companies. However, Deming, who is a great admirer of Taguchi, is critical of ASI and its focus on quality techniques, rather than the more all-encompassing philosophy of quality management. Having observed nearly four decades of American apathy toward quality following World War II, Deming is skeptical about the depth of commitment U.S. companies today have for developing a rigorous, disciplined approach to quality problems. Deming is certainly correct when he bemoans the fact that real quality improvement in U.S. corporations hasn't nearly kept pace with the level of quality rhetoric. Similarly, even ASI's admirers say that the organization has grown so fast that its training is sometimes spotty. Nevertheless, ASI offers a quality curriculum that currently is available virtually noplace else in the United States (see Chapter 10). If nothing else, it is emblematic of the seriousness with which both auto suppliers and the auto industry are trying to take quality management.

HOW A FLORIDA
UTILITY BECAME AN
UNLIKELY
CONTENDER FOR
SAMURAI SUCCESS

John Justus Hudiberg's management epiphany "wasn't born in a great burst of inspirational light." Rather, it dawned on him gradually, coming into sharp focus while he was visiting a company a long way from home during the fall of 1985. Hudiberg, a native Floridian and CEO of Florida Power & Light, was desperately trying to work out a nagging puzzle. For several years now, executives at FP&L and Kansai Electric, a utility company based in Osaka, had shared information on the management and construction of power plants. They had also launched parallel efforts to improve electric utility service and reduce costs. And although both utilities had begun their quality drives at about the same time, within just five years Kansai had far surpassed FP&L's performance. By 1984, when Kansai won the Deming Prize, the Japanese utility had become, in the words of one FP&L executive, "the best electric utility in the world."[1]

An engineer by training and a Green Beret by disposition, Hudiberg wouldn't allow the disturbing conundrum to go unsolved. For one thing, he had been handed a mandate by Marshall McDonald, then CEO of FP&L's parent company, FPL Group, to improve both the quality and efficiency of the utility's electric service. He began a series of frequent visits to Japan, often making the fourteen-hour journey by jet several times each year, in order to come to grips with how TQC had made Kansai, and dozens of other Deming Prize–winning companies Hudiberg had visited, a cut above the average U.S. firm. Hudiberg's search would culminate in probably the most radical attempt to transplant Japan's quality management philosophy as it has evolved since Deming planted the seeds four decades ago. Moreover, in its quality crusade, FP&L not only created a milestone in quality management for all of U.S. industry, it also proved that TQC is as applicable to service industries as it is to manufacturing companies.

Of all the aspects of TQC, the one that came to fascinate Hudiberg the most was Japan's quality management and strategy deployment process known as "policy deployment." A twist on management by objective, Hudiberg observed that policy deployment was probably the most important mechanism for institutionalizing quality management in the holistic, all-encompassing form in which it is practiced at Japanese companies.

What appealed to Hudiberg about policy deployment was that it requires managers to be intimately involved not only in setting objectives, but also in guiding the strategies and procedures for achieving them. They do this in two ways: First, TQC companies create an efficient, corporatewide information feedback system that is meant not only to update management on important changes in operations, but also to create a closer link between management goals and the major problems and opportunities facing the company. Second, they create a systematic way of rolling corporate objectives throughout the organization by enlisting the problem-solving skills of management and by defining the jobs of individual employees in terms of logical priorities everyone can understand. Moreover, because of its intense focus on analyzing and understanding the process, policy deployment makes it much more difficult, according to one FP&L manager, to "manipulate the system by setting loose objectives and easy targets."[2]

The more Hudiberg probed, the more he began to understand that through policy deployment, Japanese companies used the same statistical, analytical approach that had made SPC an integral part of the manufacturing process to work out both long-term strategic issues and everyday business problems. It was during one of his Japanese reconnaissance missions in September 1985 that he finally saw clearly the method behind policy deployment and TQC, which Hudiberg has come to refer to as "the single issue of highest importance to American management." Not surprisingly, the light went on while Hudiberg was visiting a Kansai nuclear plant—nuclear plants being the costliest and most quality-sensitive part of a utility's operations.[3]

This is how Hudiberg remembers the occasion:

"I was over there trying to understand this policy deployment. I had trouble understanding. Finally, I got to one of Kansai's nuclear plants. We [in the utility business] have problems with what we call scrams—when one of many thousands of instruments, sensing mechanisms, detects what appears to be an abnormality and shuts the plant down. If there really was an abnormality you'd want it to shut down, but almost invariably it's a false signal, in which case you have to find out why, what triggered the problem. Then you have to fix it, and it takes three days to fix, and meanwhile your plant's not running, plus you've put the whole system through a rather severe test. So you don't want false scrams.

"We were having seven per year, per plant. And we'd set a goal for [1985] of five per plant. And it looked like we were going to achieve that goal—big achievement, right? Well, [Kansai] operate[s] nine nuclear plants. And I asked how many scrams they'd had by that time in September. They said none. I thought there was a translation error. [We] worked on that for a while and finally realized we were in fact talking the same language. So I asked how many they had the year before. They said two. So they had operated eighteen plant-years with only two scrams. I was impressed. I knew that only six years earlier they had had terrible problems with their nuclear plants. We had better operations than they did six years earlier. By then I had some inkling of how they had done it."

That inkling developed into full-blown understanding as Hudiberg made the rounds to other, nonnuclear operations and saw a standard approach to quality. Whether visiting a district office, which dispatches meter readers and repair personnel to local customers, or watching crews of linemen who install electrical cable, Hudiberg saw the same vigilant approach to quality and to the process practiced throughout the company.

"I visited a district office," continues Hudiberg. "They had these charts on the wall. Now by that time I [had seen plenty of these] and could read the vertical axis, and it said one, two, three, four, five. And across the bottom were twelve characters, which obviously signaled the months. It showed a bar chart that started off at six, held at five, and went down to four. So I asked 'em what it was. They said it showed meter reading errors—'very bad, you know, if you misread meter it's very embarrassing, great loss of face, blah, blah, blah.'

"I understood that. I'd been a district manager in an earlier life, and we worked very hard to reduce meter-reading errors, and if we'd do a good job, we'd make about one every two thousand customers. So I asked 'em what the vertical axis represented, knowing they had four hundred thousand customers in the district. Again we had a translation problem. But finally I realized the numbers were an absolute. They had four meter reading errors per month, that is, one per one hundred thousand customers. They were doing fifty times better than we were! So I went through quite a thing trying to understand how they went about achieving that. Again it was a policy deployment, [it had to do with the way they were organized to meet] the corporate goal to reduce meter readings errors.

"Then I went out with a crew working on a project, replacing faulty wires. They had analyzed the causes of the interruptions and they had systematically identified with data the source, the root cause of interruptions, and had come up with schedules, goals, and projects to remove 'em. They found the wires were giving them some trouble, so they were in the process of replacing 'em. I found out how many interruptions they had, and it was about six minutes per customer per year. At that time we had about eighty minutes per customer per year of interruptions.

"I was impressed."[4]

By then, Hudiberg had gathered how the whole thing worked. He had carefully studied the way Japanese managers organized their companies always to be up to date on both the weaknesses of their processes and the progress they were making in every department and division. What Hudiberg had discovered was the Deming cycle as it is applied to corporate management. Although FP&L would not undergo a formal reorganization, Hudiberg, who had never worked anywhere but FP&L since he had begun as a student engineer in

1951, would use the model to radically alter the company's standards of management and the way he measured its progress. To help rally his troops, Hudiberg set his sights on the Deming Prize. As a result, in 1989 the Florida utility would become the first U.S. winner of Japan's highest award for corporate excellence. (McDonald would retire in 1989, and Hudiberg would resign as soon as FP&L clinched the prize.) During the years since Hudiberg's trip in 1985, the company's preparations for the competition have made it "the benchmark of U.S. quality," says Norman Rickard, vice president for quality at Xerox. They have also placed FP&L at the forefront of a belated worldwide awakening to Demingism, and a corresponding recognition of the benefits of Japan's holistic, process-oriented management approach.[5]

The Florida utility is an unlikely vanguard of U.S. management. "We've been producing sixty-cycle electricity for sixty years, and in sixty years the product hasn't changed one iota," chuckled Kent Sterett, the company's quality director at the time. "A bucketful today looks the same as a bucketful looked then." Indeed, FP&L doesn't have to spend heavily on new product development. Moreover, being heavily regulated, the electric utility faces little of the cutthroat competition that plagues manufacturers.[6]

Yet even power companies have their challenges; FP&L was spurred into action by the energy crisis of the 1970s, "That was the culmination of the environmental craze, the oil shock, the antigrowth movement, the antinuclear movement, and inflation," says Marshall McDonald. "None of which had been anticipated a decade earlier." As oil prices drove up utility rates in the 1970s, Florida's largest power company became the target of both disgruntled consumers and regulators. FP&L was, for example, the first Florida company forced to cut back sharply on its sulfur emissions, one of the by-products of burning sulfur fuels. Consequently, FP&L needed to recoup its loss due to the extra expense. But McDonald feared that by attempting to raise rates once too often the utility might one day suffer a backlash similar to California's controversial effort to roll back insurance rates a decade later, after the insurance industry had let premiums skyrocket. "Even a utility can be brought to its knees if regulators won't allow you to recover your costs," says McDonald.[7]

It was during the second oil shock that McDonald seized on the quality movement as a way both to boost the company's public image and to control costs. In 1979, while McDonald was still president of the utility, he was invited to give a speech at a personnel conference in Chicago. As it happened, the speaker before him was lecturing on the remarkable transformation that had occurred at a Motorola television plant soon after it had been bought by a Japanese company. McDonald doesn't remember much about the anecdote except that the Japanese firm had promised not to fire any workers at the factory and had then brought battalions of Japanese workers to help their American counterparts improve the company's performance. By the end of the year, the former Motorola factory had doubled productivity and had seen its reject rate drop from 17 percent to 3 percent. Recalls McDonald, "This was the first experience I'd heard of that showed an American labor force capable of doing the same thing as the Japanese."[8]

While it would be several years before FP&L finalized a plan, it was during that meeting that McDonald decided to reshape FP&L with a quality management strategy. What makes FP&L's experience such an instructive one is the total commitment with which management approached the challenge. Over a period of five years, it has incorporated most of the key elements of Demingism, including

- Careful analysis and redefinition of customer requirements
- A process improvement effort led by top management
- Establishment of improvement teams among the rank and file
- Extensive training of management, labor, and suppliers in the use of statistics and problem-solving techniques

Most important, what set FP&L apart from many other would-be practitioners in the United States is the total commitment of management and the absolute consistency with which quality principles, especially the disciplines of statistical analysis and problem solving, were woven through the entire fabric of the company. FP&L established strict procedures for improvement to ensure that the right improvement projects were chosen and that their results could be applied elsewhere in the company. Periodic management reviews check that the projects stay on track and serve as a means of constantly reevaluating their relevance to the customer and the company.

One of the ways FP&L made sure it was practicing "management by fact" was by adopting a Quality Improvement (QI) Story format (see Chart 3, pages 170–71). In the course of conducting an improvement project, the team responsible would have to answer some twenty-five process-related questions. These include the reason a project was chosen, a chart showing the potential root causes that might be responsible for the problem in question, and a cost-benefit analysis for the proposed solution.

FP&L's efforts were helped by the intrinsic process orientation of its top managers. Most of FP&L's top executives have engineering degrees, not M.B.A.s. While Marshall McDonald was an exception to that rule, the former CEO had spent his formative professional years in the oil business and was comfortable with the demands of a technological, capital-intensive business that requires plenty of long-term planning. Moreover, despite a laid-back style, which includes wearing a sort of modified, open-necked guayabera and Top-Siders to the office, McDonald has a reputation for discipline and consistency. When he took over as the president of FP&L just before the first oil crisis, for example, he surprised subordinates by choosing, as his first company car, a Toyota Tercel because of its high gas mileage. Even during his days as an oilman, McDonald was a stickler for consistency. "In the oil business, it struck me that petroleum engineers [would] quibble about figures two points to the right of the decimal, while making assumptions two points to the left of the decimal," recalls McDonald. "Most people don't realize the assumptions on which they then try to be very precise. In business we *assume* things. The normal American way is to take step number one, step number two, and then jump to step number 10. The TQC process forces you to spend time determining the facts. It forces you to be rational and to make decisions based on the facts, instead of on assumptions."[9]

McDonald's conviction, however, wasn't enough. He had to find a way to sell the concept to the rest of the organization. And in this effort, he got an early boost from an impressive quality management coup in FP&L's own nuclear division. In 1983, not long after the near meltdown at Three Mile Island and the fiasco at the Washington Public Power Supply System (WPPSS) in Washington State, FP&L's second St. Lucie power plant became the first U.S. nuclear plant to be completed on time and under budget.[10]

Construction of St. Lucie began well before FP&L had started pursuing a companywide quality strategy. But in tackling the St. Lucie project, FP&L demonstrated an enthusiasm for the sort of rigorous problem analysis that would make the utility an ideal candidate for Japanese-style TQC. St. Lucie's management was under intense pressure from McDonald to keep the cost of nuclear energy from spiraling out of hand as it had at other utilities. Since construction delays were the single factor that tended to drive up the cost of nuclear plants the most, the St. Lucie engineers focused on ways both to complete construction and to have the plants meet Nuclear Regulatory Commission (NRC) standards without causing any delays.

The key reason for St. Lucie's ultimate success was that, while the NRC requires nuclear plants to employ an army of independent quality inspectors, FP&L made a conscious decision to "make sure there was nothing for them to do." St. Lucie rejected the conventional build-and-fix approach that had been institutionalized by the government's inspection requirements. Instead the plant pursued a strategy that focused far more attention on initial planning in an effort to gradually eliminate the need for the sort of last-minute changes that inevitably caused delays. For example, while other utilities abdicated management of their nuclear plants to independent architect-engineers, FP&L maintained an unusual level of control over the process and worked closely both with the design and construction firm it had hired and with its own rank and file. In so doing, the utility inadvertently hit on one of the key elements of Japan's success with quality management: Instead of delegating quality to quality experts, the company placed responsibility for quality in the hands of line managers.[11]

The effort produced a host of time- and money-saving dividends. For example, when a hurricane swept through southern Florida, damaging the plant while it was still under construction, a team-based problem-solving effort helped drastically cut what could have been more than a three-month delay. St. Lucie engineers even cut

QI STORY

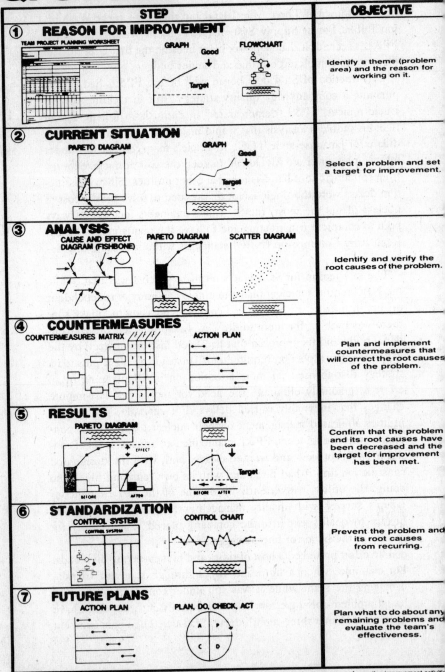

STEP	OBJECTIVE
① **REASON FOR IMPROVEMENT** TEAM PROJECT PLANNING WORKSHEET GRAPH Good FLOWCHART Target	Identify a theme (problem area) and the reason for working on it.
② **CURRENT SITUATION** PARETO DIAGRAM GRAPH Good Target	Select a problem and set a target for improvement.
③ **ANALYSIS** CAUSE AND EFFECT DIAGRAM (FISHBONE) PARETO DIAGRAM SCATTER DIAGRAM	Identify and verify the root causes of the problem.
④ **COUNTERMEASURES** COUNTERMEASURES MATRIX ACTION PLAN	Plan and implement countermeasures that will correct the root causes of the problem.
⑤ **RESULTS** PARETO DIAGRAM EFFECT GRAPH Good BEFORE AFTER Target BEFORE AFTER	Confirm that the problem and its root causes have been decreased and the target for improvement has been met.
⑥ **STANDARDIZATION** CONTROL SYSTEM CONTROL CHART	Prevent the problem and its root causes from recurring.
⑦ **FUTURE PLANS** ACTION PLAN PLAN, DO, CHECK, ACT A P C D	Plan what to do about any remaining problems and evaluate the team's effectiveness.

Adapted from the concept of the QC Story, originally named by Mr. Nogawa, president of Komatsu, for the purpose of reporting improvement activities. Professor Ikezawa and others expanded the procedure to include its use as a guide for solving problems.

HELPFUL TOOLS/TECHNIQUES:	KEY ACTIVITIES

• Graph
• Control Chart
• Process flowchart
• Control system
	• Research for themes:
	  — Review department indicators.
	  — Survey internal/external customers.
	  — Interview individuals from the work area.
	• Consider customer needs to help select the theme.
	• Set indicator to track the theme. #1
	• Determine how much improvement is needed. #2
	• Show impact of the theme. #3
	• Schedule the QI Story activities. #4
	• Describe the procedure used in the problem area.

• Checksheet • Histogram • Pareto diagram • Control chart • Graph	• Collect data on all aspects of the theme. • Stratify the theme from various viewpoints. #5 • Select a problem from the stratification of the theme. • Identify the customer's valid requirements. #6 • Write a clear problem statement. #7 • Utilize the data to establish the target. #8
• Cause and effect diagram • Checksheet • Pareto diagram • Histogram • Graph • Scatter diagram	• Perform cause and effect analysis on the problem. #9 • Continue analysis to the level of actionable root causes. #10 • Select the root causes with probable greatest impact. #11 • Verify the selected root causes with data. #12

• Cost benefit analysis
• Barriers and aids
• Action plan
• Structure tree
	• Develop and evaluate potential countermeasures which:
	  — Attack verified root causes. #13
	  — Meet customers' valid requirements. #14
	  — Prove to be cost beneficial. #15
	• Develop an action plan that:
	  — Answers who, what, when, where and how. #16
	  — Reflects the barriers and aids needed for sucess. #17
	• Obtain cooperation and approvals.
	• Implement countermeasures.

• Histogram • Pareto diagram • Control chart • Graph	• Confirm the effects of the countermeasures, checking to see if the root causes have been reduced. #18 • Compare the problem before and after using the same indicator. #19 • Compare the results obtained to the target. #20 • Implement additional countermeasures, if results are not satisfactory.

• Control system
• Control chart
• Graph
• Procedure
• Training
	• Assure that countermeasures become part of daily work: #21
	  — Create/revise the work process.
	  — Create/revise standards.
	• Train employees on revised process and/or standards and explain need.
	• Establish periodic checks with assigned responsibilities to monitor countermeasures. #22
	• Consider areas for replication. #23

• Action plan
  P D C A
	• Analyze and evaluate any remaining problems. #24
	• Plan further actions if necessary.
	• Review lessons learned related to problem solving skills and group dynamics. (Team effectiveness): #25
	  — What was done well.
	  — What could be improved.
	  — What could be done differently.

NOTE: The tools/techniques are shown in step where they are most often used. Some can be used in several different steps. Numbers #1 to #25 refer to the checkpoints on the QI Story Review and Feedback Form.

through the usual NRC red tape by eschewing formal petitions in favor of sitting across a table with NRC engineers—usually without any lawyers present at all—and giving detailed, in-person presentations of St. Lucie's capabilities and safety features.[12]

The well-publicized success of St. Lucie gave McDonald's quality vision the hook it needed. In April 1976 Kent Sterett, who had developed a cost and scheduling system for St. Lucie, was put in charge of the corporate quality department. For the next few years, Sterett's group built a track record within FP&L by helping different businesses emulate the improvement methods that had been tried at St. Lucie. And by 1981 Sterett had generated enough interest among top management to form a quality council, headed by McDonald, that would develop a quality management blueprint for the company. The utility began by studying the strategies of other U.S. companies. FP&L invited the leading U.S. quality gurus to make presentations and asked managers who attended the meetings and seminars to evaluate them on the basis of how applicable their ideas were to FP&L's business.

It was in the course of this talent search, in 1982, that FP&L sponsored its first four-day Deming seminar with the University of Miami. For the next several years, the company would regularly send its executives to the seminars. The utility's employee training material, as well as the quality presentations that are held each month for seventy-five or so executives from other companies, are infused with Deming's philosophy. And by the late 1980s one of Deming's closest disciples would give FP&L high marks for their understanding of quality management.[13]

What had begun as a jury-rigged quality drive developed into one of the most disciplined efforts in the United States, in large part because FP&L made the unique and fateful decision to work with the Japanese. FP&L chose this route in part because of its close relationship with Kansai Electric. The decision was also undoubtedly driven by the fact that FP&L was more insulated from the not-invented-here syndrome and the Japan bashing that had infected more beleaguered manufacturers, such as Ford and Xerox, which also had close ties to Japan through its affiliate, Fuji Xerox (see Chapter 7). Ironically, by choosing to hire Japanese counselors in its drive for the Deming Prize, rather than seeking Deming's advice exclusively, FP&L would never join the elite club of Deming clients whom the guru honors with monthly personal visits. While FP&L employees continued to attend Deming seminars, the guru, who demands undivided fealty from his followers, never considered the company among his growing group of disciples.

Nevertheless, FP&L is as firmly grounded on the twin foundations of Deming's philosophy—statistical analysis and a cooperative, management-driven approach to process improvement—as any other U.S. company. FP&L selected twelve line managers whose job it was to develop the company's quality management strategy. The group of twelve was freed from its routine responsibilities, given thirty days of intensive training in a variety of quality management theories, including those of Deming and his two U.S. rivals, Joseph Juran and Philip Crosby, and sent to Japan. When they returned, the team advised the utility's top executives to set FP&L on the course of TQC, a recommendation that was accepted by the quality council. At the same time, FP&L also organized the rank and file into literally thousands of teams that would work on individual improvement projects ranging from the development of better procedures for hooking up new homes to transformers to finding ways to prevent birds from short-circuiting transmission lines.

One of the first lessons the company learned was that rank-and-file initiative and top management support aren't of much use if middle management doesn't feel it is part of the process. "We practically had a revolution on our hands," recalls Kent Jones, who worked with Sterett, recalling the mistake FP&L made by encouraging workers to make suggestions without clarifying what middle management's role would be on the new agenda. Adds Sterett, "While we were asking employees to do something fun, we were asking middle management to change their style—that's personal and intrusive."[14] The company moved quickly to rectify its mistake. First, Hudiberg announced that no one would lose his job as a result of the changes. The company also revived a sporadic company institution known as the "situation conference." This was a biannual forum in which the members of the executive suite would share their strategic planning ideas with middle management. After the presentation, the middle managers were organized into groups of twenty and given a chance to respond and offer alternatives; their suggestions were recorded, reviewed by the top brass, and, when appropriate, used to amend the company's plans.[15] FP&L also enrolled middle managers in training courses that lasted at least thirteen days and that were designed to teach them how to coach, rather than just to delegate.

As FP&L firmed up its quality strategy and scored a few initial victories, it also discovered that the more improvements a company makes, the more difficult it is to find new avenues of progress. "First you can run [the quality improvement effort] like a police dragnet," says Sterett. "Line up large numbers of employees, march them across a field, and have them pick all the money up off the ground. Everyone knows it's been lying there. But once you've made the first pass, passing back with the same techniques isn't much use." Adds Sterett, mixing his metaphors, "You can pass through the orchard and pick off the low-hanging fruit, but soon you have to start getting ladders and other techniques and tools and get more sophisticated in your approach."[16]

By the mid-1980s the company determined it would have to define the needs of its customers more clearly and do a better job of linking FP&L's business objectives and its improvement projects to those needs. "We thought we had a good MBO program," says Mike Beale, another member of the quality staff. "But we found that the goals set by management often didn't filter down to the employees. And we found that we weren't stating our goals in meaningful, measurable terms." Like most U.S. companies, FP&L's approach to management by objective had emphasized setting strategic goals but had neglected the means of achieving or even evaluating their feasibility.

For one thing, management had to change its definition of customer satisfaction. For years FP&L had congratulated itself for keeping electrical service up and running 99 percent of the time. But the company's record didn't reveal the irritation FP&L prompted among its customers by taking hours to restore power whenever an outage did occur. Nor did it "show you the opportunities for improvement," says Marvin Howell, a manager at FP&L.

In 1985 the company conducted its first extensive market research effort. It determined that reducing downtime, improving the rate at which power is restored when outages do occur, was a top priority.

As a result of that survey, FP&L focused its efforts on the frequency and duration of power outages. Management established several other key indicators, including the number of complaints registered with the Florida Power Service Commission per thousand customers, the number of nuclear scrams per thousand critical hours, and the number of accidents per hundred employees. Once the criteria were established, management assessed the capabilities of its myriad electrical systems and set about establishing goals for improvement. The results were charted and analyzed on a monthly basis. If one group fell behind, or exceeded, the goals set by management, the executive in charge would be responsible for analyzing the process to determine the reasons for the change and for charting an appropriate response. The goals would be redefined based on a factual assessment of the system's capabilities. And throughout the company middle managers and teams were encouraged to find projects within their own work areas that would have the greatest impact on the corporate goals. FP&L was learning that with policy deployment, "the process is as important as the goal."[17]

The case of the red-tailed hawk droppings shows why process has become everything at FP&L. In the late 1970s, the utility began experiencing a chronic problem with its main transmission lines that many FP&L engineers attributed to the state's frequent lightning storms. The incidents were frequent enough, however, that FP&L's chief engineer decided to conduct a detailed analysis of the problem. The assignment fell to Harry Hansen in the general engineering department, which is responsible for designing poles, wires, transformers, and the like.

FP&L couldn't have chosen a better candidate for the job. Hansen, who was then in his late forties and who spent much of his free time painting, devoted the same love of detail to his new research project as he normally does to a portrait. Hansen also happened to be an aviation buff. He had served in the air force during the early 1950s and had worked at McDonnell Douglas before coming to FP&L. And he wasn't long into the transmission line project before he began to suspect the trouble had nothing to do with the weather at all. Instead he surmised that the problem involved the same nemesis that often plagues pilots—birds. Certain birds, he knew, migrate from the north along the path of the pylons.

Guesswork wouldn't do, however. Hansen hired an ornithologist. And he began studying the patterns of interruptions and determined that most of them occurred at night. The former aviation engineer also got himself a book on ornithology, and in the course of his research he ran across a case in Oregon, in 1936, when red-tailed hawks were discovered to have shorted out transmission lines. When these hawks relieve themselves, Hansen learned, they let go a five- to seven-foot stream of fluid, which creates a highly conductive bridge between the conductor and the grounder on a transmission line, causing a short circuit.[18]

Although his bird consultant disagreed, Hansen guessed that birds roosting on the transmission lines at night might be causing the problem. He obtained a night-viewing telescope and took to wandering along the transmission lines through the Everglades, charting the frequency of lightning storms. At the same time, he learned of a group from the University of Miami that was doing a lightning study for the space program that was intended to help protect the space shuttle from lightning. However, the researchers at the University of Miami had no way of verifying how good their methods were at pinpointing where, and at what time, lightning had struck. Hansen teamed up with the researchers, and by comparing notes on when lightning hit FP&L's equipment, both Hansen and the researchers were able to verify the exact time and place lightning occurred. In so doing, Hansen was able to confirm conclusively that lightning *wasn't* responsible for the chronic outages. He then talked a friend into taking him up in a helicopter so he could hover over the pylons, watching them from a bird's-eye view. Says the bird stalker, whose suspicions of fowl play proved correct, "I needed a different perspective. I would never have seen it from the ground."[19]

To solve the problem of the bird droppings, Hansen devised an umbrellalike shelter that could be placed over the top of individual pylons to redirect the "stream" produced by the hawks. He then studied the most efficient way of installing the umbrellas, and again enlisted the help of his friend, the helicopter pilot. Hansen says it took sixteen days to install the umbrellas from a helicopter. Had they done it from the ground the way most repair work is done on transmission lines, Hansen estimates, it would have taken a year. Hansen, who completed his project in 1981, would be recruited as one of the company's first in-house quality consultants to assist on other FP&L improvement projects.[20]

A cumulation of such small, process-minded improvements has reduced FP&L's average outage rate per customer from 75.8 minutes in 1983 to forty-eight minutes by the end of 1988—and the company is shooting for less than forty minutes by 1992. FP&L has occasionally come under fire for the amount of time and money it spent winning the Deming Prize. In fact, the utility learned what the Japanese discovered long ago: that the economics of quality management are such that spending time and money on improvements can generate huge savings in repairs and errors. Quality director Kent Sterett estimates it cost FP&L $2.48 million in the first six months of 1988 to notch up service reliability and productivity. At the same time, he calculates, earlier improvements bolstered the bottom line by $13.5 million.[21]

By fostering process-mindedness, FP&L was able to get groups throughout the company to answer its corporate objectives. For one thing, it recruited Hansen and several other process junkies to form a cadre of facilitators who would help both management and the rank and file "stay honest," that is, keep their attention focused on the root causes of improvement projects rather than the symptoms. The company also established a training organization to educate workers and managers in the new approach.

Indeed, nothing shows how deeply the process craze at FP&L penetrated the organization as does the detailed procedure for finding and tackling individual improvement projects that the company launched as a key element of its TQC strategy. The QI Story format, a method for reporting improvement activities that was originally developed by the president of Komatsu, is literally a blueprint everyone at FP&L must use every time they undertake an improvement project. It is designed to ensure that the improvement process they have chosen is as efficient and as accurate as possible. The story format requires improvement teams to cover some twenty-five process-related questions, including the reason for the improvement, identification of the root causes of the problem, and a cost-benefit analysis (see chart on p. 169). It would also serve as the mechanism by which FP&L would spread innovations developed in one part of the company to the rest of the organization. To help employees learn how to create their own QI Stories, FP&L spent lavishly on training programs and on coaches who would work with the teams on their initial projects. In judging a story, management places as much emphasis on the telling of the tale as it does on its ending. At any given time, hundreds of QI Stories are under way at the electric utility.

HOW WORKERS USED THE QI STORY PROCESS TO IMPROVE CUSTOMER SERVICE

The experience of FP&L's Stuart Service Center, near Palm Beach, shows how a small group of workers created an important new operating standard for FP&L with the help of a manager who made sure the team accomplished its goals. For the six men and one woman in the group, who spend most of their days installing and fixing electric cable in the hot Florida climate, the opportunity at first seemed like "just a way to get out of the sun." In 1986 the group formed a team and was given two days of training to prepare them for the group decision-making process and the analytical skills they would need to study their process and to gather the data for their QI Story.

Working together should have been easy for the close-knit group of workers, most of whom had grown up in the working-class neighborhoods behind the white neo-Greco mansions of Palm Beach. Two of the team members, Lyle Yingling and Ed Bozone, had known each other since they were children. And two others, Tom and Kimberly Quigley, were married to each other. Yet the group foundered for several months, struggling to come up with an appropriate improvement project. "We spent three months spinning our wheels," says one team member. "We had all this information that we came up with, but didn't know what to do with it. Our boss saw that we weren't getting it." What the group lacked was a coach. Originally, just one facilitator worked with FP&L's entire Treasure Coast district, which includes the service center where the Stuart team worked as well as some fifty to sixty additional employees, most of whom were also trying to organize their own improvement projects.

Management made sure the Stuart team got the help it needed. The district general manager, whose responsibilities had come to include not only monitoring the performance of the service center but also helping his employees achieve their improvement objectives, decided to hire additional facilitators. "That was a big spurt for us. We had all this pile of stuff and she showed how to use it, how to refine it, show it better, put it on graphs. We respected her." The quality coach helped the team identify a project, showed them how to hold meetings, and helped them meet the problem-solving requirements of the QI Story format itself. There are no shortcuts to FP&L's improvement methods.

The visual presentation of the QI Story was crucial to the team's success. As one team member puts it, "It helps you make sure you're working on a problem, not a symptom, it helps you speak with facts. The only way you're going to get anything implemented with management is to prove it to them. For a field worker to tell a vice president that he has to start buying this or changing that, if you can show him with facts, he's going to listen." The message is a powerful one. What the QI Story format does is not only offer the corporation opportunities for improvement, but give workers a forum for shaping their own work environment and for beginning to control the quality of their own work. "The biggest change has been that now, if there's a problem, they can do something about it," says Hansen. "Before it was kind of a macho thing not to complain. The supervisor lived with [the problems], the workers were expected to live with 'em. If they got frustrated the most they could do is phone in sick."

The Stuart team, which would come to call itself the Templations, after the device it designed to shorten the duration of transmission outages, had considerable leeway in choosing its project. Although teams are given guidance, the final decision is left up to them. The assumption is that lower-level employees often have the clearest understanding of the details that are undermining the system. As they become better educated in what the company's objectives are, and as they become more comfortable with an activist role, the rank and file are expected to identify ever more pertinent projects. In case teams miss projects management thinks are important, the company has established special task forces to work on top policy priorities.

Through the training they received, the Templations learned to focus their attention on the needs of their customers. In the tradition of TQC, FP&L's expanded definition of the customer meant "any person who receives the work product of anyone in the company." Thus, customers would include both an FP&L employee whose ability to do his job depends on how well his predecessor did his, and the ultimate electricity user. Says one Stuart team member, "Our corporate goals are service reliability and customer satisfaction. Our district is one of the worst in terms of service reliability, so a lot of our teams are [trying] to figure out why. It's not our fault, it's our location," he adds, referring to the region's problems with lightning, hurricanes, and overgrown foliage. For example, in parts of ritzy Palm Beach, including the neighborhood where President George Bush's mother lives, residents are part of the problem because they object to having their trees pruned. By focusing on systemic issues, however, FP&L has transformed the concept of "a problem" from a gremlin that can undermine careers and must therefore be swept under the rug to an opportunity for change and progress.

The Stuart team improvement project would, in fact, change operating procedures at service centers throughout FP&L. The group set out to build a device that would make it possible for linemen to work on high-voltage underground cables without constantly having to disconnect electric service. The jumbled way in which underground cable is laid is a source of endless frustration both to the servicemen, who have to spend extra time working with the cables, and to homeowners, whose electricity might be shut off for as long as an hour while the linemen hook up a new house to a transformer. The problem is particularly acute in high-growth areas like Florida, one of the fastest-expanding areas in the country. What were woods and swamps one day would become a golf course with several hundred homes popping up from it the next. And with each new home that is added to an existing cluster of houses already feeding off of a single transformer comes the need for a new electrical hookup and the possibility of a break in service.

The problem also illustrates why engineering drawings and "building to specifications" can be meaningless when it comes to improving the quality of service. For one thing, the electric cable is laid in pipes that often are installed by the real estate developer or an independent contractor who doesn't always follow the blueprints carefully. A look at the specifications for building underground cables shows why. The drawings call for a neat configuration of ten pipes—one each for the eight secondary cables and the two primary cables, which are meant to be separated by an inch or two of space. What the specifications don't show is that once the cables are laid into the ground and backfilled with soil, the pipes move out of place. The specifications don't specify a procedure for making sure the pipes maintain proper spacing.

Outages occur when there isn't enough room between the pipes for a lineman to draw out the secondary cables, which connect to individual household meters, without fear of electrocution or flash burns. To work safely with jumbled secondary cables, which feed off the two primary, 7,000-volt lines, the lineman must first turn off the power, rejigger the pipes, pull out the cable, and then turn the power back on. This reworking process can take as long as two hours and can cost as many as eight households that draw their electricity off the same transformer an hour's outage.

As a solution the Stuart team devised a simple, inexpensive template that would be used during the pipe installation process to act as a brace and maintain a proper distance between the pipes. The templates, which cost less than fifty dollars apiece, are becoming standard issue at the company. The group experimented with about half a dozen template designs before settling on the final wooden version, at a total development cost of $260.80. The Stuart team calculates that aside from reducing the number of service interruptions, the device saves each service center about $5,561.28 per year in the time and cost of reworking sloppy pipes. With about sixty service centers throughout the company, this translates to a $333,676.80 savings per year!

Aside from the savings, FP&L also gained a more enthusiastic work force. The challenge of the project got all those in the group more involved with their jobs. Although each team is given an hour a week to work on improvement projects, several of the team members took prototype templates home to work on in their basements after hours. Even Yingling, a wisecracking redhead who doesn't like to admit that he did any work on his own time, confesses to having worked on one of the wooden models at home, only because the team didn't have the right type of saw at the service station. Other team members would run some of the graphs and charts for their QI Stories on their kids' computers. And Bozone, who as a "trouble man" often spends time in the station when there is no emergency to call him out, would work on the QI Story during quiet times at the service station.

The efforts of the Stuart team won the group recognition throughout the company. Each year, in an elaborate management review, all of FP&L's QI teams are critiqued by management. The best projects are standardized throughout the company. And the best teams are given special rewards. In 1988 the first prize, including steak dinners, a weekend in Fort Lauderdale, and a company-sponsored trip to Japan, went to the Templations. Several of the team members—including Bozone, who had never been on an airplane, and Yingling, who had never traveled farther than Pennsylvania—took their families with them. Only the Quigleys, who were expecting a child, were unable to go.

It's worth noting that while they are extraordinarily proud of their achievements and have gone on to form other improvement teams, none of the Templations have particularly grand ambitions or see themselves as star performers. "This is a reflection on our district general manager," says one team member, referring to the accomplishments of the group. "It was good management commitment that helped us do it." In fact, the team acknowledges that it's often difficult for management to pick just one team as the winner, and that for "winners" and "losers" alike the real sense of accomplishment occurs when a team's ideas are picked up by the company. "There are two kinds of rewards; one is that they take your ideas and implement them companywide—that's the ideal reward," says Yingling, who points out that the ideas of many of the teams who come before corporate reviews are adopted. What made the Stuart team stand out, he adds, "is that we not only came up with a good idea, we followed the process."[22]

With the introduction of policy deployment, the greatest change at FP&L has been in the managers' jobs. John Hudiberg, whose desk is littered with charts showing the month-to-month progress of the company's quality indicators, says he spends 99 percent of his time on QI. And he expects his lieutenants to do the same. In fact, the higher a manager's rank, the more his compensation and bonus are linked to the quality indicators for which he or she is responsible. "Obviously, a manager who doesn't participate isn't just affecting himself, but is affecting the entire department or section," explains Hudiberg.[23] Adds Kent Sterett, "This thing is driven by leverage, not by numbers. [Management must] start modifying existing structures, processes, procedures, and mind-sets, and mind-sets, and mind-sets. The role of manager [must] shift from one who does the thinking and conveys answers to one who does the listening and helps with the implementation."[24] Indeed, by setting his sights on the Deming Prize, Hudiberg would test the mettle of his management team far more than that of his work force. While the rank and file might put in an extra few hours each week on an improvement project, the utility's parking lots still pretty much empty out at five o'clock. Managers, however, are putting in longer hours than ever, including working full days on Saturday—unheard-of dedication in a utility company before 1980—in order to prepare for the grueling Japanese-style management reviews that are part of the Deming Prize and TQC process. Today FP&L managers are reviewed not just on how they perform, but on how they make decisions. And they are expected to develop a far greater command of the processes they manage than they have ever had to before.

To become a contender for the prize, Hudiberg hired one of Japan's quality "counselors." The difference between a counselor and a consultant, explains Hudiberg, is that a counselor is like a coach; he stays with you. If you lose, he loses too." FP&L began working with several of the more junior counselors who are affiliated with JUSE, and at the same time began courting Professor Tetsuichi Asaka, a professor emeritus at Tokyo University, who, reflecting Japan's love of hierarchy and status, has become the country's most sought-after quality counselor among aspirants for the Deming Prize. Working with Asaka was important to Hudiberg because the professor's standards and reputation are so high that a passing grade from him is considered almost a guarantee of winning the Deming Prize. One Japanese who knows Asaka once compared the professor's approach to the training of a weight lifter: "If the Deming Prize calls for a hundred fifty pounds, he'll ask you to lift two hundred pounds."[25]

But getting Asaka to agree to an alliance with an American company was almost as unlikely as getting Hirohito and Mike Tyson to pump iron together. A major in the Imperial army during World War II, Asaka speaks no English and is reputed to harbor a deep dislike for foreigners in general, and for Americans most especially.[26] Although Asaka won a Deming Prize for individual achievement in 1952 and must have been awarded the prize by Deming himself, the American guru has no recollection of him. Indeed, Asaka is one of the few leading lights of Japanese quality who does not pay homage to Deming during the guru's visits. And while he has been the chief counselor for many of the leading Japanese companies that have won the Deming Prize, including Fuji Xerox and Kansai, he had never worked with a company outside the main islands of Japan.

Hudiberg won an introduction to Asaka through his connections with the heads of Fuji Xerox and Kansai. During a series of meetings, Hudiberg had to prove to Asaka his commitment to quality improvement because, as Sterett puts it, "the more senior counselors have more business than they know what to do with." Over time and the course of several meetings, FP&L managed to persuade Asaka and several junior professors who worked with the *sensei* to assist the utility in its quest for the Deming Prize. The counselors paid monthly visits to Florida, and teams of FP&L executives made numerous trips to Japan. But Asaka himself didn't make his first trip to Florida until November 1988, when he gave his final blessing for the utility to submit its application for the Deming Prize. In January 1989 FP&L filed its process improvement documents, a stack that measured about three inches thick, with the Deming committee for evaluation.

FP&L would have to win the approval of its Japanese tutors over and over again. On the occasion of the counselor's monthly trips to Florida, managers must submit to reviews that can be more daunting than a Ph.D. dissertation. For managers like Armando Olivera, FP&L's construction chief, who supervises the building of transmission lines, the change has been dramatic. Five times in the two years or so before FP&L formally applied for the Deming Prize, Olivera had to stand up on stage, in front of an audience of as many as a hundred of his peers and subordinates, and present the improvement projects tackled by the construction and engineering departments that report to him. The counselors and five FP&L executives conducted the reviews, questioning him in virtual Talmudic fashion about lightning, birds, and the age of his cables and transmission lines—in short, anything that might affect the frequency and duration of blackouts and brownouts, no matter how brief.

The reviews frequently lasted several hours, and attendance by top executives, including Robert E. Tallon, the president of the utility, or John Hudiberg, was a must. In addition, at each management review ten vice presidents sat quietly on stage during the presentations to study the review process and to learn to probe and analyze Japanese style. The idea was to train managers at every level to dig, spot faulty logic, and ultimately to suggest workable alternatives. Says one manager, "Before, most top executives wouldn't have had the knowledge to ask in-depth questions, let alone to give any guidance."

Demonstrating an understanding of the process was the principal purpose of the reviews. Sterett recalls an uncomfortable moment in Tokyo, just before Asaka approved FP&L's application for the Deming Prize. He and several managers were showing Asaka how they had exceeded one of their targets. Asaka wanted to know how they had overreached the target. The group, however, had left that particular piece of documentation in Miami and couldn't explain the reason for the results. If the group couldn't explain how they had exceeded their goal, how could they know if they would meet the next target? Asaka demanded to know. "Asaka can be very severe, he's one tough old boy," confirms Sterett, recalling the event the way a schoolboy might after getting his knuckles rapped for some infraction. "I can remember some times when he used some dramatic effects to get the attention of our executives. It was very effective. He has a masterful control of voice, intonation, body Japanese. You don't have to understand Japanese to understand when he's absolutely seriously intent on a point. He doesn't yell, but he gets extremely intense."[27]

Increasingly, these process-oriented reviews have become FP&L's principal method of management. Today Frank Thompson, construction services manager, for example, spends one or two of the meetings he has each week with his two top-ranking subordinates going over various indicators relating to service reliability—and as many as two meetings per week with his superior, Dotty Norton, briefing her on the division's progress.[28]

FP&L's experience has served as a catalyst for other U.S. companies. The same executives who flocked to Deming's seminars in ever-increasing numbers during the 1980s were also showing up at the monthly show-and-tell at FP&L's Miami offices. Representatives from companies such as Xerox, Coors, and Alcoa have made the pilgrimage to Miami to learn more about the company's strategy. For companies such as Procter & Gamble, which held its first private seminar with Deming in the spring of 1986,[29] FP&L's success has been an important confirmation of the company's decision to work with Deming and gradually to embrace TQC.

Nevertheless, the totality of the Japanese quality management approach, especially policy deployment, remains a mystery for most U.S. managers. Indeed, as of 1980 few Americans who hadn't spent extensive amounts of time in Japan could have been exposed to the concept since not a single article had been written in either the major business press or general-interest publications about the Deming Prize or its role in Japanese industry. And many of those who were familiar with the concept considered it too alien and formalistic. For many companies the question boils down to "How Japanese do you want to become?" says Peter Kolesar, who teaches an introductory course in quality management at Columbia Business School and advises a number of companies, including Alcoa.

Ironically, with the exception of the company's adherence to a performance appraisal system based on numerical rankings, FP&L probably comes closer than any other major U.S. company to fulfilling Deming's Fourteen Points. As he approaches the end of his ninth decade, Deming's pride often gets the better of him. He refuses to discuss FP&L, apparently interpreting the company's Japanese course as disloyalty, rather than as the logical evolution of his teachings. Having created what is virtually a personality cult, he occasionally lashes out at any suggestion that the most accomplished Japanese quality practitioners may today be as knowledgeable as he. Deming does not realize that by turning to Deming's students, the utility was simply doing its best to save itself from the conflicting

U.S. signals on quality management. When an October 1988 FP&L visit to Japan coincided with a trip by Deming, Hudiberg tried in vain to meet with him—despite repeated phone calls to his hotel room, Deming would not meet with the utility executive. However, when FP&L received its award in the fall of 1989, it was, in fact, following in the footsteps of Deming's most successful, and beloved, disciples.

Although the company won the Deming Prize, the final verdict on FP&L's quality experiment isn't in yet. The three key architects of TQC, Florida style, retired or moved on to new jobs before the close of 1989. So the true success of the FP&L experiment will become evident only a few years hence, when it becomes clear whether the company's yen for improvement has survived the men who inspired it.

7

XEROX'S QUALITY
STRATEGY: TWO
STEPS FORWARD,
ONE STEP BACK

ompany lore has it that the quality movement at Xerox got started on a Sunday afternoon in November 1979, when Charlie Christ, who would go on to become the company's head of manufacturing two years later, was reading his *New York Times*. He ran across an advertisement for Canon copiers being sold at 47th St. Photo, a discount electronics retailer in Manhattan, that gave him the jolt of a lifetime. Canon copiers were being priced at less than what it cost Xerox to *build* comparable models. Christ sent a study mission to Japan and began the company's first effort to benchmark Xerox's processes and products against the best machines than available from the competition.[1]

Changes initiated by Christ in Xerox's manufacturing operations would help to dramatically improve the quality and cost-effectiveness of production and product development in Rochester, New York, the seat of Xerox's manufacturing and design operations. Indeed, during the 1980s, Xerox has undertaken one of the most ambitious quality drives of any major U.S. company. The copier pioneer spent years formulating a corporate quality blueprint that was intended to do nothing less than reinvent TQC by giving it a decidedly American twist. Today Xerox credits that strategy with making it the first U.S. company to recoup lost market share from the Japanese without a government bailout. An MIT study on U.S. productivity, entitled *Made in America*, notes: "The history of the Xerox case is an important one because it provides a view of a prototypical U.S. company, hugely successful in its early days when it pioneered a rapid growth market and then faltering as the market matured and as manufacturing costs, product differentiation, and customer satisfaction became crucial in a highly competitive marketplace. What makes the Xerox case particularly interesting is the company's success in reversing its decline."[2]

Xerox has sought to transform its quality movement into nothing less than a corporate cult. Once a month chairman David Kearns and other executives explain the company's quality progress to major customers and suppliers. And each year the company organizes a quality fair, where dozens of Xerox teams from Tokyo to Rochester—some of them decked out in costumes of matching jogging outfits or overalls—set up booths and displays to show off their improvement projects. Cheerleading Xerox's annual teamwork day are the company's top executives. Like TV evangelists preaching to the converted, they are beamed by satellite from the company's offices in El Segundo and Dallas to two enormous monitors in the vast auditorium of the Rochester convention center, which is filled to SRO capacity by thousands of applauding Xerox-ers.

But behind the boosterism and some real progress made during the past decade by America's premier copier company, as of late 1988 the news from Xerox's quality front was still a resounding so-so. "Our very best unit, which is probably our supplies division, which . . . makes money and can compete effectively anywhere in the world, is at least a year behind where we thought we would be when we put our [quality] plan together," David Kearns confessed to a gathering of half a dozen major customers and suppliers at Xerox's Stamford headquarters in 1988. "We've made a lot of progress in identifying and analyzing problems, but we're not good implementers, we don't have the discipline. Implementation is boring, it's the trenchwork."[3] While Xerox has made major strides in cost and quality improvement and has exceeded the progress made by many other U.S. companies until the late 1980s, most of its major gains were the result of changes initiated before 1983 by its manufacturing and engineering community. While even the company's harshest internal critics report a sudden burst of improvement in the year preceding November 1989, when Xerox clinched a Baldrige award, many of its efforts to improve quality and productivity during the mid-1980s floundered.

More important, throughout the decade Xerox's quality plans looked particularly uninspired when compared with the accomplishments of Fuji Xerox, its Japanese offspring, which won the Deming Prize in 1981. The lowest-cost copiers in Xerox's line still come from the Japanese company, a joint venture between Fuji Photo Film and Britain's Rank Xerox. And Xerox engineers are unabashedly in awe of recent Fuji Xerox product designs. Fuji Xerox's financial results also far outshine those of its U.S. parent. In the early years of the joint venture, in the 1960s, Fuji Xerox and Rank Xerox together accounted for less than 10 percent of Xerox's revenues, but even then they made up 25 percent of the U.S. company's bottom line. By 1973 the two foreign units made up 45 percent of Xerox's $300 million in profits.[4] And by the end of the 1980s, although Fuji Xerox's $3.9 billion in revenues were less than one quarter the $12.4 billion its U.S. parent was making from its document processing business, the Japanese company's net profits of $179 million totaled more than one third of Xerox's $488 million in that business. Moreover, close to one third of Xerox's profits in document processing came directly from Fuji Xerox; according to Xerox's joint venture agreement, the U.S. copier maker receives 33 percent of Fuji Xerox's profits each year, or $59 million in 1989, plus a license fee for the use of xerographic technology, which amounted to $71.1 million during the same period. In addition, the earnings of Fuji Xerox have grown by 30 percent or more annually for the past several years. By contrast, Xerox's profits from document processing actually plunged in 1986 and didn't surpass the $410 million earned in 1985 until four years later. (Indeed, Xerox insiders believe that the company's 1989 returns—the best rate of growth the company had seen in years—signal the long-awaited turnaround that had eluded the copier maker earlier in the 1980s.)[5]

At the crux of both Xerox's stop-and-go performance during its decade-long quality quest, as well as its business failures during the 1970s, is the lopsided expertise of the company's top executive cadre. Xerox may have been built on technology, but for the past two decades it was led by salesmen. Not only have Xerox CEOs hailed from sales and marketing, they selected for their inner circle men with either marketing or finance expertise. Peter McColough was brought to Xerox by former chairman Joe Wilson, the man who had created Xerox's copier business, because of his abilities as a salesman, and Archie McCardell was chosen by McColough to serve as president because of his financial expertise. (It's worth noting that only in 1988 did CEO David Kearns, who retired in 1990, break that pattern by bringing in Bill Lowe from IBM to head product development and manufacturing.)

The Xerox executive salesmen are far more sophisticated than Arthur Miller's memorable archetype, Willy Loman. But they have been plagued by an inability to recognize key innovations in either management or technology, a weakness that has all too often made them seem "way out there in the blue, riding on a smile and a shoeshine." In their book *Fumbling the Future*, Douglas Smith and Robert Alexander wrote of McColough and McCardell, Xerox's leaders in the 1970s, "The two men were destined to go awry, reinforcing each other's weaknesses as they steered their corporation toward diversification without direction and change without commitment."[6] Ironically, because large U.S. companies fish for their executives from the same pond, many of Xerox's financial experts, including McCardell, had been recruited from Ford, and the copier company's managerial problems would, in many ways, mirror those that had dogged the automaker a decade before.

Deming and the top quality practitioners know that success in quality management in large part rests on how well a company can coordinate and extract synergies from all its parts, including marketing, research and development, and finance. Yet Xerox's top management ranks suffered a fundamental imbalance in its knowledge base. Like Ford, Xerox was strong on finance but weak on operations. As a result, the same management deficiencies that in the early 1970s would derail its plans to become a major player in the computer business would, a decade later, still cast a shadow over the company's efforts to develop a quality management strategy.

"Xerox was spending hundreds of millions of dollars a year on research, development, and engineering. Yet there was no one, literally, in top management who had ever run a product development program, who could say to the engineers that such and such should cost less or should be doable faster, and who would know, from their personal experience, that they were right," said Jack Crowley, a former executive vice president.[7] During the 1970s, even the chief of manufacturing and engineering at Xerox was a Ford-schooled finance man by the name of Jim O'Neill. When, in the late 1960s, McColough embarked on the biggest, riskiest, and ultimately most ill-fated move of his career, the acquisition of a computer company, he did so without consulting his newly selected chief of R & D.[8] McColough would pay $900 million for Scientific Data Systems (SDS), an astronomical ninety-two times more than the computer company's earnings at the time. Yet the company probably doomed the project when, in 1972, it effectively robbed SDS of a leader by grouping both the copier and computer operations under the aegis of Ray Hay, an executive with plenty of expertise in copiers but none in computers. SDS came to be known as "McColough's folly," and after suffering massive losses Xerox would write off SDS in 1975.[9]

More than one computer debacle would underscore the flaws in Xerox's management structure. McColough also failed to recognize a crucial innovation made by another Xerox unit, the Palo Alto Research Center (PARC), for the product coup that it was. Years before Steve Jobs came up with a personal computer named Apple, PARC had developed one that was known as the Alto. Ironically, while McColough had the insight to fund PARC's computer efforts with a $100 million annual research budget, he failed to include among his closest advisers someone with the *practical knowledge* to both evaluate and champion the work of PARC. Moreover, problems at both SDS and PARC were exacerbated by rivalries between the two groups. "There was no one at the helm—no decision maker with the exclusive, full-time responsibility and authority to set direction, coordinate activities, and resolve competing claims among the different groups building and selling computers."[10] Today many companies market word-processing programs for laymen and a "mouse" inputting device, but Xerox, the company that invented them, isn't among them.[11]

The fate of one process-minded engineer at Xerox offers perhaps the most telling insight into how antithetical the principles of Demingism were to the Xerox regime of the 1970s. Jim O'Neill, the finance executive in charge of engineering, was able to force out a man who would go on to become one of Deming's principal disciples. Widely regarded as a brilliant engineer, Myron Tribus had served as a former assistant secretary of commerce in the Nixon administration and had been dean of engineering at Dartmouth before coming to Xerox in 1970. Although he was not yet acquainted with Deming, Tribus already had all the intellectual earmarks of a Demingite. At Xerox, "Tribus railed against a system that produced copiers in haste and fixed them later. . . . Tribus hoped to establish technical standards and practices in order to eradicate what he perceived as rampant sloppiness. . . . His demise marked a major drop in engineering productivity at Xerox." Tribus went from Xerox to the MIT Center for Advanced Engineering Study, where he is said to have angered the faculty by becoming an almost fanatical advocate of Demingism. He has since become an independent consultant.[12]

McCardell would retire in 1977, followed a decade later by McColough. But the same management culture that had rid itself of Tribus would have difficulty adopting Demingism. Resentful of the advances made by upstart Japanese companies, Xerox rejected the Japanese TQC model and was even slow to study the methods of Fuji Xerox. While the U.S. company has found it relatively easy to wring productivity out of inefficient manufacturing operations, it has failed to master many of the fundamentals of quality management in other areas of its business, such as marketing, sales, and finance. One reason is that a decade after the company began pursuing quality management, its sales-oriented executives have failed to appreciate the importance of variation control, and are no more inclined to study statistical methods than they would be to master Chinese. Another problem, according to company insiders, is that Xerox has emphasized short-term cost cutting rather than quality improvements, which might have reaped greater cost savings and increased sales in the long term. In addition, when Xerox set out to create a quality blueprint for the corporation, it drew on the expertise of a variety of outside experts but failed to develop a strong theoretical base and ultimately struck some entirely wrong notes.

Thus, the Xerox quality movement was characterized by an initial spurt of improvement in the early 1980s, stagnation in the mid-

1980s, and, toward the end of the decade, a conviction that the company would have to completely rethink its quality strategy once again. Nearly a decade after it embarked on a quality management drive, Xerox is recrafting that vision and attempting to integrate sophisticated quality concepts throughout the company. But even as Xerox regroups its quality efforts, Fuji Xerox is pushing the boundaries of TQC deep into its sales and marketing organization. This chapter begins by exploring the goals and missteps in Xerox's pursuit of quality. It concludes by showing why cleaning up its quality house will depend on how well the company assimilates the lessons of Demingism and the TQC experience of its Japanese offspring.

XEROX: REINVENTING THE WHEEL

By the late 1970s, Xerox was fighting for survival. The weaknesses of its management structure, problems with SDS, and a relentless barrage of antitrust suits by both the government and Xerox competitors had taken their toll on the company's copier business. Between 1976 and 1982, America's premier copier maker watched its market share plunge by a half, to 41 percent.[13]

Spurred into action, Xerox's manufacturing mavens, under the leadership of Christ, began meticulously measuring the company's production processes against those of its rivals and came up with a variety of innovations. For example, to foster a close relationship with suppliers, the company slashed their ranks from 6,000 to 400 and brought the remaining suppliers into the design process. The company urged employees to form quality improvement teams.[14] And a reorganization in 1981 established a program management approach in which each new product was handled by a product development team, which in turn was headed by a single chief engineer. These project managers were responsible for orchestrating every phase of product development from initial product plans through prototype production. The new system marked a dramatic departure from the traditional approach in which such areas as optical engineering, paper handling, the design of frames and drives, and document handling were part of fifteen separate functional organizations, a structure that had created major coordination problems and driven up costs.[15]

By 1983 the improvements initiated by Christ had reaped significant rewards. Manufacturing costs had been cut in half.[16] And the number of defective parts, which had been ten to thirty times higher at Xerox than at the factories of Japanese copier manufacturers, were brought into line with the competition. The company even developed a phototype desktop copier in the early 1980s at a cost of about $300, which was comparable to those of the competition. But Xerox management never approved the project, preferring instead to acquire its low-end boxes from Fuji Xerox.[17]

After those initial accomplishments, Xerox had trouble keeping up its quality momentum. A new quality strategy, launched in 1983 and known as Leadership Through Quality, was initiated as a way "to take us a quantum leap toward becoming a total quality company," says Barry Rand, president of the U.S. marketing group. But the company, which had planned to integrate process improvement throughout the company by 1987, would fail to meet that objective. Two years after that deadline, Xerox was rethinking its quality strategy once again.

Leadership Through Quality lacked both a cohesive theoretical foundation and an effective implementation plan. The company's quality strategy was pieced together out of the ideas of three principal quality gurus, Deming, Joseph Juran, and Philip Crosby, with a dollop of behavioral theory thrown in on the side. Deming lectured at Xerox during the early 1980s, and several of the company's quality experts claim to be his admirers. In fact, the early improvements made in manufacturing and engineering can be attributed to the fact that they adopted the disciplines of statistical analysis much more readily than did other parts of the company. Even the quality strategy authored by Xerox in 1983 echoes several of Deming's favorite themes, including the importance of differentiating between common causes—those inherent in the system—and special causes. States the document: "Common causes constitute 85 percent of the problems; they are faults of the system. . . . Attempts to improve individual performance are in vain when the problem lies in the system, where only management can eliminate or reduce the impact of the problem."[18]

However, while Xerox's quality bible mandates "the application of a basic set of statistical tools," by 1989 much of the company still wasn't using them. An aversion to statistics among a number of key executives would lead the company initially to reject Demingism as well as the Japanese model in its own backyard. In 1983 Xerox set up a team of executives from a variety of disciplines and departments to outline the company's quality strategy. This council was manned by nine executives, more than half of whom were involved in the service or marketing side of the business. There were only two members whose professional backgrounds might have made them receptive to statistical thinking and the theory of variation. "I believe [the quality council] did not, and does not, appreciate the rigors and discipline of statistics," says Hal Tragash. "We must have had three workshops on basic statistics . . . their eyes got glassy. The real decision not to go with Deming was theirs."[19]

Instead, Xerox pieced together a hybrid strategy that initially drew most of its lessons from Deming's nemesis, Phil Crosby. Crosby is the most controversial of the four leading quality experts. (Armand Feigenbaum must be added to the list mentioned above). While Deming respects Joseph Juran, who followed him to Japan in the 1950s, he is a scathing critic of Crosby's prescriptions. His detractors call the former ITT executive, who proudly declares his Crosby College in Florida the biggest quality institute in the world, and who sports jewelry encrusted with precious gems (including a ring with diamonds in the shape of a cross), a showman. And even former clients who speak well of him say that his principal talent is in conveying the importance of quality, not in defining a theoretical blueprint for achieving it. Crosby, his fans acknowledge, is great at getting the troops excited before the more sophisticated experts come in to teach the theory and methods of achieving quality management systems. Indeed, an executive from GM recalls that while John Z. DeLorean was still at Pontiac, he brought Crosby in to lecture to his management team; subsequently, a unit of GM decided to create a zero-defects inspection system. Relying on inspection to weed out defects is, of course, antithetical to the concept of quality taught by Deming and practiced by the Japanese. While Crosby has long considered statistics to be nothing but a tool, after Deming's popularity gave new credence to the importance of variation control in the late 1980s, Crosby is said to have begun teaching more of the subject at his seminars. GM still uses some of Crosby's concepts. But some of GM's Demingites snidely joke that Crosby's most lasting legacy at the auto company, which invested $4 million to acquire a 10 percent interest in Crosby College in 1984, a stake it sold back to Crosby a few years later, was the quality Koala bears—a quality recognition gimmick—he had distributed at Pontiac. [20]

In 1981 several groups of Xerox executives went to Crosby College. Even David Kearns flew down for a specially designed, intensive one-day session; Crosby's seminars usually last three days, but he was persuaded to organize a one-day session for Kearns. [21] Yet Xerox's engineering community was said to have written Crosby off as a lightweight. [22] "The thing about Phil," says one Xerox executive about Crosby's edge there, "is that he knows how to talk business-ese. Deming and Juran don't." [23]

Moreover, on Fuji Xerox president Yōtaro (Tony) Kobayashi's recommendation, the company hired an outside consultant, someone who could tell David Kearns "to go to hell." Xerox signed David Nadler, the president of Delta Consulting Group. A soft-spoken man who was in his mid-thirties when he began working with Xerox, it is unlikely he ever called Kearns onto the carpet for sloppy thinking. And although he has taught courses on research methods and written one book on the use of survey data, he is an expert in organizational behavior, not process management. It is therefore difficult to imagine that Kobayashi, who routinely subjects himself and his company to the imperious judgment of Professor Asaka, the eminent JUSE counselor, could have had Nadler in mind. In fact, Xerox insiders concluded that top management was not yet ready to accept the level of no-holds-barred criticism that Japanese Deming Prize applicants, as well as FP&L, have come to expect as a constructive and necessary part of the improvement process.

Xerox absorbed bits and pieces of what it heard from the gurus and jerry-built a quality strategy that was finalized during a three-day meeting in August 1983 at a retreat in Leesburg, Virginia. It's not that Xerox's commitment and progress don't outshine most of the quality initiatives undertaken by U.S. companies; it's just that the copier pioneer is far behind where it might have gotten, and where it still may go if it follows the instincts that are now prompting

Kearns to reexamine the Japanese model. With Fuji Xerox in its backyard, Xerox should have been able to come up with something better than "Leadership Through Quality." This ninety-two page document identified four major corporate quality initiatives:

- First, it prescribed a nine-step improvement process that aims to identify a customer's requirements and the best way of achieving those requirements, in every task undertaken at the company. The nine-step process, which is a modified version of Deming and Shewhart's PDCA cycle, is predicated on a systematic problem-solving model and mandates the use of statistical tools of analysis.
- Second, it sought to institutionalize the competitive benchmarking system that already was being used by manufacturing and engineering.
- Third, it called upon each of its business units to establish key quality indicators to help measure its progress. This step called for substituting customer satisfaction data for technical and operational measurements wherever possible.
- Fourth, it sought to assess the cost of quality by calculating everything from the cost of lost opportunity to the price of prevention.[24]

After competitive benchmarking, which was initiated before the Leadership Through Quality (a Xerox directive prohibits the use of an acronym) program was started, the nine-step improvement process was probably the company's most important initiative. This was essentially a reinvention of the Deming wheel, with a few extra spokes added on for good measure.[25] Beginning in 1984, every Xerox employee has been required to identify precisely who his customers were, be they buyers of copiers or a Xerox colleague in another department whose output depends on the quality of all the jobs that precede his or hers in the process. The mandate led to a great deal of job analysis and fostered team improvement projects. Says Don Clausing, "That did lead to significant improvement. I remember one senior manager said, 'These people never came to talk to me before.' It integrated people more, got them more focused" on what their customers wanted.[26]

Xerox also launched an ambitious quality training program. Within the first few years of Leadership Through Quality, most of the company's 100,000 employees had undergone at least one week of quality indoctrination. The one-week course covered such things as problem solving, including ways to encourage employee involvement and competitive benchmarking. It also included a rudimentary discussion of the use of basic statistical charts and graphs, such as control charts and histograms, which are widely used in Japan to create a picture of processes so they can be more easily analyzed. To encourage the use of the process, the training course culminated with a directive that every unit pursue one improvement project. Moreover, the education process was structured so that each manager went through the process at least twice, once as a trainee and once as a coach.[27]

Yet as a blueprint for a quality strategy, the Leadership Through Quality document fell short in a number of ways. Although the group was meant to outline a set of analytical tools for measuring process capability, it did no more than tuck a list of basic statistical tools into an appendix of the document. Rigorous factual analysis, based on the concept of variation control, was by no means central to Xerox's vision of Leadership Through Quality. As mentioned earlier, the quality council, which drafted the document and which included few participants with engineering or mathematical degrees, was simply put off by statistics. And one participant in the quality planning process notes that the council spent so much time reinventing the Deming cycle, they simply didn't have time to think through the measurement portion of the document.[28]

Similarly, the one-week training course was but half a cake. While it certainly communicated the company's commitment to quality, it was too superficial to effect major change by itself. Some engineers, for example, would have liked to have seen such specific quality engineering techniques as Taguchi methods and QFD standardized through the Leadership Through Quality program. The techniques, however, were deemed too technical to merit inclusion.[29]

Moreover, one of Xerox's principal quality initiatives may have served to muddy the waters of understanding. Specifically, Xerox's desire to measure the costs of quality may be one of the more ill-conceived aspects of Leadership Through Quality. The concept of "cost of quality" is a Crosby favorite. It may sound great, but it can deflect a great deal of management attention from the business of improvement. Xeroxers contend that measuring cost of quality helps them justify, both to their own managers and to customers, short-term expenditures that they expect will lead to long-term improvements. While this may be so, it can easily focus attention on problems that are easy to quantify, rather than the ones that are most important to change. For example, because solving small problems is the most effective way to show quick results, teams set up to analyze the cost of quality have sometimes seized on relatively minor issues, such as deciding whether to purchase a particular piece of equipment, rather than broad systemic problems. Consider the obvious difficulty of trying to measure, on any sort of systematic basis, such things as the cost of lost opportunity. For example, one Xerox team estimated the cost of quality in unresolved customer problems at $1 billion, a figure Rand says is "not factual."[30] "This is a typical American approach," says Clausing, who openly criticizes the focus on cost of quality. "The Japanese don't mess with measuring the cost of quality; they know it's important, and they just focus on improvement."[31]

ZEROING IN ON THE CUSTOMER

Recognizing some of the shortcomings of Leadership Through Quality in its current incarnation, the company is taking a number of steps to improve on the blueprint. For one thing, Xerox has taken some recent initiatives to break down its segmented approach to management and problem solving. Most significantly, the company has launched a new partnership process that aims to better structure, at its branch offices, the decisions made by salesmen, servicemen, and administration around unique customer needs. The partnership was designed to make "customers believe they are the number one priority of every . . . employee" at Xerox's U.S. marketing group.[32]

Specifically, this consensus-building effort was designed to help the branch sales offices adapt more quickly and accurately to rapidly changing customer needs. It does so primarily by tying together the rewards and responsibilities of sales, service, and administrative staff that previously reported to different organizations within Xerox.

In particular, the partnership was designed to overcome a major flaw in the MBO process that often led sales and service to operate at cross-purposes. Previously, the head of sales and the head of service would each establish goals based on corporate objectives. "As you went down three or four levels the goals would be interpreted differently," says Bob Graham, vice president field customer service operations. "Each function within the districts has always had its objectives. But the emphasis was different depending on the function." For example, in the old environment, a new product would generally be introduced in major metropolitan areas, and wouldn't be available in many rural communities until much later. Sometimes, however, a major corporation in, say, Chicago, might ask Xerox to install the copiers both in its Windy City location and at one of its operations in rural Illinois. To do so, the salesmen would have to plead for the servicemen's cooperation. [33]

The problem was that while salesmen were rewarded on the basis of the number of copiers they placed, the servicemen were not. In fact, sales got the revenue each time a new model was introduced, but service got the expense. Because service, by definition, couldn't show any sales, Xerox devised a measurement system that imputed revenue for the maintenance of a product but failed to adequately account for the vast differences in servicing new and old copiers. While a typical service call for an older model that servicemen had plenty of experience fixing might register a fifty-dollar theoretical profit, servicing a new model was an entirely different matter. New models require additional training and new tools, which have to be paid for by the service department to the tune of $10,000 to $50,000 per model, an expense that can take years to amortize! Thus, unless the service department had been specifically instructed to service a new launch, it would suffer what seemed to most district service managers an intolerable loss. Thus, the only hope of selling the new machines to the big Chicago-based customer would be if the service manager had "broad shoulders" and was willing to take a gamble for the long-term good of both the district and the company, and if he had a good relationship with the sales manager. "In the better districts the sales and marketing managers already had worked it out," says Graham. But if the sales and service managers in a given district didn't get along, "you could have real problems."[34]

Xerox's partnership strategy formally ties the fate of the three chief district managers together and gives them far more power and responsibility than ever before. Today responsibility for revenues and costs is shared jointly by the three functions in each district, as is much of the bonus pool. And while routine decisions on returns and discounts used to have to be approved by Xerox headquarters, those decisions are increasingly being delegated to the district partnerships. "We want the partnerships to work like franchises," says Barry Rand. "As they mature and prove their good business judgment," Xerox plans to broaden the parameters of responsibility. In addition, under the new system, the sixty-plus district offices are meant to become "the center of the Xerox universe. Every other function becomes a support to the partnerships."[35]

The district partnerships are just one of the improvements that have grown out of a recognition that for all of Xerox's talk about being obsessed with customers, the traditional organization didn't do enough to bring the company close to its market.

FLIRTING WITH STATISTICS

Making better use of analytical tools, especially statistical ones, in the sales and service area is the next major frontier. Service personnel already have a jump on their counterparts in sales. For years Xerox had tried to deliver uniform service to its customers, aiming to respond to calls within two hours. When customer satisfaction surveys revealed that customers were dissatisfied with the servicemen's response to calls for help, the company began to reexamine this strategy. While Xerox shortened service time across the board by about 1.5 hours during the late 1980s, the company decided to tailor response time to the needs of individual companies and began to study closely the frequency and pattern of usage among its customers. Thus, companies with the lowest usage rates might have to wait a day for help, while businesses that might literally grind to a halt if their copiers or printers malfunction are given top priority and may receive service in as little as an hour or two. For example, several phone companies generate bills on Xerox's 9700 laser printer. If the machine goes down, it can affect the phone company's revenues because bills that go out late are also paid late.[36]

Teams of servicemen have also begun to use statistics to analyze such things as parts usage, an exercise that used to be conducted only at Xerox headquarters. Parts usage is a principal indicator for controlling parts inventory, determining budgets, and, most important from a quality standpoint, analyzing the skill level of service teams. One of the basic theorems of the service business is that the better a serviceman is at spotting the precise nature of a problem, the fewer spare parts he'll need to use. That's because an inadequately trained serviceman, working on a machine as complex as a copier, might randomly substitute new parts until the problem appears to be solved without ever pinpointing precisely what went wrong. Improving the diagnostic skills of servicemen not only saves time, labor, and the cost of new parts but generally improves the rate of service. Graham points out that by learning to use the simple charts and diagrams that facilitate statistical analysis, the service staff can more easily find the patterns of service and usage than by trying to scrutinize long columns of numbers. "Your memory just can't deal with three hundred numbers on a page and remembering all the relationships," he says.[37]

To get the salesman to appreciate what a statistical picture can do, the company's quality staff are searching for a "high-leverage" vehicle that will overcome the pitchman's innate resistance to the analytical process. Xerox has begun experimenting with using a fishbone diagram, also known as an Ishikawa diagram, to map out the account management process and to show how the sales rep is doing in the six key steps of the sales cycle. The trick to getting consistently good sales results, says Rand, is to stagger prospects so that a sales rep always has a new opportunity in the earliest stage of the pitch process even as another prospect is getting ready to close a deal, and while still other customers are spread evenly throughout the cycle. Eventually, to improve their sales technique, Xerox reps may start building charts and diagrams that show the amount of time they spend on such activities as cold calling, the care and feeding of clients, and chasing orders with administration, says Carolyn McZinc, the marketing group's vice president for quality.[38]

However, Xerox's best chance to make quantum leaps in improving its performance could rest on how well it learns its lessons from Fuji Xerox. That isn't something that comes easily to the U.S. copier pioneer. Since 1979, when Xerox first decided it had to pursue a quality strategy, the company has assiduously avoided modeling its strategy on that of its Japanese counterpart. The U.S. company's determination not to copy Fuji Xerox was born partly of an emotional, not-invented-here syndrome, and partly of legitimate concern about whether a "Japanese management" system can effectively be transferred to a U.S. company. Jeff Kennard, the liaison executive between Fuji Xerox and Xerox, notes that when Fuji Xerox began to pursue its quality strategy, the president of the joint venture company, Yōtaro Kobayashi, "promulgated this to everyone. Everyone in the organization plugged in except [U.S.] Xerox. It fell on deaf ears for a while and led to several false starts." Adds Don Clausing,, "If they had copied Fuji Xerox they would have been ahead of the game."[39]

FUJI XEROX: TESTING THE LIMITS OF TQC

In many ways Fuji Xerox was an unlikely company to serve as a quality management model for its parent company. Although Fuji Photo Film had won the Deming award in 1956 and had spread the principles to many of its subsidiaries and affiliates, Fuji Xerox had had no qualtity control experience whatsoever.[40] Indeed, until 1971, when Fuji Xerox formally acquired two manufacturing plants, it had served largely as a marketing organization. When the company finally began to adopt quality ideas, it did so first in its new engineering and manufacturing departments, relying to a great extent on the formation of quality circles.

The company was driven to pursue the Deming Prize for the same reason it made the transition from a marketing to a full-fledged manufacturing concern: The market demanded it. The expiration of xerography patents, which had given Xerox a lock on the copier business until the early 1970s, opened the way to nearly a dozen Japanese competitors. One of Xerox's chief challengers was Ricoh, which won the Deming Prize in 1975. Moreover, Xerox wasn't responding fast enough with the sorts of compact, high-quality products the Japanese wanted, while Fuji Xerox was building small copiers to keep its share of that market. At the same time, the joint venture's expansion into manufacturing created new quality management demands and nearly doubled the size of Fuji Xerox's work force to 5,220 in the early 1970s, making it more difficult for the company to manage change. Finally, with the first oil price shock Fuji Xerox's manufacturing costs soared by more than 20 percent, while profits, despite price increases, tumbled in 1971 and 1976, fueling the company's need to develop more efficient systems.[41] By 1978 Fuji Xerox had expanded its commitment to TQC throughout the company, and in October of that year a new president, Yōtaro Kobayashi, announced his plan to enter the Deming competition.

Through its competition for the Deming Prize, Fuji Xerox consolidated a series of process improvements, many of which grew out of Deming's early teachings (see Chapter 2). The company adopted policy deployment as its quality-oriented strategic planning process. It also learned to use a variety of sophisticated quality techniques that had been pioneered by the Japanese, including Taguchi methods and QFD (see Chapter 5).

These changes paid off in steady gains in quality and efficiency. By 1978 Fuji Xerox was supplying low-end copiers and key components to both Xerox and Rank Xerox, providing a much-needed defense against the corporation's principal rivals, Ricoh and Canon. The 3500 copier, which was introduced in 1978 and until recently was the company's best-seller, took just two years to develop, half the time it had taken Fuji Xerox to build its first copier and less time than most Xerox machines would spend in the development cycle a decade later.[42] Notes Don Clausing, who left Xerox temporarily in 1976, "When I went to Fuji Xerox in 1977, I was going as an expert to teach them about product development. It never occurred to me that they were doing things I should learn from." In 1984 Clausing visited Fuji Xerox again, this time to learn about such techniques as QFD, which he brought home to Xerox.[43]

The company's quality strategy was, to a great extent, the creation of Yōtaro Kobayashi. The articulate and urbane son of a man who had served as president of both Fuji Photo Film and Fuji Xerox, Kobayashi was the ideal candidate to redefine the management agenda of this hybrid Western and Eastern company. Kobayashi was born in London in 1933 at the end of his father's tenure there as a sales executive for Iwai Trading Company, which founded Fuji Photo Film. And it was through his father, Setsutaro Kobayashi, who is credited with honing Fuji Film's customer-driven product development approach, that his son is said to have developed an appreciation for quality management. Known as "Tony" to his American colleagues, the younger Kobayashi was educated at Wharton and Tokyo's Keio University and speaks English with barely a hint of an accent. This patrician Japanese, who took over the presidency of Fuji Xerox when he was only in his mid-forties, has emerged as one of the country's foremost business leaders. When the heads of Keidanren, the Japanese Federation of Economic Organizations, were looking for someone to head a committee of Japanese firms with foreign affiliations, they turned to Kobayashi, making him the youngest member of the prestigious business group to head a policy committee.[44]

For Kobayashi, the Deming competition is a management prerequisite that is as important to a modern Japanese company as is the purchase of the latest office technology. Nearly a decade after winning the prize, Kobayashi still goes to great lengths to understand the problems and processes behind the company's results. For example, like many Japanese presidents, Kobayashi conducts periodic, in-depth plant tours to assess the progress and processes of the company's operations. When he began to discover, in the mid-1980s, that managers were pulling their punches in the formal presidential reviews and presenting only the "good" TQC stories, Kobayashi began to focus more of his attention on the conversations that took place during the drinks and dinner that follow the formal reviews.[45]

HOW TQC HELPED SALES AND MARKETING TAKE BETTER CARE OF THE CUSTOMER

For Kobayashi, entering the Deming competition represented nothing less than a commitment to redefining the company's culture, to questioning "the raison d'être of the company itself." To make sure it started out on the right track, Fuji Xerox brought in Tetsuichi

Asaka. And it permanently adopted the comprehensive management reviews, including policy deployment, that characterize the advanced stages of TQC and that are an integral part of winning the Deming competition.[46]

It was perhaps inevitable that as a company that had its origins in marketing, Fuji Xerox would come to pay a great deal of attention to integrating marketing and sales into the quality improvement process. In 1980 over half of Fuji Xerox's 8,100 employees were salesmen. And one of the principal preoccupations of the company's quality movement centers on such questions as "What is the definition of a good salesman? Does each newly developed product reflect input from the sales division?"[47]

Improvements in sales were initially focused on the importance of meeting the needs of a growing base of Japanese customers who prefer to buy small, inexpensive copiers and facsimile machines. The needs of this burgeoning group of small customers couldn't be met by a cadre of account executives whose job traditionally had been to cultivate large clients and to furnish them with pricey rental units. In 1976 the company decided to sell, rather than to rent, certain models. But it was not until Fuji Xerox established a separate sales network a year later that it was able to improve its market share in small copiers.[48]

The first step was to establish which markets were the most important to the company. "Before TQC, Fuji Xerox had some segmentation, but we [had assumed that] only the major accounts were important," says Takamichi Hatanaka, managing director of Fuji Xerox's marketing business. "We organized a special function to focus on major national accounts, the equivalent of the U.S. *Fortune* 500, and those customers were covered very well." While the company's five hundred or so major national accounts were well cared for, there was no other segmentation. Regional salesmen handled all manner of accounts in their territory. Moreover, the pitchmen operated on a single principle: Sell as many boxes as possible during a six-month period. And while individual salesmen understood the prospects in their territory, management never did.[49]

To better service small customers, the company launched a mass-marketing strategy that was based on the establishment in 1981 of twenty-nine joint-venture sales companies. The joint ventures were struck with local firms that had strong ties to their communities, in cities like Fukuoka, Sapporo, and the prefectures of Saitama, Kyoto, and Hiroshima. Fuji Xerox retained a controlling interest in the companies and set up special training programs for the executives selected to head the joint ventures. The company established the joint-venture sales strategy because it was confident that "once [it] was successful in relating itself closely to a community, support from customers would naturally grow, and the company could expect an increase in the number of sales."[50]

When Fuji Xerox had nailed down the general approach to improving its sales strategy, it began to focus on improving the service process and on upgrading the input from individual salesmen. In particular, the company sought to develop a system that shifted the emphasis from one that let salesmen decide when, and how, to pitch to clients, to one that would focus strategically on top-priority accounts. Before the "TQC era, the marketing department operated in terms of its internal interests, except when it came to major national accounts. We had a product-oriented approach," says Hatanaka. "Neither the territory or headquarters staff thought about the customer and what the customers want. Before we started to use TQC in marketing, [the salesmen] stopped by [the] customer whenever he wanted, maybe because he liked a particular customer. Even if the company wants to push one product, the salesman [might] push another product. It was all based on the salesmen's willingness; the attitude was based on [whether the product] is easy to sell and easy to explain to the customer."[51]

Many of the changes Fuji Xerox made in its marketing organization flew in the face of conventional notions about sales. "Before TQC, marketing saw sales as a kind of experience business," says Hatanaka, who notes that servicemen "like to sit and talk. They don't like to write reports." With TQC, however, they would have little choice. The company instituted process control procedures that required salesmen to document their business. Fuji Xerox pitchmen were issued small cards on which they were constantly to update the vital statistics of every client. They were to document carefully such information as the number of people employed by the client, the type of document-processing products they used, and the number of copies they generated on a monthly basis. In addition, when a salesman made a call, he was expected to write down the actual process of his pitch; for instance, whether he made a sales call to the company, if he invited a client to see a new product at the regional office, or if he took a client to dinner. He was to note how the meeting transpired and when he would make the next sales call.[52]

Demingism in sales developed into a detailed information-gathering process designed both to create an accurate picture of the market and to enable managers to help their subordinates improve their sales strategies. "Through this kind of daily control system, you can [figure out] how long since a customer bought his last piece of equipment." If a customer had been generating five thousand copies per month, and Fuji Xerox discovers it is now generating ten thousand copies, the company knows it's time to sell another copier. The company has developed a detailed list of two hundred thousand prospects that will go either to Fuji Xerox or to a competitor. The system is designed to increase the odds that they will go to Fuji Xerox.[53]

Fuji Xerox has also established a sophisticated system for speeding marketing information to the product development department.[54] Whenever a customer voices a complaint or product requirement, salesmen make a note of the request on one side of a special product form they take with them on sales calls. The forms are sent to headquarters, where someone from either manufacturing or administration *must* respond to the comment. For example, in 1987 the sales department generated 1,429 comments from its customers about problems or new requirements pertaining to copiers. The company distilled the comments into a list of about forty key areas that needed to be studied. These in turn were narrowed down to nine categories of improvements that would be tackled by the product development department, including a copier that can feed postcards and tracing paper, one that will clearly reproduce pencil impressions, and one that will copy photographs better. The technical problems and demands inherent in this requirements list define the QFD process and drive the strategies that are established for the research department and for suppliers. Similarly, manufacturing reviews the forms and considers the production implications of the requirements.[55] This process was introduced to U.S. Xerox by Don Clausing in about 1985, but it is only now beginning to catch on there.[56]

Hatanaka credits this customer-driven process with perfecting Fuji

Xerox's successful 5030 copier. The sleek, narrow machine is about the size of a miniature refrigerator. The 5030 has a front-loading option and the ability automatically to choose the proper paper size from five separate trays. It also has an editing function—once the paper that is to be copied is laid on the machine, portions can be deleted or highlighted in different colors by touching the portion of the document that needs to be altered with a special wand. While Fuji Xerox was not first on the market with a copier boasting this mix of features, the machine is known for its level of reliability, according to John Grattan, a quality expert from Xerox who was visibly impressed when he first saw the machine during a trip to Japan in 1988.[57]

Fuji Xerox's process control system is also designed to establish realistic targets for salesmen. Explains Hatanaka, "The corporation and marketing staff understand the market potential in each business unit and in each geographic area. When a business unit gets a target, it is based on detailed information" on the market. In the United States, the Fuji Xerox sales system, in which salesmen spend a third of their time updating data on their customers and analyzing it with their supervisors, is probably unprecedented. The company's emphasis on the collection of sales and marketing data by salesmen has been so intense, in fact, that Hatanaka says the next quality improvement task will be to find ways to streamline the procedure so that it takes less of the salesman's time.[58]

A DOWN-UP-DOWN APPROACH TO MANAGEMENT

Fuji Xerox's sales and marketing systems are an integral part of the strategic planning process the company adopted in the course of competing for the Deming Prize. At Fuji Xerox, corporate and quality strategies converge in a process that is defined by a series of product- and process-driven management reviews and that culminates in the annual presidential review. In 1988, for example, the annual review focused on an assessment of the 5026/5030 family of copiers, its shortcomings, future product plans, and potential process changes that could enhance future service of the next family of copiers. In sessions that typically begin at 1:30 P.M. and last into the early evening, Kobayashi, the company's top thirty-four executives, and two JUSE consultants, including Professor Asaka, who shepherded Fuji Xerox through the Deming Prize preparation, preside over these annual reviews. At the end of the reviews, in which executives from operations present the company's year-to-date performance and its plans for improving products and processes, the professors critique the presentations and point out flaws in the reasoning.[59]

The reviews are also attended by Kojiro Akiba, who heads Fuji Xerox's quality improvement office, known at the company as the New Xerox Movement promotion office (the name of the department is intended to convey how important the quality office's role is to the culture and functioning of the entire corporation). Akiba and his corporate staff of about ten full-time quality experts and two additional quality experts in each of the company's divisions help the operating units implement the improvement strategies that have been approved during the presidential review.

However, it is important to note that the presidential review isn't an end in itself; rather it is one of the principal vehicles of a tightly coordinated cycle that links every discipline in the company around a common set of improvement goals. Japanese refer to it as a down-up-down approach to management. The policy deployment process, with its reviews, is designed to accomplish a number of goals. First, it is intended to tie new product development to the needs of the market based on information gleaned by marketing and product development. It is also meant to reinforce the sales effort and to reduce costs by streamlining upstream processes. And, finally, it is structured to incorporate new technologies easily. In short, it is a management system designed to be as precise as Toyota's production system, in which every task is measured for ultimate efficiency, to be performed as quickly as is humanly possible without sacrificing quality.

The strategies that are finalized during the annual review cascade down to every operations unit and are buttressed by a series of monthly reviews that are meant to strike a pragmatic balance between blue-sky goals and the realities of a business's process capability. The system attempts to guard against the setting of unrealistic goals, since every objective must be supported by a detailed account of process capability. At the same time, the demands of a competitive marketplace lead teams of managers and their superiors to search for ways to constantly improve their products and processes. In addition, a failure to meet goals is subjected to meticulous problem solving during monthly reviews and ultimately at the year-end presentations to the president. Like the presidential reviews, the monthly sessions are designed specifically to identify problems and solutions relating to management, process, product development, and marketing. The quality promotion office assists wherever necessary.

Most important, the process is designed to coach, not to police. An internal Fuji Xerox document referring to a new product review in 1988 identifies as one of the principal goals of the review the opportunity to "define the items for improvement of the division . . . and discuss [them] with top management, division managers and program team. And decide [the] solution to the problems with the cooperation of top management and the division personnel."[60]

Policy deployment has become the principal method of strategic planning at many Japanese companies by establishing both annual and long-term goals, and by creating a management method that helps to evaluate and achieve those objectives. One problem Fuji Xerox is still working on is an attempt to build flexibility into the rigid system that was spawned by the Deming Prize. Historically, Fuji Xerox has not been a market innovator.[61] As a result, one of the company's goals is to improve research and the development of new technologies. To do that, executives at Fuji Xerox suggest they may have to loosen the reins of TQC. Traditionally, policy deployment has fostered a system of Talmudic questioning in which every decision was subjected to a litany of "Why? Why? Why? Why? Why?" To foster creativity, Kobayashi is experimenting with a modified approach that is intended to get the organization to replace that question with an equally insistent "Why not? Why not? Why not? Why not? Why not?"[62]

WHY XEROX IS BEGINNING TO SAY "WHY NOT?" TO FUJI XEROX

For Xerox, however, the problem is too little discipline, not too much. The company badly needs a pool of experts who are well versed in both quality theory and the teaching of user-friendly statistical analysis. Having passed up the chance to work closely with Deming, the company will find it difficult to find this particular mix of expertise—so common in Japan—at home. Indeed, many of Xerox's quality executives, including Norman Rickard, Xerox's vice president for quality, and Carolyn McZinc, come from unrelated disciplines such as finance, and are largely self-taught.

These days the company is finally beginning to look at Fuji Xerox's TQC model. Ironically, it is the quality crusade at FP&L, which studied Fuji Xerox closely and unabashedly followed the Japanese example, that has prompted Xerox to give its Japanese joint venture's strategy a second look. In recent years, dozens of Xerox executives have visited the Florida utility. During the last two years, Xerox has sent roughly eight hundred key executives of ever higher rank to visit the joint venture.[63] In June 1989 Paul Allaire, the company's president, chairman David Kearns, and the entire top executive cadre of the company visited Japan to receive a "week of intensive Japanese TQC indoctrination." A few months earlier, Kearns had authorized Fuji Xerox to approach Professor Asaka to ask whether he or any of his colleagues would be willing to work with Xerox. While the company isn't ready to subject the entire organization to the education process of the Japanese yeshiva bochers, one group—the company's West Coast printing systems business—has volunteered to serve as an experiment in policy deployment. Printing systems, says one Xerox insider, are an ideal candidate because they are a key strategic business and encompass both product development and manufacturing.[64]

But in late 1989, Asaka declined Xerox's offer, saying he would not work with a single division unless the entire company commits to the same process. While Xerox says it is committed to TQC, Kearns wasn't willing to plunge the entire corporation into an Asaka-style regimen. Indeed, the copier company is choosing a much more difficult course: According to one insider, Xerox will try to implement policy deployment without Asaka, by drawing on Fuji Xerox's expertise and by sending employees to JUSE seminars, as well as to Deming seminars.[65] Thus, it is likely to be years before Xerox reaches its full quality potential.

PERESTROIKA AT
GENERAL MOTORS?

t isn't the same Detroit smog wafting over West Grand Boulevard; there is the smell of genuine change in the air at the monolithic General Motors headquarters building in the heart of Motown. It is 1989, CEO Roger Smith is one year away from retirement, and Bob Stempel, the new president and soon-to-be CEO, is talking a lot about quality these days. "Ten years ago we had a different concept of quality," concedes Stempel. "The concept that we embrace today is continuous improvement. Now we are working to change our corporation into a total quality corporation based on quality people and guided by a consistent set of quality policies."[1]

What is remarkable about Stempel's assertion is that during the course of Detroit's most difficult decade, neither employees, consistency, nor quality seemed to have been much of a priority for GM's top management. Nineteen-eighty was a pivotal year for the Motor City. All three major U.S. automakers were awash in red ink. GM's $762.5 million loss was its first since 1921. By virtue of its size, GM was not hit as hard as Ford and Chrysler, both of which hovered on the brink of ruin. Yet the more enlightened leaders in the bowels of GM were beginning to understand the sorts of management changes that would be needed to design and build competitive cars for the 1980s and beyond. Indeed, as Ford executives were seeking a dialogue with Deming that year, managers at GM's Pontiac Division were also beginning to develop what would be a long, close relationship with Deming.

But changing GM would prove to be much more difficult than changing Ford. The corporation, which rang up revenues of $42.8 billion in 1980, was less desperate than America's number-two automaker. Moreover, GM lacked a companywide consensus regarding the true source of its problems. In 1981, even as Pontiac was beginning to work with Deming and to seek a new cooperative approach to management, Smith made this assessment of the company's problems: "Without question, noncompetitive labor costs represent the single biggest disadvantage we must overcome."[2]

GM's fixation with labor costs diverted its attention from fundamental product development problems. During the next several years, a dizzying array of policy and organizational changes, as well as capital investments, were aimed at thinning the workers' ranks. These strategies would succeed in dramatically altering GM, but they would do little to address the fundamental problem facing the company, which as Deming puts it, was to "build a product that not only will satisfy customers, but get them to come back."

The relative magnitude of the changes facing GM in the 1990s are extraordinary, particularly in light of the upheaval that plagued the automaker during the last decade. In the early 1980s, driven in large part by Smith's belief that people themselves were the problem, the company spent nearly $70 billion on new technology and acquisitions. But the nature of many of Smith's investments showed that the CEO didn't understand the underlying causes of GM's problems. Ventures like the $600 million Detroit-Hamtramck plant, which had been built to assemble GM's smaller luxury cars such as the Cadillac Eldorado, and which had once been hailed by Smith as "the most modern automobile plant in the world"[3] would cast a long shadow over GM's high-tech strategy. The GM flagship, which opened in 1985 and was to be 96 percent automated in its painting and welding operations, became a model of mismanagement in large part because it was planned without adequate input from the employees who would have to operate the new equipment.[4] In late 1986, it was still taking forty-one man-hours to put together a midsize GM car, while Ford was building Taurus Sables with just twenty-five man-hours of labor. Even that production rate was about 40 percent longer than it took to put together a Honda in Marysville, Ohio.[5] Moreover, productivity at New United Motor Manufacturing Inc. (NUMMI), the joint venture between Toyota and GM that produced the Chevy Nova and Toyota Corolla, was about twice that of the average GM plant—and the old Fremont, California, facility, where the compacts were produced, wasn't even endowed with as much robotics and high-tech gadgetry as other GM plants![6]

The company launched what was to be the $5 billion Saturn Corporation, its first new division in decades, and one that was to define the essence of future car manufacturing at GM.[7] But the project was started without the backing of several key GM executives, and it became clear the company wouldn't be able to sell 500,000 Saturn cars per year. So CEO Smith halved both Saturn's production projections and its budget.[8]

Smith acquired Electronic Data Systems and, to inject a fresh management perspective, got its founder, Ross Perot, to sit on GM's board. But having latched on to one of America's most maverick entrepreneurs, Smith couldn't stomach Perot's pointed criticism of his regime. GM's chairman wound up paying $700 million to rid himself of the company's only activist board member.

Throughout these costly maneuvers, GM conducted a host of layoffs, plant closings, and personnel and compensation policy changes that were aimed at cutting costs but that also succeeded in devastating morale and hampering the company's ability to achieve its product and quality objectives.

No amount of cost cutting or technology fixes seemed to solve GM's biggest problem—its bevy of "look-alike" cars. Trailing the standards of innovativeness, distinctiveness, and quality that were being set by the competition, GM just couldn't get its customers to come back. By 1987 GM's market share had slipped nearly ten percentage points since 1980 to 36.6 percent, even as Ford's market penetration jumped 3 points to 20.2 percent during the same period. And for the first time since 1924, Ford's profit outstripped GM's, reaching $785 million in 1986, a 9 percent increase over its performance a year earlier.[9] According to a 1986 index of consumer satisfaction compiled by J. D. Power & Associates, a market research firm in Agoura Hills, California, in 1986 Cadillac was the only GM car that was not ranked below the industry average. And warranty costs on new Cadillacs were said to run $360–$400, more than ten times the warranty costs of a new Honda.[10]

Worse, GM was plagued by a glacial decision-making process. As with Ford, the big problems at GM had started in the 1960s, with the ascendancy of a financial cadre led by Frederic G. Donner, who was CEO at the time. As the beancounters took hold of GM, they dismantled the balance of power that had been carefully crafted by Alfred P. Sloan, the company's legendary chairman. Sloan's vision had been to create a system that would give individual car divisions the autonomy they needed to maintain relatively entrepreneurial operations, while the corporate staff kept control over broad policy functions. Thus corporate staff would oversee finance and general product policies, such as deciding that there was a market need for, say, a new small car. But once such decisions were made, Sloan believed, the execution of the new car should be left in the hands of the individual car divisions. This system worked best, according to Sloan, where cooperation among various operations within GM was stressed, where management moved through persuasion rather than fiat, and where decision-making was delegated to the lowest level at which it could be made intelligently.[11]

In the 1960s, the beancounters gradually robbed the divisions of their responsibilities. In 1971, in one of the biggest blows to operations, the corporation transferred manufacturing from the car companies to the General Motors Assembly Division (GMAD). That decision, born of a misguided belief that the resulting economies of scale would pay off in huge cost savings, contributed in a major way to the look-alike syndrome that would come to dog GM cars in the 1980s. Product decisions were increasingly divided between the individual car divisions, such as Oldsmobile and Chevrolet, which had become little more than marketing units, Fisher Body, which was responsible for product engineering, and GMAD, which controlled manufacturing. Concedes Roger Smith, "If Bill Mitchell [the former head of GM's design staff] didn't like a car division manager, that guy wouldn't get a good car . . . he'd [get] an awful looking car."[12]

And the buck never stopped until it hit the president's desk. Cost became the paramount priority. Quality and the customer were a distant second. As John DeLorean observed, "It seems incredible, but sound, long-range and comprehensive business planning was almost non-existent at General Motors when I was there. . . . I got the empty feeling that 'what I am doing here may be nothing more than perpetuating a gigantic fraud,' a fraud on the American consumer by promising him something new but giving him only surface alterations—'tortured sheet metal' . . . or a couple of extra horsepower and an annual price increase. . . . Committees were constantly being set up, usually stacked with financial types, to study the dimensions of the industry ten or fifteen years ahead. . . . But on the whole these studies were heavily weighted with financial data. They lacked depth and a sensitive feel for the market. In the end, management usually did not act on this information but instead reacted to developments in the marketplace as they occurred. . . . The excessive emphasis on cost cutting has permeated the organization as the first, and sometimes the only, precept of management."[13] GM was paying the price for refusing to undertake a serious reevaluation of its organizational structures and policies, something that Peter Drucker had advocated since the 1940s in his seminal book *Concept of the Corporation*.

One of the last and most obvious casualties of the post-Sloan era was the GM-10 program. A power struggle between marketing, engineering, and manufacturing helped stymie the midsized car project.[14] It dragged on for seven years, twice the time it takes the Japanese to bring a new car to market. And GM wasn't able to get the line's four-door Lumina, which debuted in 1989, ready in time to battle Ford's Taurus and Sable, launched in 1985.

In the early 1980s, to help fix GM's product problems, Smith convened a study group of GM executives and brought in McKinsey & Company, a management consulting firm. After two years of soul searching, the group concluded that one of GM's biggest problems was a glacial pace of change: "It didn't pay to take too many chances in General Motors culture, because the penalties for failure were rather severe." In the words of Gerald P. Hirshberg, a former chief designer for Pontiac and Buick who is now director of design for Nissan Design International in San Diego, "The company was full of executives, including designers, who only had to keep things going. The muscles of creativity atrophied."[15] GM executives in Detroit had entirely lost touch with the tastes of customers outside the Midwest, who increasingly came to prefer foreign cars.[16]

The answer seized on by the study group was to launch a massive reorganization of the company in 1984 that would divide GM's five car divisions and its Canadian operations into two groups.[17] The reorganization of 1984 was meant in part to improve efficiency by centralizing all the manufacturing and engineering for both big and small cars into two organizations, Buick-Oldsmobile-Cadillac (BOC) and Chevrolet-Pontiac-GM of Canada (CPC), respectively.

The reorganization threw the corporation into years of turmoil. It did little to address GM's core product problem or to bring the company closer to its customers. Employees whose loyalty to particular divisions was legendary were shuffled around the company like properties on a monopoly board, and little was done by GM to ease the shock of the moves. Final decisions were still made high up in the company by the two executives responsible for the two car groups, and the power of GM's financial cadre remained strong. Cost pressures can still send GM "scrambling to change a decision that was made a year ago," notes Jim Perkins, who left GM in the mid-1980s to work on Toyota's new luxury car, the Lexus, and who returned a few years later to head Chevrolet. Persistent product problems were underscored three years after the reorganization by another restructuring that restored to the ailing Cadillac division the manufacturing and engineering responsibilities, which had been assigned to the BOC group. While a complete restructuring of Chevrolet is unlikely in the near future, Perkins is searching for ways to pull marketing, engineering, and manufacturing closer together at GM's largest divisions. Says Smith, "We're just right now reorganizing the engineering department out at CPC to get stronger platform control."[18]

Today executives throughout GM are beginning to understand that the secret of building better cars has more to do with the way the company is managed than the way it is organized. Stempel is talking about "trying to force cultural change without having organizational change drive everything."[19] Behind the rhetoric, there is emerging at GM a concerted and remarkably centralized quality strategy that takes its vision from Deming and that is attempting to create a framework for institutionalizing a customer-driven vision of quality throughout GM.

Behind this vision is the realization that GM must fix the processes by which it builds cars. For one thing, GM must temper the run-amok individualism of its culture, which led every factory and every division to reinvent the wheels of management and manufacturing, while at the same time constructively harnessing individual initiative. "At GM there isn't even a mechanism by which someone could learn about an innovation that worked someplace else" in the same company, says Maryann Keller, a leading auto analyst at Furman, Selz, Mager, Dietz & Birney and author of *Rude Awakening*, a book on GM.[20] Thus, the most crucial elements of the company's new quality strategy involved identifying and improving the best processes within the corporation, and breaking down the barriers of institutional rivalry to foster the dissemination of new standards throughout GM.

Those barriers were so great, it took Deming eight years to gain an entree to GM's executive suite. Indeed, the history of Demingism at GM offers a stark reminder that change and improvement can come only with the commitment of top management and a consistent vision of change, what Deming refers to as constancy of purpose. It is the story of missed opportunities and of a belated awakening to the discipline of quality management. It is also the tale of how a few committed managers and executives created, against great odds, a model of change that is shaping the direction of the corporation.

Deming's influence gathered steam gradually over a period of a decade, gaining strength out of the remnants of failed ventures, playing its first role in the ill-fated Pontiac Fiero. It was carried on to one of GM's most troubled plants in Van Nuys, California, saving the Chevrolet Camaro and Pontiac Firebird assembly facility from imminent demise. And it ultimately won its fullest expression in two of the corporation's most important product areas—one of the divisions that produces GM engines and Cadillac.

THE RISE AND FALL OF THE FIERO

To a great extent, the origins of GM's quality odyssey and its belated shift to Demingism are reflected in the genesis, and the ultimate failure, of the Fiero. Had it not been for the utter lack of consistency and commitment by GM's top management, which nickle-and-dimed the car to death, Fiero could have capitalized on the huge success it enjoyed during its first year on the market. It was the brainchild of a group of managers who would become the company's most ardent Deming advocates and one of the first testing grounds for Deming's ideas at GM. Yet Fiero was also the victim of a bureaucratic product development process, exacerbated by political infighting, that had doomed several earlier GM car programs. Many of Fiero's woes could be traced back to the same dysfunctional management systems that had produced the infamous 1959 Corvair, a disaster chronicled in Ralph Nader's *Unsafe at Any Speed*, as well as the snail's-pace development of the GM-10 cars.[21] As a result, when Mazda introduced the Miata, a low-cost, sporty two-seater that was one of the biggest successes of 1989, the Fiero had just been discontinued and many former Fiero hands could be heard lamenting, "That could have been the Fiero."[22]

Fiero was to help revive the flagging fortunes of Pontiac, which had been hit especially hard by the double whammy of management problems and the energy crisis of the 1970s. Slow to react as the industry sped past the power-and-styling-conscious 1960s and into the fuel-obsessed 1970s, Pontiac lost its youthful image and for several years failed to replace it with a compelling new identity. Though Pontiac had once been known for engineering prowess and high performance, by 1980 GM was even considering dropping it as a nameplate, writes Gary Witzenberg in *Fiero*.[23] The Fiero was to be a key element in the Pontiac Division's renaissance. Pontiac's market share had dropped from close to 10 percent in 1967 to below 6 percent in 1974 and 1975. The division's performance recovered somewhat through 1978, when its market share crept to above 7 percent. But with the next oil shock, Pontiac's piece of the industry began to slide, and by 1982 its share was again below the 6 percent mark.[24]

At the start of the 1980s, Pontiac was determined to recover lost ground by building cars that would "put the fun back into driving." Cars like the 1982 Firebird and Trans Am helped restore Pontiac's image as an "exciting, affordable car." But it was the Fiero, which was introduced in 1983, that was to be, in the words of William E. Hoglund, at the time general manager of Pontiac, "the most *inno-*

vative new General Motors product since the first Corvette."[25] In anticipation of three-dollar-a-gallon gasoline, GM aimed for Ferrari-esque styling and Volkswagen-like pricing and fuel efficiency in creating its two-seater commuter car.

Fiero would, in fact, set new standards in both manufacturing and management within Pontiac. What was immediately evident on entering the Fiero factory, part of an old Pontiac facility that had been newly renovated for the car, was the revolutionary machinery used to build its widely hailed "space frame." This technology had been designed to create a near-perfect fit for the car's plastic body panels, to allow for easy repair and service, and to let both manufacturer and owner easily change the look of the car by popping in new panels.[26] Less obvious was the Deming-driven management revolution that was taking place on the plant floor. While GM had begun a feeble quality-of-work-life program in the 1970s, Fiero was one of the first GM projects that gave workers a genuine opportunity to participate in improving the carmaking process.

The cooperative spirit at Fiero owed a lot to Bill Hoglund. In his early forties at the time, Hoglund was young enough to have avoided falling victim to GM hubris, but old enough to have developed the experience and savvy that would be needed to rescue the Fiero from immediate demise. Hoglund had grown up in the shadow of GM. His father, Elis Hoglund, had risen to group vice president of overseas operations at the company. His brother had worked at GM, as had two of his children. Hoglund, says Maryann Keller, is representative of a "new generation at GM, who were not brought up in that company in the 1940s and 1950s when GMers believed that the company could do no wrong. He was part of a GM generation that had been hit by a big dose of humility."[27]

While Hoglund believed that the Fiero's design was crucial to restoring Pontiac's image, he had also come to recognize that a new look wouldn't by itself suffice—Pontiac would have to begin to reverse the dismal reputation for quality that GM had developed during the previous decade. For example, in 1977 the company came under attack for powering its relatively expensive Oldsmobiles with engines from less expensive Chevrolets.[28] The company was also plagued by recalls.[29] And its chronic failure—one that continued into the 1980s—to iron out the kinks in its new models *before* they hit the road gave credence to the cliché that you should never buy a car in its first model year. For example, although the company's new $55,000 Cadillac model, the Allante, was given reasonably good marks by 1989, in its first year on the market it had less power than a Honda. The car was so weak that it sold only a fraction of Cadillac's original 1987 estimates.[30]

Hoglund was among the first Detroit executives to seize on the message contained in NBC's 1980 documentary *If Japan Can, Why Can't We?*, which touted Deming's role in the revival of Japanese industry. "As the Japanese well know, there's no point in having any sort of image at all unless it begins with quality," Hoglund said in a 1982 speech to the auto industry. *"Quality is the ticket. You have to buy to play the game."*[31]

Shortly after the documentary was aired, Deming was invited to Pontiac. Twenty managers, including Hoglund, showed up at the first meeting with Deming, whose age and confrontational manner didn't inspire immediate confidence. "When we shook hands I had a feel for how old he was," recalls Hoglund. "He seemed like Artie Johnson on a tricycle on *Laugh In*. You had the feeling if he got up he would keep right on going. [But] we had nothing to lose." Adds Ernest P. Schaefer, who would become plant manager for the Fiero, "His status in Japan gave him credibility. Had he been an unknown consultant, he wouldn't have gotten past the first meeting."[32]

Soon Deming's philosophy would come to shape a new management culture at Pontiac. "We embarked on a bold new course of action . . . no gimmicks . . . no slogans, no thirty-day programs . . . but a *total*, long-term commitment that involves the entire organization," Hoglund says.[33] In June 1982, as part of a five-year business plan, the division authored a mission statement and a quality philosophy that are both vintage Deming, and that began "Pontiac Motor Division commits itself to quality as our number one business objective. We are dedicated to operating under Dr. Deming's philosophy of management, including extensive application of statistical techniques and team-building efforts . . ."[34]

Moreover, Pontiac's actions were as determined as its rhetoric. In January 1982 Ronald D. Moen, a statistician and Deming disciple, became Pontiac's director of statistical methods. Moen clinched the job because in addition to his academic credentials the young statistician's résumé credited "inspiration from W. Edwards Deming."[35] Moen's hiring signaled the beginning of a new process orientation similar to what had been launched at Ford and Nashua Corporation. Moen's duties included everything from conducting classes in SPC to advising managers and workers on the use of statistical tools and the proper methods for conducting customer satisfaction surveys.

In 1980 Pontiac needed all the help it could get. It had to improve both the quality and the image of its cars. At the same time, it had to close the $2,000-or-so gap that existed between what it cost to build a car in the United States and in Japan.

Many of the early applications of statistical techniques were aimed at streamlining the bloated bureaucracy that had made routine administration unwieldy, time-consuming, and costly. Each staff area, for example, was expected to establish a quality budget that would target measurable improvement objectives and would monitor progress. One indication of Demingism's widespread acceptance at Pontiac was that one of the most vigorous improvement efforts was launched within the finance department. For instance, the accounts payable, audit, and data processing departments brainstormed ways to produce a more streamlined method for processing accounts payable. What had been a four-part process was boiled down to one. Not only did the system save money but, according to an internal Pontiac memo, "by going to the one part form, we eliminated or reduced manual effort in hand matching checks and remittance [forms]. Machines can now fold the forms and stuff them in envelopes. The information is microfiched directly off the computer."[36]

Pontiac also used SPC to streamline the processing of employee expense reports. Official Pontiac policy had been to require three authorized signatures and receipts for any item, no matter how trivial. An analysis of the expense system established that missing receipts and the omission of an authorizing signature accounted for a 13.2 percent rejection rate of employee expense forms. The rejections doubled the work of both the beancounters and the employees trying to collect their expense money. The group recommended that the rules on signatures and receipts be modified so that fewer signatures would be required, and so that receipts for expenditures under $25 would not be required at all.[37]

Similarly, Pontiac wanted to shortcut the process of reviewing the tax codes assigned to purchase requisitions, which heretofore had been subjected to 100 percent inspection. The tax department plotted twenty-five weeks of data showing the number of incorrect tax codes that had required correction and plotted it on a control chart; the data showed an average error rate of 5.58 percent. A brainstorming session revealed three major causes for the mistakes: first, human error, resulting from lack of training or misinterpretation; second, errors in the data itself, which were due to either lack of information or wrong information; and third, systems errors, which included programming mistakes. On closer scrutiny the tax department concluded that human error due to inadequate training had the greatest impact, signaling the need for better training courses.[38]

Fine-tuning each of these processes produced a ripple effect throughout Pontiac's administration. "Most of the applications . . . impact more than one of the areas within our framework, therefore, the potential for costs savings is increased accordingly," concluded a division study.[39]

It was in the plants, however, that the most radical changes would take place. Even before the first cars began rolling off the assembly line at NUMMI, Pontiac was combining SPC with a more participative approach to production. While work-together notions had been bandied about at GM for years, Deming lent the idea a clearer focus. "The concept of helping employees do their jobs was the most important thing I got [from Deming]," says Hoglund. "We had been working with quality of work life for eight or ten years, but in my opinion the approach was always too touchy-feely. The purpose of the quality-of-work-life programs was never very clear. They were based on the understanding that happy employees make better products. But they never focused on the business of business . . . part of the problem of U.S. industry, especially middle management, is that it has lost touch with employees."[40]

Pontiac found itself on the cutting edge of both SPC and labor relations. The Deming experiment that proved to be Pontiac's inspiration took place at engine plant No. 18. Only a year or so before Deming's arrival, another consultant had written off the plant's management as incompetent and suggested that it be replaced.[41] Clayton Williams, the superintendent of manufacturing, knew his job was on the line. To Williams, a God-fearing Southern Baptist, Deming's brand of quality evangelism with its belief in the fundamental goodness of people, coming at that particular moment in time, must have seemed like a sign of divine redemption.[42] Williams became an ardent Demingite. "Within five months he had dropped his inventory $600 million, dropped scrap rate eighty percent, increased his throughput four times," recalls Hoglund. "He went from goat to hero in about eight months. It was just flipping from a very traditional approach to this very human give the people the opportunity, controlling the process. . . . When we saw this, we saw the power of what Dr. Deming was doing."[43] An internal GM memo shows that between 1981 and 1983 the combination of SPC, worker involvement, and management support at plant No. 18 reduced total production costs by 33.2 percent, including an overall 72.5 percent drop in the production of scrap.[44]

In 1983, to make sure such efficiencies wouldn't be perceived as a threat to the jobs of either workers or managers, Pontiac authored a job security policy that stated, "when our joint efforts to improve quality and productivity result in excess employees, these gains will be covered by the Pontiac Motor Division policy of job security. Specifically, manpower gains resulting in excess employees, either salaried or hourly, caused by improvement in work practices, competitive edge, employee . . . suggestions and SQC/SPC activities will be handled by attrition and new business opportunities, rather than employees being laid off."[45] While the policy didn't guarantee jobs in the event of a volume decrease in production or the closing of a business operation, it was one sign of Pontiac management's efforts to establish a relationship of trust between management and the rank and file. The policy would become another victim of the 1984 GM reorganization.[46]

In many ways Fiero was the prototype of Pontiac's efforts at cooperative management. Yet Pontiac had enormous obstacles to overcome with the car. Fueled by indecision and interdivision rivalries, the corporation pinched pennies on the Fiero, keeping it alive, but just barely. Chevrolet managers, led by Lloyd Reuss, who would later rival Hoglund, Stempel, and a handful of other GM executives for the succession in 1990, were said to have fought hard to kill the Pontiac car, afraid that a successful Fiero might hurt Corvette sales.[47] Fiero had gotten a go-ahead to develop the car in 1979. But just as

Bill Hoglund was taking over as the new general manager of Pontiac, GM's corporate beancounters issued the first of three "kill orders," which were intended to stop development of the car.[48]

Still, the Fiero survived the numerous cancellations, delays, and top personnel changes largely because of the determination and cooperation that developed within a core Fiero group. The Fiero evolved as a sort of automotive skunk works. Although top GM management, in particular E. M. ("Pete") Estes, then president of GM, winked at the project, Pontiac never received formal approval to build a prototype. Funds for the Fiero were pinched and shaved off of other Pontiac budget items. As the Fiero's development was an unofficial project, Pontiac engineering couldn't make room for it. So Hulki Aldikacti, at the time Pontiac's chief of advanced engineering, moved the Fiero design team twelve miles southeast of Pontiac to Entech, an independent drafting-engineering company in Troy, Michigan.[49] "The effect was to provide unusual creative freedom and also to isolate and insulate the program from detractors and 'helpers' alike," writes Witzenberg. At Entech, Aldikacti built a close-knit design team that, in contrast to the traditionally compartmentalized design process at GM, included the early involvement of representatives from manufacturing, service engineering, and reliability, disciplines that "typically never got represented this early in a car program."[50]

Even as Deming was beginning to lecture Pontiac management on the importance of working with a single supplier and using the brains as well as the brawn of the company's work force, Aldikacti was beginning to break with traditional GM design and manufacturing practice. "[Hulki] recognized that the design had to be built. If you're going to have a competitive vehicle, you have to have some pretty strong interface not only between manufacturing and engineering but between all elements, including sales, marketing and so forth. He got deeply involved in manufacturing very, very early. We were working on plant layouts at the same time they were working on a car," says Schaefer.[51]

Deming helped strengthen Fiero's cooperative approach by encouraging the Fiero team to bring both suppliers and production workers into the design process at an early stage. Fiero not only dispensed with competitive bidding and settled on using a single supplier with the best history of quality and reliability for most parts, it also launched a presourcing program. Fiero began working with its suppliers on the design and specification of parts *before* blueprints were completed and *before* an agreement on price had been reached. The aim was to devise components that would be easy to build from the beginning, without having to make the usual round of costly changes. As a condition of doing business with Fiero, suppliers had to submit to an ongoing quality monitoring program. Rather than having vendors submit samples for approval, GM had a team of Fiero inspectors visiting plants to approve tooling and production procedures, as well as the quality of final parts.[52] Budget constraints that forced the Fiero group to use some components from existing car models would ultimately hurt the performance of the car. But at no time did the value of the supplier alliance become as clear as when GM's "kill" orders, which continued through December 1982, were issued. Aldikacti kept telling the Fiero team, including some five hundred people from its supplier organization, to ignore "rumors" that Fiero was being discontinued. And everybody did.[53]

Nowhere was the break with traditional GM practice more apparent than on the factory floor. "The whole key to the manufacturing process was to get the union on board," says Hoglund, who even laid the Fiero's books open to the local union leadership. Adds Schaefer, who was to become one of Pontiac's most ardent Deming disciples, "One thing we insisted on very early was to get some union people into planning how we were going to run that plant."[54] To improve the production process and get the most creative talent out of its work force, Pontiac recognized that it would have to break down the traditional system of job stratification, in which workers typically were divided into 260 distinct work classifications. To forge those splintered groups into a cohesive team, Schaefer began by slashing the number of job classifications to thirty. The teams were also organized along cross-disciplinary lines. Thus, the body shop team would have responsibility for both production and maintenance, which under the previous organization would have been part of two separate bureaucracies. Schaefer even formed four management teams to replace the usual plant hierarchy.[55]

Team leaders and team members were trained in SPC, and a culture of strict process vigilance was fostered throughout manufacturing. Schaefer, for example, credits Deming's influence with virtually eliminating the need for repairs. Because the Fiero group operated in cramped quarters, there was no room to park faulty cars outside and little room for a repair area. So the cars had to be built right the first time. With the new statistical methods and an organization that assigned individual teams responsibility for each part of the production process, high manufacturing quality quickly followed. When Fieros began rolling off the production line, they zoomed to the top of GM's monthly quality audits.[56]

Schaefer's faith in his work force paid off in worker initiative as well. When the assembly line's output needed boosting, for example, Schaefer convened a team of workers on a Saturday. They figured out a way of increasing the number of cars produced per hour using fewer additional workers than the industrial engineers had initially thought would be necessary.[57]

The relationship between management and union members blossomed. "The unprecedented levels of team spirit and cooperation that developed between union and management might have been born out of desperation, but it flourished out of mutual respect and a common goal."[58] Long after the Fiero had been discontinued, Maryann Keller would say of the Fiero workers, "They were a very highly motivated, responsive, wonderful work force, people who broke their backs trying to make the car right."[59] Many of the Fiero workers, as well as some of the managers, would get jobs working for Japanese auto plants in the United States after the car had been discontinued.

Fiero would be responsible for a whole series of cooperative precedents at GM. In the early 1980s, Fiero developed the most progressive union contract in the GM system, one that made it possible, for example, to have team leaders elected by their peers instead of being chosen on the basis of seniority. Another unprecedented experiment, one that Schaefer calls "the most valuable," was a one-and-a-half-week trip to Japan taken by a group of about fifteen Fiero managers and union people. The group visited the operations of Isuzu, Toyota, Nissan, Fanuc, and the Japan Productivity Center. "We got a lot of benefit from seeing the Japanese factories, from seeing how the teams worked and the quest for quality," says Schaefer. But the most important breakthrough had to do with getting to know one another. Workers and managers ate together, stayed in the same hotel, and in many cases learned one another's names for the first time. From that standpoint, says Schaefer, "We could have gone to Toledo and gotten the same benefit."[60]

The team-building process, however, was fraught with obstacles and was continuously bumping up against GM's bureaucracy and its cobweb-encrusted traditions. Schaefer confronted problems when he tried to rid the plant of symbols of hierarchy by banning neckties on the plant floor and closing down the heated garage that was reserved for salaried staff. The maverick necktie policy brought criticism from some of Schaefer's superiors and the personnel department, and snickers from Pontiac people outside Fiero. Finally Bill Hoglund interceded and the no-necktie policy was adopted. When Schaefer broke another rule by introducing coffeepots to the factory floor to create a "homier" environment, he again had to negotiate with the personnel department's policy wardens. Schaefer also ran up against objections to his proposed trip to Japan—the personnel department felt the trip should be a Pontiac-wide excursion. But when the rest of the division failed to organize its ranks for a trip, Schaefer prevailed in organizing an all-Fiero outing.[61]

While the necktie-garage controversy may seem relatively trivial, Deming followers insist that such gestures are part of the delicate process of building trust between traditionally adversarial union people and their managers. "Where there has been union resistance [to innovations], that's due to management," says a former Fiero manager. "The management has to take the first step to create the proper environment. . . . At GM we have a culture that says we're in this to make money. . . . But we have focused too narrowly on the end result, instead of recognizing that we're dealing with people with very broad desires. We've become managers, not leaders."[62]

The naming of the Fiero is one indication of how far teamwork extended. Management was already calling the car Sunfire—a darling of the salesman, until two hourly workers called Hoglund. They explained that they'd been talking it over, and the guys on the floor agreed that "Sunfire" was a terrible name—it was too old-fashioned. The call set into action a brainstorming process that extended from the factory through to the product designer's office—practically every group at Fiero proffered a name. Although Aldikacti was holding out for a Turkish name, almost everyone else agreed that an Italian moniker would best suit the sleek European styling of the car. One Saturday, John Schineella, Pontiac's chief designer, finally came up with the name Fiero while leafing through an Italian dictionary. The following week, at a meeting packed with people from every corner of the Fiero organization, "Fiero" beat out both "Fiamma" and "Sunfire" in a naming contest.[63]

By the time Fiero was ready to hit the pavement in late 1983, Pontiac's perseverance seemed to have paid off. Fiero hit the top of GM's quality audits and in the coming several years occasionally outranked even the NUMMI plant in Fremont, California. The car won a long series of awards, including *Time* magazine's "The best of 1983: Design." In 1984 it was named American Car of the Year by the Detroit Auto Writers Group and one of the Ten Best Cars of 1984 by *Car and Driver*. That year Pontiac sold 93,485 of the cars, nearly 20 percent more than the company had originally projected. It was the country's hottest-selling two-seater ever. "Not since the Mustang had there been this much public interest in—and demand for—a new car," concluded Witzenburg.[64]

The Fiero saga, however, was not to have a happy ending. For one thing, although the car's appearance was an unqualified success, the concept itself had some serious flaws. For all its innovative styling and production techniques, the mixed signals from top management and halfhearted support during the crucial product development stage would ultimately translate into serious shortcomings that eventually drove off buyers.

Product development for the Fiero was a far cry from the sort of customer-driven decision making that characterized Japanese cars and even the Taurus Sable, which was being developed by Ford across town at about the same time. "The Fiero was a reflection of the way product development was done in the past," says Keller. Instead of making an analytical decision about the kind of car the customer wanted, what he would pay for it, and then deciding whether it would be worth GM's while to build a car to those precise specifications, the company never developed a clear vision for the car. "Visually it was what the public wanted," says Keller. "But it was half a cake."[65]

Competing objectives and inadequate planning doomed an otherwise promising automobile. Several management decisions undermined GM's intention to build a sporty commuter car. First, management endowed Fiero with a fuel-efficient but slow and fundamentally unsporty engine. The decision was based on a mistaken prediction that high gas prices would continue to drive auto sales throughout the 1980s and a completely unrelated decision to use the fuel efficiency of the Fiero to help GM meet the government's corporate average fuel economy (CAFE) standards, which establish an average fuel efficiency target that all of GM's cars put together must reach. Lobbying by Chevrolet may also have kept Fiero from acquiring a more sporty engine. Not only did GM fail to change the engine design when gasoline prices dropped, but the company wouldn't go the extra mile and spend money on such crucial details as power steering. Thus, the car that drove like a tortoise parked like a truck. Moreover, Chevrolet managers, afraid of what a successful Fiero might do to Corvette sales, were said to have fought hard to kill the Pontiac car. And finally, design problems in the 1984 Fiero caused one in every five hundred cars to catch fire, forcing GM to recall 125,000 vehicles and to place a warning label on the recalled 1984 cars.[66]

As word of the car's deficiencies spread, revenues soon came to reflect the problems. Sales volume dropped to 76,371 in 1985, and although it recovered slightly in 1986, the Fiero would never match its first-year showing.[67]

GM might, however, have saved the car. The company made dozens of improvements throughout the 1980s. Pontiac even set to work on a power steering system, but the car was discontinued before it could ever be utilized. By the time the Fiero was phased out at the end of 1988, it was a far better car, but its name was battered, and it would very likely have required a dramatic image-building relaunch.

Ultimately, Fiero's fate was sealed with the GM reorganization. Just as the competition was coming on strong with a raft of two-seater imports, including the Toyota MR2, the Mazda RX7, and the Honda CRX,[68] Fiero was stripped of its most important asset, a committed management team. With the reorganization in 1984, throughout GM the management ranks were being reshuffled completely. "The whole Pontiac organization was destroyed in the reorganization," said Thomas J. Donnan, the former director of reliability at Fiero shortly before the car was discontinued. "Not one of the old management people are still [at Fiero]."[69] Hoglund was transferred to a series of jobs before landing at the head of the BOC group. James B. Fitzpatrick, an ardent Deming follower who had been Pontiac comptroller, and Bob Dorn who was then chief engineer at Pontiac were both transferred to BOC. And Ernie Schaefer, who was relocated to a Pontiac plant in California, was followed in quick succession by two other plant managers, neither of whom understood the Deming philosophy.

Despite the Fiero's demise, the sporty commuter car's legacy as a test bed for quality and management innovation would not go to waste. As Fiero alumni fanned out around the company, they planted the seeds of Demingism in their new domains. In a move that would reverberate throughout the company in years to come, former Pontiac managers made a place for Deming at BOC. Thus, GM's most innovative engine in decades would come from a group of Demingites inside the big-car group. Dorn would apply the principles of Demingism in his efforts to revive Cadillac. And although intracompany rivalries would never allow CPC to become a Deming stronghold, Schaefer would take the lessons he had learned from Deming to save a Van Nuys, California, assembly plant known among GMers as the most troublesome operation in the corporation. A version of Fiero's plastic space-frame design was used in Chevrolet's all-purpose van (APV), which debuted in 1989, and is being considered for use on a future Firebird. And as quality has increasingly become the rallying cry throughout GM, former Fiero hands are resurfacing to lead GM's quality training efforts into the 1990s.

THE POSSIBILITIES AND LIMITS OF TEAMWORK

Not long ago, the Camaro and Firebird assembly plant in Van Nuys, a northern suburb of Los Angeles, seemed to embody all that was wrong with American manufacturing. Wildcat strikes plagued it. Security guards toted Mace and handcuffs. Tensions ran high, quality and productivity low.

Ernie Schaefer left the Fiero plant for California in 1984 to change all that. He was the perfect man for the job. Bill Hoglund, now executive vice president for both the automotive components groups and the power products and defense operations group, sums up the key to Schaefer's management style: "Ernie [is] somewhat of a revolutionary . . . he believes in the quality of his people."[70]

Schaefer is in many ways typical of the young men who have become Deming protégés. Reared in a small midwestern town with a strong technical education, the towheaded Schaefer looks as though he could be Deming's grandson. During Deming's visits to Pontiac in the early 1980s, Schaefer had the job of chauffeuring Deming on the one-hour journey between the Fiero plant and the Hyatt Regency hotel, where Deming then stayed. "Deming was a major influence on me," says Schaefer. "We had many discussions, and it took some time to understand him, but his absolute conviction got to me after a while." Deming taught Schaefer that the power of statistical tools wasn't just in their ability to analyze a system, but also in their ability to predict its future capability. The guru also insisted, recalls Schaefer, that "management's job is to work on the system, not to build cars." Deming's insistence that management make better use of production workers really hit home with Schaefer, whose first work experience had been in the entrepreneurial environment of his father's lawn equipment business in Tremont, Illinois. "I was always amazed at the lack of use we made of people in the [GM] organization," says the plant manager.[71]

For Schaefer, a GM man since his days as a student at the GMI Engineering and Management Institute, cooperation and team building offered the best hope for the future of both Van Nuys and the corporation. When he arrived in 1984, Schaefer faced a salvage operation. Van Nuys's quality record had been dismal. Its costs of production were four hundred dollars more per car than those of a sister plant in Ohio that also assembled Firebirds and Camaros.[72] With GM market share slipping, one of the two plants would have to go. And Van Nuys looked to be the likely loser. Schaefer was determined to improve that record and to save Van Nuys by transferring to the plant the team concept ideas he had championed at Fiero.

But on the floor of the Van Nuys factory, where the strains of salsa and rock-and-roll waft over a Hispanic and Anglo work force, breaking the management-labor divide would be a much tougher proposition than it had been at Fiero. Van Nuys was a far cry from the model of innovation Fiero had in many ways become. More important, while team concept was a novelty during the heady days of the Fiero's development in the early 1980s, a few years later it had become a political pawn in the struggle between an angry union and a battered corporation.

In many ways, the Van Nuys experience would underscore the fragility of participative management as it is practiced at GM and the long road the company has to go before the totality of Demingism becomes a reality there. The Fiero story demonstrated that changes in the factory, without changes in management policy and product development, can save neither a product nor a work force. The Van Nuys experience underscored management's inconsistencies and showed just how slowly change has been brought about at GM.

By the time Van Nuys was struggling with the question of introducing the team concept, GM's malaise had reached a new low. Although fully one third of GM's thirty-one car and truck assembly plants had introduced this participative management approach by the mid-1980s, none had achieved NUMMI's consistent record of high quality and productivity. In 1986, with its market share declining, GM's per-car production costs remained the highest of any major automaker. GM's cost problems were in large part attributable to its huge base of internal suppliers. GM produces 70 percent of its components, compared with 50 percent for Ford and 30 percent for Chrysler. And although GM insisted it was committed to remaining vertically integrated, many experts argued that the company would have to begin shedding many of its component plants—a prospect the union could not have found comforting.[73]

The reorganization and GM's financial hardships set the company and the UAW on a collision course in the 1987 contract negotiations that would test the company's tenuous experiments with participative management. GM hoped to get an endorsement for team concept in its national contract. But with the union fighting to win greater job security and GM moving to close more plants, there seemed little basis for agreement. Moreover, team concept threatened the sacred seniority system. Team leaders were increasingly being chosen on the strength of their leadership skills and not according to how long they'd been on the payroll. And by giving workers a variety of duties, the new method threatened the system by which the best jobs were reserved for employees with the longest tenure and heightened the sense of instability among the rank and file. Moreover, when it came to layoffs, team leaders were sometimes more protected than high-seniority team members.[74]

Schaefer knew that his only chance of introducing team concept at Van Nuys would be gradually to build a culture of trust. Drawing on his experience at Fiero, he tried to foster goodwill by establishing a costly second exit to the parking lot to ease congestion at quitting time. He banned preferential parking for managers. He accompanied teams of workers and managers to a seminar in Michigan to meet the workers who had worked for him at Fiero. But Van Nuys wasn't going to give in easily. The union leadership demanded a guarantee from GM that the plant would get a new product line—one that would ensure the plant's survival in case Firebirds and Camaros were phased out. It is a measure of the confidence Schaefer inspired in his work force that the local union narrowly delivered Schaefer its support for the team concept in 1986, although he says he never gave a guarantee.[75] One result: Van Nuys stayed open, while its rival plant in Ohio was closed.

To turn Van Nuys into a team, Schaefer set up a training program with a $20 million grant from the state of California. Everyone in the plant, managers and workers alike, went through a week of team training on an array of subjects, from statistics and financial systems to safety and conflict resolution. Leaders of teams got an additional five weeks of training. Even before team concept began to be implemented, enough goodwill was generated to improve the plant's performance. Van Nuys, for years at the bottom of GM's quality audits, shot up to the number-three ranking for a time. Repairs dropped nearly 15 percent.[76]

But GM's troubles continued to cast a shadow over the plant. In 1986 GM executives got bonuses totaling $169 million, even though the company's profits had continued to decline; at the same time, union workers received no profit sharing and faced layoffs that would affect close to 10 percent of the work force.[77] Suddenly support for team concept fell off. In the spring of 1987, union members in Van Nuys elected a president who favored the concept, but for the chairmanship of their powerful bargaining committee, they chose Peter Z. Beltran, who was thoroughly opposed to the idea. A dissident UAW group led by Beltran filed a charge with the international union claiming that GM had improperly introduced the team concept at Van Nuys without providing a new product line. Both the union and the courts dismissed the complaint.[78]

However, the team concept has raised thorny questions at other plants. In several factories GM imposed the plan on unwilling workers. Critics charge that the company focuses too much on making workers more productive and too little on changing the management systems over which workers have no control. "Management needs to fix itself before it tries to fix us," says one UAW official in Detroit. "Team concept is not a substitute for poor management."[79]

Despite persistent suspicion and tension between GM management and the UAW, well into the late 1980s a sort of industrial survival instinct continued to foster support for the team approach among the rank and file. Indeed, most of the local union officials who helped introduce the idea at their plants were being reelected. Many reflect the views of Jerry Shrieves, who served as president of the Van Nuys local in the late 1980s: "Job security is the only game in town. Team concept is a matter of survival."[80]

As the Fiero experience showed, however, team concept alone is not nearly enough to guarantee any plant's survival. In January 1989 analysts were predicting that the institution of team concept at the California plant had done nothing but delay the inevitable, that the plant would close by the early 1990s. "Van Nuys has no economic basis for existing—sixty percent of the components of the cars are shipped in from east of the Mississippi, and sixty percent of the cars themselves are sold east of the Mississippi," says Maryann Keller. "Moreover, the land on which the plant is sitting is very valuable."[81] If the critics are right, then the irony of Van Nuys is that by rewarding the California workers for embracing team concept and punishing the Ohio workers who, though better positioned to supply its market had initially rejected the idea, GM's management may have doomed both plants.

Fiero and Van Nuys suffered because to a great extent they were trying to superimpose new manufacturing ideas on an outdated product management system. Hoglund and several of the executives who went with him to BOC understood this. By inviting Deming to the newly formed big-car group, which ironically makes few big cars, they were hoping Deming's philosophy would spark a change in management culture. But they also understood that in light of Deming's age and the recent upheaval at GM, building a BOC-wide program around Deming could backfire. "We're trying to make a concerted effort not to make too big a play out of Deming, because we don't want to have his philosophy thought of as a program," said Arvin F. Mueller, who served as product manager of BOC Powertrain after the reorganization. "We're trying to get away from the pill-taking approach" to quality.[82]

During the 1980s there were many at GM who avoided Deming because it simply wasn't politic to be seen with him. In 1983 Deming had given Jim McDonald what was probably the dressing-down of his career as a senior manager in front of a conference of auto executives at the Society of Automotive Engineers. In what is by now a familiar Deming lament, he blamed McDonald for 85 percent of GM's problems. "McDonald was furious," recalls one GM manager. "Something happened when he got to be president, he couldn't take public criticism." Among the GM executives who now support Deming, but were said to shy away from him because of McDonald's antipathy, was Bob Stempel. Indeed, while Stempel claims to have brought Deming to Pontiac, he left Pontiac in the summer of 1980, just about the same time the NBC documentary was aired and well before Deming's first visit there.[83] The executives who deserve the credit most, GMers say, are Hoglund, who succeeded Stempel at Pontiac, and his lieutenants.

At BOC Hoglund favored a more gradual, experimental approach and encouraged Deming to become involved first with one small but strategic part of BOC, the Powertrain division, which builds engines and transmissions. In so doing, BOC stood to gain the most mileage out of its guru without foisting Demingism on the entire organization all at once. In this latest era of cheap gasoline, high performance has again become the rage, making powerful engines one of the most important selling features of a new car. Engines, however, have also been an Achilles wheel of the U.S. auto industry. In Japan and Europe, a dearth of speed limits and tax penalties for large engines and gas guzzlers have encouraged constant engine innovation, but lacking such incentives, U.S. automakers have been building more or less the same engine designs for decades.

To end the engine apathy at GM, Powertrain embarked on an ambitious new product development program. The focus of the division's project was the Quad 4, a cornerstone in GM's strategy of overcoming its reputation of building lackluster, look-alike cars. The Quad 4 was to be the soul of a whole family of new GM machines. Indeed, in addition to the Saturn project, the Quad 4 would turn out to be the least derivative, cleanest-sheet project GM had undertaken in decades.[84] It was first offered as an option with the Pontiac Grand Am in 1987. (BOC-developed powertrains are available in some cars made by CPC.) It has since become an option on the Buick Skylark and the international series Oldsmobile Cutlass Calais. The new engine is so popular that more than half of those buying a Calais pay extra for the Quad 4 option.[85] And the company is working on new versions of the engine, including a modified, lower-cost model and a V-6.

The design of the Quad 4 became a study in detail and design innovation unparalleled in a U.S.-built engine. It is the first U.S.-designed engine to boast two intake and two exhaust valves, resulting in more power and fuel economy. By achieving a "new standard for roundness" in its cylinder bores, GM also achieved exceptionally low friction levels. Another unique feature was that the engine design did away with distributor and spark plug wires; instead a computer triggers sparks from coils that are mounted on the plugs.[86]

The engine would turn out to be BOC's test bed for new management and quality ideas. "We did a lot of veering away from traditional business practice," says Beth Hubbard, the manager of supplier development for Lansing Powertrain. "Because we had a whole new product, we could challenge every way of doing things."[87] During the course of about four years, Powertrain would make dramatic changes in everything from its purchasing policies to its performance appraisal and compensation system, based largely on Deming's influence.

Deming, it turned out, had landed in the right place at an opportune time. "Within Powertrain, we have tried to confine ourselves to the teachings of Dr. Deming," says N. L. ("Norb") Keller, who was director of materials management and product assurance at Powertrain during the mid-1980s and who has since gone on to work as the group director of statistical and process improvement methods at BOC under Deming's protégé Bill Scherkenbach, who moved to GM from Ford in November 1987.[88] Because of the self-contained nature of the engine's product development effort, Deming would be able to exercise the sort of wide-ranging influence on Powertrain that he was never able to exert on Fiero. The subsequent success of the Quad 4 would not only give several cars at both BOC and CPC a boost, it would also be a pivotal factor in gaining acceptance of Deming's philosophy among GM's top executive ranks.

Deming's influence at BOC was typical of his relationship with clients in that he functioned more as a teacher than as a traditional consultant. While Deming never made specific suggestions about how to build a product or change an organization chart, he did make some policy suggestions. He also hammered away at his Fourteen Points, questioned, and probed.

Even before the guru arrived at BOC following the reorganization, Powertrain was ripe for Deming's brand of transformation. In 1982 Powertrain was drawing up plans for the Quad 4 and had already begun to do some presourcing. The division recognized that the best place to control the cost of quality of the engine was through the purchasing department. While only half of the cost of a finished automobile is in the componentry purchased from suppliers—the other half going toward such things as labor and advertising—the purchased parts of the Quad 4 would account for fully 80 percent of the engine's costs. "The Quad 4 was somewhat of a pilot; we had an opportunity to get all brand-new equipment and a brand-new plant, with an experienced work force," says Hubbard. "We were thinking in terms of reducing suppliers and reducing variation. The time was ripe."[89]

Purchasing would lay the groundwork for the success of the Quad 4, as well as create a high-profile forum for Deming's theories on supplier relationships. To find suppliers for the Quad 4, Powertrain not only dispensed with the usual GM competitive bidding practice but launched the most rigorous search in GM history. Rather than allow the purchasing department to dominate decision making, as was customary at GM, Powertrain established an audit team that would include managers from purchasing, materials, quality control, engineering, and finance. Before its search was complete, these auditors would review no less than forty different foundries. To narrow the choice to the eight best candidates, all audit team members were instructed to write a confidential report on their findings, without comparing notes with their colleagues. Three additional reviews were conducted before a single company was selected for each component, in keeping with Deming's dictum of working with just one supplier. And the suppliers who were finally selected, including J. L. French Company, which had learned its quality ropes from Ford (see Chapter 5) and would build the Quad 4 front covers, both built the components and helped redesign them for manufacturability. "We tried to develop a philosophy for the program based on long-term relationships," says Hubbard. "We wanted to find the right supplier for each part. And we traveled the world for years" doing so. Powertrain ultimately wound up with just seventy-four suppliers for the Quad 4, compared with 200 to 250 for a typical engine program.[90]

To help deliver a consistent message to its suppliers, Quad 4 developed a supplier manual. The manual was important because of Powertrain's high performance expectations and because of the division's insistence on closely monitoring the design and production work of its suppliers. It provided a clear set of criteria for both the Powertrain judges and the vendors being judged. Ultimately, because of the success the division achieved in controlling the cost, quality, and delivery of the parts its suppliers produced, Hubbard was asked to revise the manual for the entire BOC organization. Although the original guidelines had been authored while Deming was still focusing most of his attention on Fiero, the statistician would collaborate closely with Hubbard on developing the criteria for the BOC version.[91]

"We rewrote the manual because of Dr. Deming," says Hubbard, who counts six key changes Deming made in the supplier criteria. For one thing, "Deming didn't think we did a good enough job making the suppliers understand how critical they are in the design process." So the manual encouraged vendors to take a more active role early on in the design of component parts. Deming also objected to the way the manual focused on process control, rather than on the need for management to understand how to use process analysis as a means of achieving improvement. "He told us, 'Your emphasis is on controlling the process, but what about management? How does management run the business, do they chart scrap, re-work, absenteeism . . .'?" According to Deming, collecting data on such things as scrap and absenteeism can be counterproductive if management fails to search for the root causes and variables that *produce* scrap and absenteeism in the first place, and that therefore hold the key to overall improvement.[92]

Deming also prevailed on Hubbard to eliminate some of the rigid inspection requirements that she had been planning to require of BOC suppliers. To eliminate the need to inspect parts once they get to GM, suppliers conduct sample inspections to make sure they aren't shipping defective products. Picking just the right population size for this sample inspection is important because too small a sample can miss defectives, while too large a sample adds unnecessary cost. Hub-bard originally wanted to require every vendor to conduct a blanket sample inspection of 225 parts but was won over by Deming. "Every situation is different," says Hubbard. "For some suppliers, inspect-ing thirty pieces would be enough. Others need to inspect four hun-dred pieces. Deming doesn't like [quotas], and he's right."[93]

In a far more radical effort to banish arbitrary targets, Deming has encouraged Powertrain to revamp its performance appraisal system. In January 1988 GM instituted a forced-distribution system in which managers were required to rank employees on a bell curve, placing each employee into one of four categories. The plan required, for example, that ten percent of any work group be singled out as inadequate performers. The move was part of a national trend that aims to link compensation more closely to an employee's actual performance.[94] However, this pay-for-performance approach runs contrary to Deming's theory of management, and Powertrain won a partial exemption from the new appraisal system and began devel-oping an alternative that was aimed at virtually eliminating rankings.

Deming's ideas about performance appraisals and compensation are one of the central and undoubtedly most controversial elements of his philosophy. "The most powerful inhibitor to quality and pro-ductivity in the Western world is the so-called merit system or annual appraisal of people," he says. He argues that from the viewpoint of statistical theory and the nature of variability, pay for performance is an inherently unfair and therefore destructive system. "The basic fault of the annual appraisal is that it penalizes people for normal variation of the system," he says.[95] In other words, it is management's job to control the system: to hire the best employees and to create an environment that will allow them to do their best work. If the system is in control, most employees will perform within the system, and it will be almost impossible to separate their performance from other factors that contribute to variation of the process. Employees who perform below the control limits should be retrained. Those who perform above the control limits should be studied by management because their superior work practices can provide a clue to how to improve the system.

Powertrain parted with GM practice and has established a new performance appraisal system (known at GM as a "personal development" system) designed to be "consistent with the teachings of Deming on variation."[96] The system has eliminated rankings and represents a dramatic departure from past GM practice. Powertrain has tried to shift the emphasis of performance appraisals from what is essentially an after-the-fact grading system to a process that is intended to help employees understand and improve their work over time. For the first time employees will be evaluated in part on the basis of comments of both peers and subordinates, and they are encouraged to help select fellow employees who will contribute to their appraisal. The division also tried to decouple performance appraisals from the compensation system, basing raises largely on experience and expertise, and it is now being emulated by other GM divisions.

It is a measure of Powertrain's commitment to the Deming philosophy that when the division began revising its appraisal system, it stood virtually alone. Chapter 9 deals with how Deming's ideas have come to influence performance appraisals at GM, as well as a number of other organizations.

A DEMING-INSPIRED COMEBACK FOR CADILLAC

Cadillac may produce GM's most Deming-driven car in the 1990s. Throughout much of the 1980s, technological snafus combined with poor design decisions gave Caddys a bad name. During most of the decade, the cars lagged behind the luxury makes of the Europeans and even Ford. And in 1985 the opening of Cadillac's much-touted assembly plant in Hamtramck became one of the biggest debacles of the Smith era.

No car is more emblematic of the problems that plagued Cadillac in the course of the decade than the Allante. The $55,000 car, with a body built by Italy's Pininfarina, was meant to compete against European luxury cars like the Mercedes SL roadster. Yet the first Allante, introduced in 1987, had less power than a Honda. It leaked. And its seat adjusters and automatic door locks were apt to break. Moreover, industry experts contend that building a two-seater at that price was a fundamental marketing mistake. According to Bunkie Knudsen, the son of a former GM president who was himself a former executive at GM and a former Ford president, the market for a luxury four-seater would have been much greater. While GM designers were said to agree with Knudsen's assessment, the corporation stuck with the two-seater concept. Ultimately, GM sold only two thousand of the cars in its first model year, less than one third the division's original estimates. "The Allante fiasco is perhaps the most searing example of the cynical attitude General Motors has traditionally had toward its customers" notes Maryann Keller.[97]

Today Cadillac is working hard to overcome that reputation. Many of the problems with the Allante, for instance, were well known to GM before the car ever left the factory. They were the result of a product development process that failed to catch problems early on in the cycle and then failed to fix them because doing so after the car was in the prototype or production phase would have been too difficult or expensive.[98]

Now Cadillac is pursuing a disciplined process management effort meant to eliminate the need for last-minute changes by carefully coordinating marketing, engineering, and production. The new Cadillac process was spearheaded by Bob Dorn, an ardent Deming disciple who is a frequent fixture at the guru's lectures and who was part of Pontiac's Fiero team in the early 1980s. At Cadillac, where he has served as head of operations and chief engineer, Dorn worked with Gary Cowger, who was the chief of manufacturing during the late 1980s, to divide the product development process into six categories: chassis, fit and finish, powertrain, and so on. Representatives of each discipline, from assembly line workers to engineers, were represented on all the body part teams. In addition, some sixty-five special improvement teams were established to refine a wide range of specific features, including sunroofs, upholstery, and window-wash mechanisms. And finally, Cadillac established monthly problem-resolution meetings that included not only a cross section of the division, but dealers as well. Cadillac is also starting a review process that will bring people from different parts of the corporation in to critique its designs.

While marketing traditionally has focused on the *entire* car, these multidisciplinary teams sought to perfect the individual components of the vehicle and to settle the vast majority of design decisions before prototypes were built. "Historically, we have made engineering changes late," concedes Cowger. "[Now] we're trying to get the voices of those different customers—whether it be manufacturing, materials management, financial, customer satisfaction—early up in the design process. It's much, much more difficult to change things once you've tooled up for [production]."[99]

For the first time, Cadillac opened direct communication lines between dealers, assemblers, and engineers. Typically, engineering and production relied largely on warranty data for customer feedback on automobiles. This was a highly flawed system, however, largely because dealers were reimbursed by GM for fixing a specific problem only once; if a given part broke down a second time, the dealers had to absorb the cost themselves. As a result, dealers resorted to creative bookkeeping, charging the cost of second breakdowns against some other, fictitious problem. Thus, warranty data never accurately reflected where the worst recurring problems occurred. Moreover, "when you talked about going to visit dealers and exploring warranty problems, they would get very defensive, because the implication was that you were there to expose some irregularity in the way the system worked."

The corporation still collects warranty data. But Cadillac has set up a separate hotline to a network of twenty-eight dealers, which is entirely independent of GM's warranty wardens, and which provides customer feedback exclusively to the engineering and manufacturing staff. Thus, when dealers register a complaint on the first cars off the production line, Hamtramck employees can correct it before thousands more are produced. Prior to Cadillac's reorganization, news of problems that cropped up in dealers' showrooms crawled through six layers of management and rarely reached engineering in time to affect production. With the new communication network, dealers are asked to relay product problems to a central data base on a daily basis. And because operations and marketing are now part of the same division, engineers and even assembly line workers collaborate with dealers on a regular basis. For example, when a dealer in Toledo, Ohio, reported a recurring problem with noisy exhausts, two factory workers got into a car and drove out to check on it. Combing over both the car and the original specifications, the workers discovered that the vendor who supplied the exhaust pipe had made an extra bend in the metal that wasn't part of the original engineering specifications. Moreover, the supplier had made the design change without notifying GM. Cadillac was then able to contact the vendor and make sure it went back to producing the exhaust pipe as it originally had been specified. Collaboration has also solved problems at Hamtramck. The plant collects data on everything from concrete problems with electrical wiring to customers' subjective impressions of workmanship. The information gives "each department a [factual] view of what their contribution is to ultimate customer satisfaction, without [resorting] to opinions." Workers, who early in Hamtramck's conception were shut out of the most basic questions relating to plant layout and equipment, are now invited to attend most management meetings. They participate in product improvement teams, and at least once a month they gather on bleachers on the plant floor to critique a competitor's car or to fire questions at the plant manager.[100]

The changes have begun to pay off. In 1988 GM's luxury nameplate was rated one of the top five brands on the customer satisfaction survey conducted by J. D. Power, a dramatic jump from its lowly number sixteen ranking in 1985.[101] The Cadillac process has also shortened product development time. And new Cadillac models have gotten good early reviews. The 1992 Seville, for example, has been hailed as "the embodiment of a design revolution now underway at GM."[102]

DEMING'S INFLUENCE SPREADS

By the end of the decade, Deming's influence was spreading throughout GM. In 1988 the corporation established its quality network, a continuous improvement strategy modeled on the teachings of Deming that even bears some of the hallmarks of policy deployment. Without making any organizational changes, GM created a framework in which employees at every level of the company work on improving four strategic areas of management: incoming materials from suppliers, factory equipment and technology, methods and systems, and management culture.[103]

The purpose of the exercise is not only to improve crucial processes at GM and to ensure the creation of customer-driven products, but to do so in the most efficient way possible by standardizing good ideas wherever they're found. "GM's number-one problem is that it hasn't standardized anything. It's a company of individuals all doing their own thing," says Maryann Keller. "No two GM plants look alike, even if they're building the same car."[104] Adds Ed Czapor, vice president for quality at GM, in explaining part of the purpose of the quality network, "We want to find the same systems at work at our Lordstown plant as we do in any other manufacturing facility."[105]

Unlike its outlook in the early 1980s, when GM looked to technological innovations to solve its competitiveness woes, by creating the quality network the company signaled a new understanding of the role "people . . . and teamwork" play in bringing about continuous improvement. Indicative of this new emphasis on cooperation, every process and problem tackled through the quality network is headed by joint teams of GM employees and representatives of the UAW. The quality network itself was set up by Bob Stempel and Don Ephlin, the now retired vice president of the GM section of the UAW. At each level of the corporation, a GM employee works with a member of the UAW on one of the four strategic management areas targeted by management. For example, heading up the project to improve materials handling was Mike Mutchler, the group vice president of the Truck and Bus group, and Larry Stevens of the UAW. One of the first projects Mutchler and Stevens worked on was procedures for instituting just-in-time (JIT) inventory control procedures for the entire corporation. When Mutchler and Stevens arrive at a new process for JIT, they must get the approval of their GM/UAW counterparts in the other three strategic groups. Only when consensus is achieved do the recommendations go to the quality council, headed by Stempel and Steve Yokich, Ephlin's successor, for final approval.[106]

The system could hold the seeds of policy deployment. It is constructed in the form of a pyramid involving every level of the organization down to the factory floor, and is based on a down-up-down approach to problem resolution. Thus GM management established the four top management priorities; GM/UAW teams throughout the corporation will cascade recommendations up to ever higher levels of management; and the recommendations are reviewed and approved by the four strategic groups and ultimately by Stempel and Yokich.[107]

The quality network seeks to expand some of the company's efforts at creating a consistent culture of cooperation. One of the earliest efforts at ending the tradition of separateness and rivalry between the various car groups, for example, was initiated by the BOC and CPC Powertrain divisions, which put together a joint long-range plan for GM Powertrain production. The plan entails a vision of the future engine, as well as a future production plan that aims to avoid the redundancies so often found throughout GM. "Two years ago there would have been two plans," says Dick Donnelly, the head of BOC Powertrain, one for CPC and one for BOC. "This is unprecedented in the history of GM. [And it's done] without forcing a reorganization."[108]

Yet GM faces numerous hurdles. For one thing, Yokich is said to be far less interested in the quality network than was Ephlin. And in the winter of 1990, before a new CEO replacement for Smith was chosen, progress on the quality network reportedly had stalled.[109] In addition, GM faced a major challenge in rejuvenating its in-house suppliers. For years the component divisions were powerful independent fiefdoms: They were GM's principal profit center and held enormous sway over the vehicle groups, who had no access to their books and little bargaining power over price. To say that the component businesses were under little pressure to improve efficiency is an understatement. In part because GM couldn't sell its vast component empire without guaranteeing the company's continued business, the company was forced to clean up its own mess. While GM has already weeded out its least competitive units and substantially improved the quality and efficiency of others, including its internal trim operations, the company still faces enormous challenges in key strategic areas such as its castings operations. "We didn't have any choice but to make our existing [supplier] assets competitive," says Hoglund, who inherited the component business in 1988. We have to "completely eliminate internal competition so that the inside component resources are working with the vehicle groups in the total product development process. . . . If we could do that, we could restore the competitive advantage of a vertically integrated company.[110]

Hoglund is confident that his lieutenants have understood the importance of managing their processes. With a new management era dawning at the world's largest automaker, GM's Demingites no longer have to hide their regard for the guru. But as the component operations struggle to redefine their business and Deming approaches his ninetieth birthday, Hoglund knows the company won't be able to rely on the guru's charisma for long. GM's future success depends in large part on how well it has absorbed the lessons Deming has taught since his early days at Pontiac. As he approached the end of his decades-long tenure as chairman of the largest U.S. industrial corporation, even Roger Smith was showing a change of heart: "We've ignor[ed] our best resources because of our autocratic style. We need to get rid of that, and we need to get down to finding out how to make decisions better and in a more timely way. . . . This is not a one-man corporation: we run as a team—and the team is important."[111]

THE CASE FOR A
PASS-FAIL APPROACH
TO EVALUATING
INDIVIDUAL
PERFORMANCE

E very schoolchild knows the fear and anxiety that comes with a year-end report card. Their parents should be able to empathize. Throughout the 1980s, grown men and women across America, whether they have high school degrees, M.B.A.s, or Ph.D.s, are hauled before their bosses for the discomfiting ritual of an annual review and performance ranking. But as companies become leaner, less hierarchical, and more competitive, the report cards themselves have been getting lousy grades.

Today some of the stodgiest companies of all, including American Cyanamid and GM, are abandoning the grading game. While managers have always evaluated employees, the competitive pressures in recent years sparked a feverish quest for scientific ways to spot stars and laggards. However, attempts to build corporate success on the toils of high achievers have often failed because a few designated winners couldn't undo the damage caused by labeling many others "losers." America's corporate star system, Deming contends, is in fundamental conflict with efforts to foster teamwork, which smart companies recognize as a key to long-term success. Now an influential coterie of rebels is putting away the carrot and stick of money and ratings in experiments that could radically change both the measures of individual achievement as well as the way employees are paid.

Appraisals have acquired a bad name because they have become no-win lotteries for meting out "merit" pay. As salary budgets tightened, companies tried to limit high ratings, and corresponding raises, by requiring managers to grade their minions on a bell curve. But bell curves, which rate people relative to one another and ensure that some are always "losers," fail to reflect the likelihood that in a typical goal-oriented work group a large number will be high achievers and incremental differences are often meaningless. At an electric utility, for example, the manager of a competent group of five found the only way to meet the rule without being unfair to his staff was to institute a "designated dummy" system in which employees take turns getting demerits.[1] Xerox also sowed discontent with a one-to-five rating scale. Says a company insider, "The source of dissatisfaction was the borderline between four and three. Each manager had more fours than allotted and a fight would develop over who would slide. It was very irrational." To make the system fairer, Xerox is now basing its rating scheme on three broad categories instead of five.[2] And at Cyanamid the bell curve was met with derision by the scientists who work for the chemical and pharmaceutical manufacturer. "Evidently there is an effort to fit the people within a section to a bell curve so they can dole out raises and not go over budget," said one scientist. "But as a scientist I know that a bell curve should be applied only when a population is large enough; and these departments are very small." Noted another Cyanamid scientist, "It's a Mickey Mouse numbers game. My superior and I just laugh at it and we get through it as quickly as we can."[3]

Individual performance ratings are no laughing matter, insist Deming and a number of other experts, who have concluded that such rankings actually degrade performance because they are perceived as inherently destructive. "A merit rating is alluring," asserts Deming. "The sound of the words captivates the imagination: pay for what you get; get what you pay for; motivate people to do their best, for their own good. The effect is exactly the opposite of what the words promise. Everyone propels himself forward, or tries to, for his own good, on his own life preserver. The organization is the loser. The merit rating rewards people [who] conform to the system. It does not reward attempts to improve the system."[4] Agrees Michael Beer, an organizational behavior expert at Harvard Business School, "The idea of trying to differentiate on some fine-grained system is ridiculous. You can't make those kinds of discriminations on total performance. Total performance is a complex collage of competency, skills, and knowledge. Most people are in the middle, and what we need to do is identify the really outstanding performers and the really poor performers and try not to pretend that one can make [fine-line] differentiations objectively."[5]

Appraisal reform is driven by the notion that if management is doing its job in terms of hiring, developing employees, and keeping the system stable, most employees will perform well. Moreover, Deming contends, within a stable system, most fluctuations in individual performance over time will be attributable to natural variation of the system within which people work; it is impossible to accurately measure individual performance within a variable system. For example, the progressive appraisal scheme pioneered by the GM Powertrain division of the BOC group cites "individual effort" as only one of ten typical factors that can cause variation in work output; others mentioned in a report by the division include training, the nature of job assignments, the availability of resources, and the performance of the supervising manager. The Powertrain scheme, which was inspired by Deming, is predicated on the belief that if the division's management processes are stable, only a very few employees will perform outside the system. Those who perform outside, on the low side, are in need of special help and probably will need to be retrained or transferred.[6]

Indeed, Deming believes that ranking employees is a cop-out for inadequate leadership. "A merit rating is meaningless as a predictor of performance, except for someone whose performance has placed him outside the system. . . . Good leadership requires investigation into possible causes that have placed someone outside the system. There is a rational basis to predict that anyone outside the system on the good side will perform well in the future: he deserves recognition. The reason why someone outside the system is on the bad side may be permanent; it may be ephemeral. Someone that cannot learn the job would provide an example of a permanent cause. The company that hired him for this job . . . has a moral obligation to put him into the right job. Likewise, someone that is worried about his health, or about someone in the family, may show poor performance. Counseling will in some cases restore confidence and performance."[7]

Deming's conviction that performance rankings are used as a substitute for leadership partly accounts for his passionate attacks on top executives. By clinging to a grading system, he believes, management perpetuates one of the principal impediments to achieving high-quality performance and high-quality products and services: "The merit rating nourishes short-term performance, annihilates long-term planning, builds fear, demolishes teamwork, nourishes rivalry and politics.

"It leaves people bitter, crushed, bruised, battered, desolate, despondent, dejected, feeling inferior, some even depressed, unfit for work for weeks after receipt of rating, unable to comprehend why they are inferior. It is unfair as it ascribes to the people in a group differences that may be caused totally by the system that they work in."[8]

But statistical theory is only part of the passion that drives Deming's intense opposition to judgmental performance appraisals. Deming, who frequently quotes from the Book of Ecclesiastes, also is driven by a religious and moral conviction that most people want, and deserve, to take joy in their work. It is management's moral obligation to create a system that enables them to do so, Deming believes. Given a chance by management and the system, most people will seek fulfillment in their work by doing the best they can.[9]

Biblical interpretations aside, secular evidence suggests that Deming is right on the money in fingering traditional appraisals as demotivators. "October used to be depression time," says William Hodgson, the British-born former director of the Medical Research Division of American Cyanamid, where he initiated the company's efforts at appraisal reform. October was when performance appraisals and raises were negotiated, and anxiety levels ran so high that performance throughout the company became erratic.[10] Indeed, as long ago as 1965, *Harvard Business Review* published a study undertaken at General Electric that was one of the only comprehensive reports ever conducted on performance appraisals. It concluded, "Defensiveness resulting from critical appraisal produces inferior performance. . . . Comprehensive annual performance appraisals are of questionable value. . . . It seems foolish to have a manager serving in the self-conflicting role as a counselor (helping a man to improve performance), when at the same time he is presiding as a judge over the same employee's salary action case."[11] Critics contend that even if ratings are accompanied by detailed comments, they are counterproductive: The employee will see only the grade, not the comments.

Moreover, insist many experts, changes in technology and the market dictate new relationships within corporations. The rapidly evolving information age increasingly involves the cultivation of legions of highly skilled employees whose expertise is vital to conducting business, but who cannot hope to achieve prominent management positions. The 1990s will be characterized by "flatter" organizations in which employees will have to find satisfaction in their present jobs rather than in climbing a ladder.[12] "When businesses were growing at a rate in excess of ten to twenty percent per year, everyone was expanding not only their responsibilities but their economic position too, everyone was a winner, even if some were winning more than others," says William Hoglund of GM. "So it was easy to maintain a team effort and [joint] goals in a growth situation." The trick, says Hoglund, is to maintain that level of teamwork in an environment of slower growth and even economic adversity.[13]

Nevertheless, the traditional performance appraisal has been slow to die in American companies. Managers, for whom rugged individualism and the entrepreneurial mystique still make up a vision of success, find it difficult to accept the economic transformation that inexorably is changing relationships inside corporations. To the extent that companies are beginning to seek different alternatives, it is because traditional grading schemes have been found to batter morale and undermine teamwork just when U.S. firms most need to rally their troops and spark dynamic change to battle foreign competition.

GM is a case in point. In less than a year the corporation went from a sweeping, companywide forced-distribution scheme to a more decentralized approach that opened the way for one division to virtually abandon employee ratings. In January 1988 GM instituted a forced-distribution system that was born in part of a lingering belief that employees could be held accountable for GM's competitiveness problems and that they could be coerced into doing better work. GM proudly announced the end of the "entitlement era" at the auto company and issued a directive requiring managers to rate white-collar employees on a curve. "To treat people fairly you have to treat people differently," Roy S. Roberts, the vice president for corporate personnel told the *Wall Street Journal* in an article that ran under the headline "GM's New Compensation Plan Reflects General Trend Tying Pay to Performance." Under the new system, managers would have to label 10 percent of their employees as poor performers. Similarly, 10 percent would be given a top rating, while the next 25 percent would be deemed almost worthy of a top rating. The remaining 55 percent were given a lower rating, albeit one that deemed them a cut above the 10 percent who were stigmatized as bottom of the barrel. Pay increases were meted out accordingly.[14]

GM's corporate Calvinists forgot that well-managed companies weed out poor performers in their hiring and promotion practices. By definition, says Harvard's Beer, "the more effective organizations will have less of a distribution than less effective organizations."[15] Indeed, within a few months, a near revolt by GM employees, who had always prided themselves on being the heartland's best and brightest, compelled the company to abandon the quota system. Moreover, a core group of GM managers began to recognize that the root of most of the company's problems lay in its systems and its culture and wasn't within the power of most individual employees to change. So even as GM began searching for ways to redefine its corporate culture, it gave a green light to experimentation in different parts of the company. The automaker's soul searching opened the way for the innovative plan that had been percolating in the Powertrain division for over two years. Powertrain had begun analysis of its appraisal system when it came under Deming's influence in the mid-1980s, and had convened a multidisciplinary committee of personnel, technical, and supervisory employees to study the question.[16] This task force sought to resolve the inherent conflict between a process that aims to coach and improve performance and one that is used as a bullwhip and a yardstick for determining compensation.

When GM instituted the forced distribution with four buckets, Powertrain got a partial exemption for a 10-80-10 distribution that would be more "consistent with the teachings of Deming on variation." Initially, the 10-80-10 distribution sought to acknowledge the existence of outstanding performers. But by the time Powertrain was finished refining the system in 1989, the division had moved even closer to Deming's vision. "It was definitely a big struggle; GM wants desperately to pay for [levels of] contribution," says Mary Jenkins, a personnel manager who helped shepherd the Powertrain performance appraisal through the GM bureaucracy. "We can all think of people we've worked with whom we feel are exceptional individuals, who stand out."[17]

By early 1989, Powertrain had hammered out an appraisal blueprint that marked a dramatic departure from the corporation's recently abandoned quota system. Compensation was completely decoupled from the performance appraisal. The new evaluation system was designed to get managers and their employees working together to identify and plan individual and group improvement projects. Recognizing that no one works in a vacuum, part of each employee's appraisal would be based on input from peers and subordinates. And rankings were eliminated.

The pioneering appraisal was one of the cornerstones of a larger experiment in cooperative management. It was part of an effort by Powertrain, which had been working with Deming for years, to foster cooperation between employees and with suppliers in building the Quad 4 engine, hailed as the best new U.S. engine in years.

The division has gone to extraordinary lengths to create a one-for-all group culture. Powertrain allowed for the possibility that the performance of an employee might be truly outstanding and sought to ensure that such a designation would indeed be the exception rather than the rule. "Exceptional, given its most elementary definition, is rare. To identify more than a very few individuals as such negates the 'exceptional' label—makes it a non-tolerable contradiction. It is more likely that a given work team will have *no* rather than *one* exceptional team member," state the Powertrain guidelines. Under the new system, singling out an individual as an extraordinary performer would require "consensus by acclamation; no debate" by all those who know the employee and are involved in the appraisal process. Such an employee must also "inarguably" stand out from the rest of the work team over a sustained period of time, according to the division's specific "leadership principles." After the first appraisal period using the new system, only 5 percent of employees were identified as being exceptional. Moreover, according to Jenkins, they were the very sort of employee one would logically expect to be exceptional: older, seasoned managers with many years of experience.[18]

The division also established a set of leadership principles, most of which mirror several of Deming's Fourteen Points, which all employees are expected to strive to meet. They include:

- Fostering trust: Employees are expected to "effectively empower others by encouraging positive performance, ensuring that people have the information, authority and resources required, and expecting others to do things right without interference."
- Fostering team involvement: The guidelines encourage employees to "participate in peer development . . . recognize others' efforts and accomplishments . . . [and] react with positive understanding to constructive feedback, suggestions, and viewpoints of others."
- Participating in the drive for quality: Employees must strive to "consider and exceed customers' expectations, improve quality while reducing cost through continuous improvement in products, processes and people, and eliminate waste. [They also must] consider long term strategy in making decisions."[19]

At Cyanamid, similar goals and logic paved the way for appraisal reform. Like GM, the company flirted fleetingly with forced distributions. And although Cyanamid has never come under the influence of Deming, an experiment in Hodgson's medical research division at the company's Lederle Laboratories unit led Cyanamid to reach very much the same insights about employee motivation as did Powertrain. Says Hodgson, who spearheaded the experiment in which all but a small percentage of exceptional employees are grouped in a large middle range as "good" performers, "Many organizations depend vitally on people who do a routine task but one which is very necessary to the company, and I saw the demotivating effect of ratings. My contention is that the people at the top [of your middle] range are self-motivators, self-starters." The focus of management, Hodgson believes, should be to challenge and motivate employees, especially those who do acceptable work but are not reaching their full potential.[20]

Hodgson's epiphany began in the mid-1970s, when he ran across an article by Saul Gellerman that challenged the accepted assumptions about performance appraisals. "The performance appraisal has two purposes," says Gellerman, the dean of the Graduate School of Management at the University of Dallas and a former management consultant. "One is administrative: How do you administer merit pay, and how do we justify ourselves in court [if we want to fire someone]? The administrative purpose is the principal one. The second purpose involves employee motivation—focusing on people's motivations. The problem is that in pursuing both purposes, if it does one well, automatically it will do the other one badly. It will create tension between the supervisor and the employee."[21] Hodgson, who himself had once had the benefit of a very supportive boss in the days when performance appraisals were optional and were left up to individual supervisors, felt instinctively that Gellerman was right. Hodgson became so interested that he even attended a conference on the subject where he was the only participant who was not a personnel manager.

Hodgson was irrevocably won over when Cyanamid instituted a forced distribution in the early 1980s and he saw what the system did to employee morale. The Cyanamid directive mandated the grouping of employees into three categories: 20 percent were given a top rating, 40 percent were rated exceptional in some areas, and the bottom 40 percent were those who "achieved expected results." (Inadequate performers were a negligible number and were not rated on this scale.) However, by simply grouping the "average" performer at the bottom of the heap, the system served as a demotivator. "Think of it," says Hodgson. "You're in the bottom forty percent. I mean, even if [the categories were] labeled A Triple Star, A Double Star, and A, you'd still be in the bottom forty percent."[22]

Moreover, the quota system made any hope of achieving an equitable ranking impossible. The fairness problem was exacerbated by what Hodgson refers to as the "halo" effect. Hodgson points out that some employees, by dint of personality or just plain luck, always wind up looking good, whether or not their work is really measurably better over an extended period of time than that of their coworkers. IBM, for example, reportedly rates as "exceptional" a far higher percentage of employees at its Armonk headquarters than in its satellite offices.[23] Does the air in Armonk make employees better performers? Or does the high incidence of positive ratings have to do with the faces Armonk executives see in the hallways each day and at local country clubs?

When Cyanamid eliminated the four-tier rating scheme and began to require managers to plan specific work projects with their subordinates, the move suddenly sparked improvements in morale and surges of creativity. For example, one aging technician in Cyanamid's chromatography labs, who for years had been considered capable of handling only tasks that were closely supervised, came up with a minor breakthrough. Encouraged by his boss to use a new computer system to test an anticancer drug, the technician discovered a destabilizing ingredient that had eluded detection and slowed the drug's development. Today the compound, known as Novantrone, is a best-seller. The case showed how, under the old system, management "for many years of a man's career had not been able to discover the extent of what he could do," concludes Hodgson.[24]

Decades ago Frederick Herzberg referred to money as a mere "hygiene factor": Not enough of it causes distress, but lucre, by itself, has little to do with job satisfaction. Today, this idea remains one of the most controversial contentions of Deming and the corporate reformers. Companies that are moving toward eliminating rankings altogether sooner or later must make hard choices about compensation if they are to maintain a consistent policy. Having eliminated ratings, Powertrain recognized it could not remain true to its convictions without changing its policy on merit pay. Says Dick Donnelly, whose management beliefs have been strongly influenced by his early exposure to Deming and by the two years he spent in Japan in the early 1980s, "We expect to approach the position of the Japanese," in which compensation will be based largely on rank, expertise, and years of experience rather than "merit." However, recognizing that previous appraisal systems have skewed compensation levels, Donnelly says it will take a few years to bring employees in comparable jobs to parity.[25]

The Medical Research Division of American Cyanamid has also made a break from performance-based pay. Although the corporation still gives managers a kitty of cash to distribute, if they wish, to employees who are identified as being on the high side of its catchall "good" category, Hodgson never takes advantage of it. In Hodgson's domain, the vast majority of employees are rated "good" performers—87 percent in 1986—and receive raises, but not special merit bonuses. It's not that Hodgson can't identify "high performers" even within this broad category of good conduct; rather, he is convinced that from the standpoint of overall productivity, it isn't useful to make those distinctions.[26]

If money were a prime motivator, contends Hodgson, there would be a lot more job-hopping at Cyanamid. "The people here in Pearl River, at the pharmaceutical research organization, they're good, they can demonstrate they're good," he says. "Any one of these people could go out of here, could answer an ad, without even having to move to a new house. [They could] go over to Ciba-Geigy across the river or down to Schering [Plough] in Bloomfield and a whole host of places around here—maybe sixty percent of pharmaceutical research is done within a hundred and fifty miles of here—and get a twenty-five percent raise. So they're not staying here because I add an extra percent to their salary this year. They're staying here because they like the work, they find it stimulating, they like the people they work with, and they see a future. And that's the reward that those people are going to get."

As for the company's best performers: "Those people you've got to reward by promotions, new responsibilities, you give them an extra salary increase with the promotion, the new assignment, the new job." Making fine-line distinctions, he says, will just "turn people off."[27]

Hodgson and other executives are discovering that employees' intrinsic motivation to do well becomes particularly pronounced when a company's quality management practices create an environment conducive to improvement. Indeed, FP&L's John Hudiberg contends that it is easier to inspire an organization around improving quality than around any other set of corporate objectives, including profits and sales. Agrees Tom Laco of Procter & Gamble, a company that is reevaluating its appraisal policy, "Real satisfaction comes from accomplishment. And what TQC does is grease the skids of accomplishment, it helps everyone get superior results. That's why one of the greatest assets of TQC is that it is a tremendous morale builder. I wonder whether compensation, per se, isn't grossly exaggerated in its impact on performance."[28]

However, by rejecting pay for performance, Deming and the corporate reformers are challenging one of the most fundamental values of American industry. From respected electric utilities to an ice cream maker with a social conscience, American companies have invested the paycheck with almost magical powers to manipulate performance. These companies are also convinced that they can measure the performance of individuals with the hair-splitting accuracy needed to make narrow distinctions in pay and perks.

"We would never decouple compensation from the performance appraisal; it's a corporate culture issue here," says R. Peter Mercer, the human resources manager for General Electric Plastics, who, however, does acknowledge that there have been problems with GE's appraisal system. For example, in the fast-changing plastics business annual assessments were found to be so out of date as to make them virtually meaningless, and the division is now encouraging managers to make more specific evaluations in shorter time frames.[29]

Duke Power Company developed a reputation as one of the best-managed utilities in the country even though it didn't have a consistent performance appraisal system before 1982, when it too tried an ill-fated forced-distribution system. The experiment "caused quite a stir" and the company quickly dropped it. But Duke Power wasn't prepared to give up its pay-for-performance compensation scheme, which continues to allocate increases based on which of five rankings an employee receives.[30]

Perhaps the most telling sign of just how much of an American icon pay for performance has become are the ambivalent policies of Ben & Jerry's. The Waterbury, Vermont, company is known almost as much for its innovative management practices as for its Cherry Garcia ice cream. The company is committed to a rule that limits the pay of top executives to five times the lowest wage, even though the policy has made it difficult to recruit a chief financial officer. And its cofounder, Jerry Greenfield, gave up his operating duties to become the company's Minister of Joy (his job now includes, among other things, arranging for a masseur to minister to overworked employees). The ice cream innovator has even taken the unusual step of eliminating commissions for its national sales reps and putting them on a straight salary. The reason: Differences in distribution from region to region are "out of the sales rep's control" and make the commission system unfair. Yet when it comes to paying supervisors and managers, the company built by the Minister of Joy is committed to paying for performance.[31]

Companies like American Cyanamid and GM, which have faced up to the shortcomings of traditional performance schemes, are recognizing that when designed properly, evaluations can serve as a way to foster improvement projects and as a way to reinforce corporate values. At both companies, developing a more meaningful appraisal system grew out of a desire to create a closer link between individual performance and corporate goals.

Even companies that aren't yet ready to abandon the grading game are trying to make it more productive. The performance appraisals at Xerox and Ford, for example, have been rewritten to help foster teamwork. At both companies ratings and compensation are based partly on the performance of the team and individuals' contributions to cooperative efforts.[32]

At GE Plastics, performance appraisals have been amended to encourage scientists to stick with tough, long-range product development projects. Until recently, managers would typically go through twenty levels, and at least as many jobs, during a twenty- to thirty-year career. GE has replaced the twenty levels with five broad bands, with much broader pay ranges than the previous levels had, so that employees can stay in jobs longer or make lateral changes without fear of limiting their career or pay potential.[33]

And in one of the most innovative incentive schemes in industry, Ben & Jerry's is rating and rewarding employees in part on "social responsibility," the company's latest, and most experimental, performance criterion. According to David Barash, the head of human resources at the company, the idea was inspired by a company tour guide (the ice cream factories are the second biggest tourist attraction in Vermont) who developed a plan for replacing Styrofoam supplies with ones made of more ecologically sensitive materials. Having rid the offices of Styrofoam, the company is now working on eliminating the substance in its packing materials.[34]

Deming and his disciples, however, caution against the popular practice of granting incentive bonus payments to employees who accomplish specific company goals. The Achilles heel of most achievement-based bonus plans is the same as that of most MBO programs, says Joyce N. Orsini, a Deming disciple and an associate professor at Fordham University: "[When] individual employees participate in setting specific objectives . . . often the negotiating environment is coercive." In other words, goals are often based on wishful thinking, not a realistic assessment of what is achievable within a given system during a given period of time.[35]

Orsini cites one stark example of the problems that can occur when a bonus system is linked to numerical goals, describing the lengths to which one personnel executive went in order to receive a year-end bonus. The personnel officer in question was informed that his bonus would be tied to reducing turnover of nonexempt employees from a rate of 37 percent per year to 25 percent per year. To accomplish this goal, the personnel officer made the following changes:

- He changed the hiring criteria. While arithmetic and communications skills had been deemed important by the company, he looked instead for candidates who were less likely to leave within a short time frame. "These often turned out to be people who had had difficulty holding or getting jobs in the past."
- Employees who didn't work out in one department were haphazardly shunted to other departments.
- And entirely unsuitable employees were retained even if they had failed to improve their performance after several warnings, and even after having been put through the same retraining program several times.

- The personnel executive changed the method of calculating the turnover ratio. Instead of the old system in which the total number of employees who left was divided by the average number of individuals employed during the year, he divided the total number of employees who quit by the total number of individuals employed at any time during the year (that is, including peak employment periods).[36]

On paper, the turnover rate seemed to decrease, and the executive got his year-end bonus. For a company concerned about turnover, a far more effective way of solving the problem, according to Orsini, would have been to look for the fundamental reason why employees didn't stay in their jobs. If the company had studied the problem instead of setting an arbitrary target, management might have learned that it was hiring the wrong types of employees, that it was not training them properly, or that there were problems with the working conditions. Any of these reasons would have dictated different solutions than the ones seized on by the personnel executive. "Executives are not stupid; they *are* creative," notes Orsini. "Given a system within which to work, they will always find a way to give the company the results that trigger the bonus, even though there may be no *real* gain to the company."[37]

Orsini notes that the least destructive bonuses are companywide "thank-you" payments, which are generally linked to company profits. Bonuses meted out for numerical achievement, on the other hand, "are destructive primarily because there is no accounting for quality or natural variability."[38]

If a definitive study on performance and motivation were ever conducted, the sales function might provide the ultimate litmus test for Deming's theories on merit pay. "Sales is the one area in which you can get some good, hard data" on performance, says Gellerman. But here too, questions of equity can be a problem. In 1988 Ben & Jerry's eliminated its incentive pay system for sales reps because of inherent problems with finding a fair measure by which to rate employees in different territories. For example, whether a supermarket decides to carry Peace Pops, Ben & Jerry's latest chocolate-covered delight, often depends on marketing and shelf-space decisions at the headquarters of major chains that are entirely out of the control of individual sales reps. Setting uniform targets for disparate territories like Los Angeles and Seattle, according to Barash, simply becomes too complicated.[39] Notes Procter & Gamble's Laco, "I'm not sure the total quality company of the future will have sales quotas. There are so many variables that contribute to what results you get that sales quotas can be counterproductive. If you don't have quotas for advertising, purchasing, finance, why have them for sales? [Salesmen] are just as motivated" as employees in other business functions.[40]

Only time will tell how Ben & Jerry's sales system will work. Although at the time the decision was made, the sales reps said they preferred getting incentive pay, Barash says they accepted the company's reasoning. And within a year of eliminating its incentive pay system, only one of Ben & Jerry's thirteen salespeople, most of whom had come from more traditional food and distribution companies, had quit.[41]

Indeed, many companies that have come to question the wisdom of judgmental appraisals have taken to hiding behind the ingrained preferences of their employees. For instance, although some Ford executives say they privately agree with much of Deming's argument on performance appraisals, the company let a committee of employees decide on a new scheme: The group, which represented a cross section of the company, voted to maintain a ranking scheme, although they suggested limiting the categories to three buckets.[42]

If pay for performance is, indeed, the result of ingrained cultural conditioning, it is no surprise that employees say they want to be rated. "Most people say they would like to be evaluated," says Harvard's Beer. "What they mean is that they want to be told they're doing well." Mary Jenkins says that introducing GM's pass-fail system was the result of more than two years of planning and education. Without having a full year of results, the new system seemed to win qualified "neutral to positive" acceptance from most employees, according to Jenkins. "Everyone feels good that the division feels strongly about something and that it would go out on a limb," she says. "The idea of being a maverick, and of being principled, and of resisting the system has appeal. GM typically is not that way."[43]

Powertrain's appraisal system is not yet a corporate prototype, but it is beginning to influence other groups at GM. The Powertrain system is serving as a model for the evolving appraisal system at BOC. Ultimately, says GM's Hoglund, "I'm not sure a complete elimination of a meritocracy is realistic or desirable. But my personal bet, and I'm probably in a minority on the executive committee, is that the real truth is closer to Deming than our traditional approach."[44]

Most executives who have considered a Deming-style review acknowledge that it places a greater burden on managers to *manage* their subordinates. Hodgson points out that the longer a manager has been on the job, the more likely it is that he has selected the employees who work for him; so if an employee doesn't work out, the onus is on the manager.

For all the widespread efforts to reform performance appraisals, most companies remain dissatisfied with their results, according to Marc Wallace, a professor at the University of Kentucky, who conducted a study of forty-six firms that changed their policies during the 1980s. Says GM's Hoglund, "Our task is to marry individualism with the importance of working together toward the same goals."[45] That balancing act is enough to stump the most seasoned executives. But if experiments such as the one at GM are successful, they will deliver not only a positive appraisal of Deming's most controversial crusade but a model for other U.S. companies to follow.

DEMINGISM ENTERS
THE 1990s

enneth Hopper arrived at the Harvard Business School about twenty-five years too soon. The young Scottish engineer, who had spent several years working in the Procter & Gamble factories in Britain after World War II, had become fascinated by the process-mindedness of U.S. companies. Convinced that the United States was on the cutting edge of manufacturing know-how, he set off for Harvard determined to study the role of the foreman in the factory. He was to be disappointed. Hopper arrived at Harvard just as it was in the midst of a decades-long romance with the study of marketing and finance. The young manufacturing maven was shunted from one professor to the next, each of whom all but ridiculed his preoccupation with operations. When Hopper was finally sent to see Fritz Roethlisberger, coauthor of the controversial Hawthorne studies, the Scotsman hoped he had finally met the one man at Harvard who might share his interest in the factory. Instead, Roethlisberger scorned Hopper's preoccupation with manufacturing and told him there was no room at Harvard for a young man of his interests. Hopper packed his bags, left the ivy-covered campus on the banks of the Charles River, and slipped into obscurity for the next several decades.[1] The same fate would befall operations-minded managers throughout American industry.

Today Harvard, the bastion of American management science, would welcome Hopper. As companies and entire industries have been battered by foreign competition and gradually grown disillusioned with financial wizardry, the business schools themselves are being forced to change. As recently as the late 1980s, a report by the business school accrediting agency, the American Assembly of Collegiate Schools of Business, made this point: The schools excel in quantitative abilities, such as advanced mathematics, but at the expense of broader management skills. Robert Hayes, a technology management expert at Harvard Business School, sizes up the challenge for academia: "If schools don't respond to the nation's problem in competitiveness, the schools themselves will become irrelevant."[2]

From Stanford and Berkeley to Harvard and MIT, that message is starting to hit home. And it's prompting what John Zysman, coauthor of *Manufacturing Matters* and codirector of the Berkeley Roundtable on the International Economy, describes as "a massive reorganization of priorities" in the nation's business schools. Not since 1950, when two critiques by the Ford and Carnegie foundations flushed M.B.A. programs from the backwaters of academia, have business schools engaged in such soul searching. Fading fast is the shopworn you-can-manage-anything-by-the-numbers approach scorned by Hayes and the late William Abernathy in 1980, in a celebrated *Harvard Business Review* article, "Managing Our Way to Economic Decline." Instead, schools are trying to cultivate a broader complement of management skills and the kind of cross-disciplinary problem solving Deming has long advocated. At Harvard, men like Hayes and David Garvin are teaching quality management concepts. The University of Tennessee is focusing its MBA curriculum on quality management. And MIT recently launched a joint management-engineering program that is designed to turn out fifty to seventy-five graduates interested in process technologies annually. Says Lester Thurow, a liberal economist and dean of MIT's Sloan School of Business, "A fair number of people in business schools have a scientific background. We have to build on that, rather than brainwashing it out. Process technology is America's scientific-and-management weakness. A manager, for instance, has to decide should he or should he not bet on powdered metals. I don't think you can make that decision by looking at the numbers."[3]

Even the business schools in Wall Street's backyard, Columbia and

Fordham, have started to incorporate Deming's teachings into their classes and curricula. Throughout much of the 1980s, Deming taught a seminar at Columbia, geared principally toward educating the business faculty. And Fordham has established a Center for Advanced Management Studies that uses Deming's philosophy as a platform. Deming has lectured at the institute on such subjects as how quality management should be taught at business schools. And Marta Mooney, one of the center's founders, is even considering calling on Kenneth Hopper, who has emerged in recent years as a chronicler of the quality management movement, to compile a detailed history of the practitioners and episodes that influenced its evolution.[4]

As the hothouses of tomorrow's management talent, business schools are a logical catalyst for introducing quality management to the marketplace. Yet Demingism is so new to the business schools that most are still ill equipped to teach it. In the absence of strong leadership from academia, a number of public and private groups are trying to fill the void, attempting to create a common quality blueprint for American industry. Consulting firms started by several of Deming's disciples, as well as the Juran Institute, which was founded by Joseph Juran, the U.S. quality expert who followed Deming to Japan in the 1950s, are playing an ever more influential role in the educational process. ASI, which was established by Ford and described in Chapter 5, has been instrumental in disseminating quality concepts throughout the supplier networks of the Big Three auto companies and related industries. A Washington arm of ASI was even established to introduce quality principles to the Pentagon's procurement process. And in one of the potentially most promising developments, a number of companies are beginning to advocate the adoption of the Malcolm Baldrige National Quality Award criteria as a common blueprint all their suppliers would be expected to follow.

THE MALCOLM BALDRIGE NATIONAL QUALITY AWARDS

In its third year, the Baldrige Awards are showing early signs of establishing a national standard in quality management. Motorola, one of the three companies to win a Baldrige Award in 1988, the first year of the prize, sent a letter to its suppliers requiring that every one of them commit to preparing for the award. Although Motorola didn't specify a deadline for its suppliers, the electronics company signaled that it would do business only with vendors who demonstrated their commitment to quality by setting their sights on the award. In April 1989, IBM, which had failed to win the award two years in a row, sent a similar letter to its suppliers. Referring to the Baldrige criteria, the IBM letter stated, "This program embraces all of the elements that IBM and other U.S. enterprises must comply with if we are to meet essential quality objectives. IBM cannot and will not continue to do business with suppliers that fail to meet these objectives. We at IBM are continuing to pursue the goals of excellence that are in the Baldrige program."[5] And following the second award ceremony, Commerce Secretary Robert Mosbacher said he expected the latest winners, Xerox and Milliken & Company, the privately held textile company, as well as AT&T, to lay down the same gauntlet in front of their suppliers.[6] Even the Department of Defense (DOD) is considering making the Baldrige criteria a standard for all defense contractors.[7]

That type of peer pressure combined with the rigorous requirements of the Baldrige Awards could make the prize a formidable purveyor of quality management principles in industry. The application guidelines contain eight broad criteria that cover most of the key hallmarks of TQC and Demingism:

- Top management involvement, including clear plans for quality leadership
- A planning process for short- and long-term quality improvement
- The use of data in spotting and analyzing potential problems and opportunities for improvement, and a consistent data management system to ensure that accurate process information is available on a timely basis
- Extensive employee involvement in the quality improvement process
- The availability of quality education and training for employees at all levels of the company
- A method for measuring customer needs and expectations, and a process for developing new or improved products that meet those requirements

- A system for selecting, auditing, and training the outside suppliers of materials and component
- A system for auditing internal quality management processes

The Baldrige committee has also set up a rigorous process for selecting winners. Inspectors and judges come from the companies and organizations with the best quality reputations. They include Brian Joiner, a statistician, consultant, and respected Demingite; Kent Sterett, the man who shepherded FP&L through the Deming awards; Blan Godfrey, a former quality expert at AT&T, coauthor of a leading textbook on quality improvement, and the new head of the Juran Institute; and Jim Bakken, the retired vice president for quality at Ford. Audits take at least a week, and auditors require access to any part of the company, from the factory floor to the boardroom.[8] At Motorola, for example, the auditors not only visited plants but spent hours interviewing chairman Robert Galvin, the company's CEO, as well as its vice chairmen, to make sure they all spoke the same quality language.[9]

Yet maintaining the integrity of the award-giving process in the long term will be a challenge for the Baldrige committee. Unlike in Japan, where the Deming Prize evolved as a sort of grass-roots effort and where a core group of highly respected academics became both advisers for and judges of the award, the Baldrige Award is essentially a peer review. In the clubbish world of American business, in which even boards of directors rarely countermand the dictates of a CEO, no matter how troubling they may be, an award so heavily dominated by the very companies it seeks to judge could develop long-term problems. For one thing, the Baldrige committee has received over $10 million from corporate sponsors. And the rules limit the number of awards that can be granted each year to two large industrial companies, two small companies, and two firms in the service sector. By placing such limits on the number of companies that can win in each category, the committee may be forced, especially in later years when candidates become more conversant with its quality criteria, to make arbitrary distinctions among several qualified companies.

Before the competition was established, Curt Reimann, who is now director of the awards, consulted with Deming. At the time Deming expressed grave reservations about creating a U.S. quality award.[10] For one thing, Deming was concerned that no U.S. company had yet demonstrated the stuff of which a true TQC company is made. Since FP&L clinched the Deming award and such companies as Motorola and Ford demonstrated dramatic improvements in product quality, which have translated into increased market share, that concern might not be as valid as it was even a few years ago. (Colleagues suggest that Deming may also have been miffed that the award, in trying to remain nonpartisan, includes no reference to either Deming or his Fourteen Points.)

Deming has a point, however. There are relatively few U.S. experts who are as well versed as the Japanese in quality theory and technique, although the Baldrige committee deserves credit for amassing a *Who's Who* of America's best quality practitioners. At least during the first few years, winners of the award are unlikely to be held to as high a standard by U.S. judges as are applicants for the Deming Prize in Japan, which has raised the quality ante every year since the award was established. For example, even executives at Xerox, a Baldrige winner in 1989, acknowledge that they still lag behind Fuji Xerox in perfecting several of their processes and in achieving some quality targets. Moreover, the scrutiny of companies by the Baldrige committee does not appear to be as rigorous as that of the JUSE committee; otherwise, it is unlikely that IBM, which withdrew its Japanese subsidiary from the race for the Deming Prize precisely because of the level of disclosure required by JUSE, would twice have been willing to subject itself to the scrutiny of the Baldrige examiners.

However, for now the Baldrige committee has demonstrated its willingness to make tough choices. In its first year, the committee granted only one award in the small business category and none to service companies; in 1989, no awards were given to small businesses or ones in the service sector. If the committee continues to fine-tune its standards and practices, it could serve as one of the most important quality management catalysts of the 1990s.

THE PENTAGON

The fledgling quality movement within the DOD, which purchases an estimated 20 percent of all the manufactured goods in the United States, offers "an extraordinary opportunity to leverage the benefits of this process throughout industry," says Thomas Murrin, who formerly presided over Westinghouse's defense and aerospace business and who serves as both the deputy secretary of commerce and chairman of the Defense Manufacturing Board (DMB), an advisory group to the Pentagon.[11] The organization that brought America the $7,600 coffeepot and $600 toilet seats has launched a major quality drive and is creating Deming's largest new constituency. What is propelling the Pentagon's quality reform efforts are deep-seated problems with the procurement process, huge budget deficits, and a belated realization that buying cheaply today can drive up costs tomorrow. By using standard industry quality practices, DOD hopes to achieve a "modest goal" of reducing costs by 30 percent, or $77 billion, in the next five years, a savings equal to more than 70 percent of the Gramm-Rudman-Hollings 1988 deficit target.[12]

No system (except perhaps Soviet central planning) is more prone to producing waste than the Pentagon. Procurement regulations have come to virtually guarantee the delivery of shoddy goods by disproportionately favoring the lowest bidder, to the point that it has become virtually impossible for military personnel to justify purchases based on quality and *long-term* cost savings. "Traditionally the emphasis has been on the procurement cost, and we have neglected the costs of maintenance, rework, repair, storage, and training," notes one Pentagon official.[13] While theoretically procurement standards leave some room for maneuvering on price, purchasing agents who pay more for quality must be prepared to justify the decision before a review committee. Moreover, military contractors have grown so used to being graded largely on price that they will slash prices even if it means severely compromising the integrity of the product. As a result, some twenty-five thousand auditors and inspectors have to oversee the DOD acquisition process at a cost of between $5 and $10 billion per year.[14]

The dilemma faced by an officer who recently went shopping for jam and jelly for military cafeterias is a case in point. The troops had long complained about the notoriously runny and tasteless goo served up in mess halls. And though the Pentagon wanted to switch to a better brand, the acquisition rules made that impossible. Knowing they were being rated largely on price, the lowest bidder, as well as the next *four* lowest bidders, all proffered lousy jam. The purchasing agent would have had to go to jam maker *number six* and pay 25 percent more than the lowest bid before he got a decent-quality product. Because quality has taken a backseat in the procurement process, the lowest bidders were able to drop their price by literally watering down the preserves. Explaining why he decided to go with the lowest bidder after all, the officer told a quality consultant, "It's easy for me to follow the rules. How would I ever justify to a reviewer jumping up to the sixth guy? [To purchase one of the better brands] I'd have to write an epistle to protect myself." Far more crucial purchases also suffer from excessive cost-consciousness and quality neglect.[15]

It is the shoddy quality of strategic components, such as the ball bearings and fasteners that literally hold together the nation's defense machinery, that has helped spur change in the procurement process. "It wasn't long ago people were saying a nut is a nut and a bolt is a bolt," says Gordon Keefe, who established ASI's Association for Defense Suppliers office in Washington. There was little appreciation for the fact that the tighter a bearing fits, the better it will hold up. In fact, loose-fitting joints caused so many problems in everything from helicopters to tanks, which have to bear up under rough conditions, that the Air Force Logistics Command launched Project Fastener in an attempt to fix the problem.[16]

The Pentagon's Total Quality Management program, which was first formulated in 1987 under Defense Secretary Frank Carlucci, considered a variety of ways to improve the quality of materiel while at the same time lowering acquisition costs. The idea was to place "the acquisition cost . . . in proper perspective as related to the total cost of ownership throughout the product lifecycle."[17] In the late 1980s, under the aegis of Carlucci and Robert Costello, the undersecretary of defense for acquisitions, a number of reforms were proposed, many of which grew out of recommendations of a presidential commission headed by David Packard. While most of the proposals were still pending approval by the Bush administration in late 1989, they give a good idea of the sorts of extensive systemic changes needed to lower costs and improve the quality of the procurement process:

- Foster multidisciplinary problem solving early on in the design and engineering of military equipment, in part by bringing suppliers into the earliest phases of product development. Doing more of the problem solving up front would also require that more money be made available in the early stages of an acquisition program. Multiyear funding for major programs would also permit longer-term planning.

- Take the DOD's shopping list out of the hands of soldiers, and give it to civilian procurement experts. [18]
- One proposal of the DMB raised fundamental questions about resource allocation at the Pentagon. Currently, DOD spends far less on manufacturing than either the Japanese, who allocate two thirds of their resources to perfecting manufacturing-related functions, or U.S. industry, which spends about one third of its resources on production. One recommendation of the DMB, according to Murrin, would be to use some of the funds that currently are allocated to scientific research to help develop better ways of translating laboratory inventions into useful, produceable products.
- In a DOD experiment with Deming's most controversial directive, some installations have eliminated traditional performance appraisals and instituted gain-sharing programs aimed at letting both employees and suppliers earn more money as they help the government save money.
- DOD is simplifying portions of the Federal Acquisition Regulations that apply to defense procurement in an effort to make them more consistent with quality management practices. Changes in the procurement guidelines are specifically intended to make quality improvement an explicit requirement in procurement contracts.
- The air force has started writing "report cards" on the work of major contractors as one screening measure in awarding new contracts. [19]

One of the more important reform measures involves DOD's determination to introduce the practice of controlling and reducing variation as one of its procurement criteria. To this end, DOD is trying to eliminate traditional specifications for Acceptable Quality Levels (AQL), which specify the number of permissible defects. AQL has led contractors to become "complacent with a 'good enough for the government' concept, and [to] los[e] sight of good business practices," writes Jack Strickland, the Pentagon's top quality and productivity official. Instead, DOD is encouraging suppliers to use SPC to reduce variation in their processes and to pursue quality improvement.[20]

To highlight the importance of variation control, DOD is modeling much of its initiative on Deming's theories. In May 1988 Deming was brought in to speak with five hundred top military officials. At about the same time, Bill Scherkenbach, one of Deming's principal disciples, addressed forty-five of the top leaders in Carlucci's office, the Joint Chiefs of Staff, and the military services.[21] Deming's name and Fourteen Points are popping up all over the government's new quality guidelines, as is the concept of process control and variation reduction. And thousands of military officers attend Deming seminars each year. The Fourteen Points were even printed verbatim in an appendix of a report by the House Republican Research Committee on High Technology and Competitiveness. And quality is being incorporated as part of the core curricula in all armed services schools, according to Jack Denslow, project officer of the Defense Productivity Program Office.[22]

Where pilot projects have been started, there are already signs of success. A quality program at the Naval Aviation Depot in North Island, San Diego, has helped reduce maintenance costs on F-14 fighter planes by about $400,000 per aircraft, and a fifty-two-week service backlog at North Island also has been slashed to just two weeks.[23] The quality efforts at the depot were spearheaded by a number of Demingites, ranging from Lori Broedling, a research psychologist who launched many of the North Island quality experiments, to retired Admiral John Kirkpatrick, who headed all six naval aviation depots in the mid-1980s. Deming himself lectured frequently to depot personnel. Similarly, the naval shipyards in Pearl Harbor, which repair ships and submarines, have saved an estimated $24 million through their quality efforts.[24] Major aircraft companies, under extra scrutiny because of the rash of airplane accidents in recent years, have also stepped up their quality efforts. McDonnell Douglas, for example, has slashed the number of defects per "aircraft equivalent" in its F-15 program from fifteen hundred in 1986 to twelve hundred a year later.[25] Boeing, home to legions of Deming followers, also offers a battery of quality seminars for both employees and suppliers.

Nor is the Pentagon the only government agency focusing on quality. The Office of Management and Budget has established the Federal Quality Institute (FQI) to serve as a quality clearinghouse and resource center for government agencies. A number of municipalities, including Madison, Wisconsin, are trying to improve government service by adopting Deming's principles. And the Internal Revenue Service has launched a quality strategy with the help of the Juran Institute.[26]

However, the obstacles that remain in overhauling the government's management practices are as numerous as fallen soldiers. The DOD procurement process is riddled with regulations that are in direct conflict with TQC principles. For example, critics charge that the Pentagon's attempt to "second source" strategic weapons systems actually raises costs and erodes quality. Trying to bring the number-two supplier up to the standards of the principal supplier inevitably causes delays. At the same time, it actually foils innovation by the number-one supplier, who doesn't want to give away advanced technology to a competitor.

In its desperation to enhance productivity, the federal government has also indulged in setting arbitrary targets—a key Deming bugaboo—only to create even worse problems. For example, by trying to mandate prompt payment of government contractors without identifying why payments are being made late in the first place, billing costs at DOD have skyrocketed. During the Reagan administration, DOD's deadline for paying contractors was shortened to seven days from the previous thirty-day timetable. To avoid paying late fees, DOD's beancounters often end up reimbursing contractors before they're able to verify whether a bill already has been paid by some other person or department. Hence, DOD sometimes pays several times for one piece of work and then has to spend time trying to get reimbursed. The rework rate in DOD's accounting departments, estimates one Demingite, is about 50 percent, and sometimes creeps as high as 65 percent.[27]

The sheer size of the military establishment and Congress's attempts to micromanage its activities are another source of endemic problems. In 1988 alone, Congress demanded some 661 reports from

DOD, up from just thirty-seven in 1970.[28] As of 1987, procurement regulations were being authored by seventy-nine different offices and monitored by fifty-five congressional subcommittees.[29] And as recently as 1988, each of the military services and the Defense Logistics Agency were planning to issue its own separate guidelines on quality, independent of the DOD's TQM strategy. These initiatives "differ in virtually every major element," charged one government report.[30]

In short, without the drastic changes quality management could bring to DOD and the procurement process, the nation's defense systems will remain in dire straits. "A confrontational atmosphere that exists among Congress, among the department [of defense], and among industry, I've never seen anything like it. I will be candid . . . and tell you that if major corporations throughout the country, either in the automotive industry or electronics industry, whether it be a General Motors or Ford or General Electric or AT&T, if they ever had the relationship that exists between our suppliers and ourselves, indeed those companies couldn't long exist," noted Secretary of Defense Dick Cheney in a 1989 speech on defense management report. Adds Tom Murrin, "I doubt that there is any other near-term, credible opportunity involving our federal government that holds as much promise" as quality management.[31]

Even if DOD arrives at a common, workable quality management policy, amassing the know-how to coordinate it could take years. When DMB suggested making the Baldrige criteria a common standard, the group concluded "that there were not enough expert judges in the United States to make those evaluations," says Murrin. DOD lacks the expertise to organize all the training that is needed. This was highlighted in a recent attempt by the FQI to solicit bids from prospective quality experts. Following federal guidelines, FQI issued a formal "request for proposals" through the *Commerce Business Daily*. Not surprisingly, most of the applicants came from the cabal of beltway bandits who regularly scan the publication for lucrative consulting contracts with the Pentagon. Most of Deming's disciples didn't even know that bids were being requested. As a result only one Demingite, Lou Schultz's Process Management Institute, which is based in Bloomington, Minnesota, became one of the finalists.[32]

DEMING'S DISCIPLES

A loose confederation of Deming followers is playing an ever more prominent role in championing Deming's quality agenda. Among those who have made the guru's philosophy their full-time vocation are both former executives who worked with Deming during the 1980s and the statisticians who have been his disciples of longest standing.

Since Deming has never established a school or consulting organization, there is unlikely to be a single individual or group that will assume his mantle in the coming years. Yet the so-called Deming Masters, the statisticians who have passed Deming's rigid standards of competency and whose names he recommends to client companies, meet on a quarterly basis to share information and ideas. In addition, five of the Deming Masters—Brian Joiner, Lou Schultz, Chuck Holland, Harold Haller, and Ron Moen—have formed independent consulting firms. This group of five meets on a monthly basis and for the past two years has cosponsored meetings with representatives of JUSE. In addition, Schultz, the only one of the Deming Masters who is on FQI's roster of federally approved statisticians, is likely to bring in other Deming Masters as subcontractors. "What the five of us will end up doing is gravitating toward [setting up] an organization like JUSE," says Schultz. "We've talked about a not-for-profit that would develop as a training organization." But because the five are competitors, it will take some time before they agree on what final form their association will take.[33]

A few who haven't formed independent consulting organizations also deserve mention. Bill Scherkenbach, who currently works at GM, is emerging as a key figure among quality management practitioners. He occasionally pinch hits for Deming on the lecture circuit, as he did in 1988 at the Pentagon. In fact, his relatively visible roles at both Ford and GM have endowed him with an unusual level of legitimacy, one that is likely to grow stronger if GM's quality efforts lead to improvements in both product and market share. Indeed, Scherkenbach has already parlayed his association with Deming and the auto industry into a series of lectures for George Washington University, which has long sponsored Deming's four-day seminars. Gipsie Ranney, who was recruited for her quality expertise by GM's BOC Powertrain division, is another respected Demingite. Similarly, Kent Sterett, who led Florida Power & Light's quality drive, has recently moved to Omaha, where he is applying his expertise at the Union Pacific Railroad. And John Hudiberg, FP&L's retired chairman, is also devoting his time to promoting the quality movement in the United States.

Many of the executives with whom Deming has worked over the years have also joined the ranks of quality consultants. William Conway, the man who brought Deming to Nashua Corporation, has established a consulting firm that counts Dow Chemical and Mc-Donnell Douglas among its clients. And Maryann Gould, the former president of Janbridge, a small Philadelphia electronics company, has also set up a company, known as the Gould Group. Gould, who has developed an avid interest in Japanese-style policy deployment, counts Hercules and the Sun Refining and Marketing Company, among the companies that have sought her advice.

A number of experts outside Deming's immediate circle are also serving to spread the quality management doctrine. Blan Godfrey, the new CEO of the Juran Institute, could well raise the profile of the organization created by Deming's principal U.S. rival. Godfrey earned his stripes at AT&T's Bell Laboratories, Shewhart's alma mater, and has sought to keep himself free of professional jealousies and loyalties to a given quality doctrine, to which many of his fellow quality experts often succumb. While Deming was a visionary, Juran was a pragmatist, a trait that would keep him in Deming's shadow. While Deming had neither the interest nor, in all likelihood, the talent to create an organization that would carry on his work, his genius and self-confidence enabled him constantly to push the boundaries of his quality philosophy. Juran's forte, on the other hand, was being a cautious and conscientious purveyor of methodologies that had been extensively proven out in industry; he was not a messiah for untested ideas. Godfrey acknowledges the importance of Deming's role as a visionary in fueling the quality movement at a pivotal time. And Godfrey, who cited both Deming and Juran extensively in *Modern Methods for Quality Control and Improvement*, a textbook he coauthored, has both the know-how and the conviction to doggedly search out new quality ideas and applications. With the backing of the Juran Institute, he also has a well-established platform from which to put his ideas to the test.

Finally, business communities from California to Pennsylvania have sprouted grass-roots "Deming User's Groups." Many of these are loose associations of managers in business and government who share ideas about quality. Typical of this movement is the Philadelphia Area Council for Excellence (PACE), which was launched by the Greater Philadelphia Chamber of Commerce. Spearheaded in the early 1980s by a group of Demingites including Gould, PACE sponsored quality seminars that were led by Deming and his master statisticians, including Ron Moen and Brian Joiner. Among the companies that got involved with Philadelphia's quality efforts were Campbell Soup, Rohm & Haas, and Philadelphia Electric.[34]

QUALITY VERSUS WALL STREET AND THE RAIDERS

One look at Wall Street, and it becomes abundantly clear that the country's quality movement has little chance without fundamental changes in the role played by the shareholders of public companies. U.S. management's myopic outlook was aggravated during the 1980s by the hit-and-run tactics of corporate raiders and by a growing cadre of institutional investors, especially pension funds, that act more like speculators than owners. Columbia University's Institutional Investor Project, which was launched as a response to the increasing dominance of institutional shareholders, arrived at the following disturbing conclusions about corporate ownership: "There is increasing tension in the United States between shareholders and corporate directors and managers which, many observers believe, is leading to watershed developments in the governance of U.S. corporations. At best, the present situation is palpably unstable. The U.S. does not have a well-defined consensus on the proper role of the shareholder of large public corporations."[35]

A proxy fight at Gillette is emblematic of the problems cited by the study. In 1988 a dissident group of shareholders challenged management's resistance to a sale or merger. Yet, Gillette, which in late 1986 had paid "greenmail" to prevent a hostile takeover by Ronald O. Perelman, Revlon's owner, wasn't under siege by its dissident shareholders for bad management. In fact, in 1987 Gillette's return on equity was about triple the 13 percent average for the *Fortune* 500. Moreover, Gillette gleaned more than 60 percent of its profits from overseas, prompting Louis Lowenstein, a law professor at Columbia University, and Ira Millstein, a prominent New York lawyer and takeover expert, to write that Gillette "might have seemed more like a national treasure than an object of dissident displeasure. . . . The Gillette question ultimately is whether the shareholders are entitled to take the money and run, or whether they have a role that entails other, ongoing responsibilities."[36]

The crisis in corporate governance at companies such as Gillette is in large part due to the power and ownership practices of pension funds. The amount of publicly traded stock held by pension funds has increased steadily throughout the 1980s, reaching 43.5 percent by 1987. And pension funds control just about half the shares traded in the country's fifty largest corporations. While pension funds increasingly dominate the shareholder ranks of U.S. companies and are thus in an ideal position to "help assure that American management takes a balanced time-horizon approach to running their companies," most fail to exercise their responsibilities as owners. Says Millstein, "Pension funds have a disturbing history . . . of abdicating their ownership responsibilities by not participating in the corporate governance process—either by not voting proxies . . . by always voting automatically with management or, on certain issues, by always voting against management without regard to the particular situation of the corporation involved."[37]

Opponents of leveraged buyouts have long advocated new tax laws that would make takeovers much less attractive. Critics also cite a number of specific changes in both the laws and the practices that govern pension fund investment decisions that would give the companies they control more leeway to manage for the long term:

- New government rules, such as the proposed section 717 (B) of the New York Corporation Law, would encourage pension fund managers to consider the impact their decisions have, not just on immediate profits but on employees, suppliers, and even the community as a whole.[38]
- Boards of directors should play a more active role in overseeing their companies' pension fund activities and in establishing pension policies. They should encourage their own pension fund managers to *avoid* doing, to the companies in

which they own stock, what they would not have done unto themselves.

- The one-share-one-vote system should be abandoned "at least as long as the company shows adequate financial results."[39]

Another force that is likely to stretch the time horizons of U.S. companies is the boom in Employee Stock Ownership Plans (ESOP), which have gained popularity, at least in part, as an antitakeover defense. Since 1987 an estimated two hundred public companies have established ESOPs. Polaroid was probably the first company to use an ESOP to ward off raiders when Stanley Gold and Roy Disney's Shamrock Holdings made a hostile bid for the company. Polaroid's ESOP holds 22 percent of the company's stock. A Delaware law prohibits a raider from completing a hostile acquisition for three years unless he gains control of 85 percent of the stock.[40] Polaroid's defense was later mimicked by Dunkin' Donuts and Lockheed, both of which used an ESOP-cum-poison-pill strategy.

While employees in most ESOP companies have neither voting power nor commensurate management influence, this is likely to change in the future. For one thing, companies that encourage employee involvement are 52 percent more productive than those that don't, according to a 1986 report by the General Accounting Office. Polaroid became one of the first ESOP companies to make a place on its board of directors for an employee. The United Steelworkers of America has become one of the first unions to demand full voting rights for members who work for companies in which an ESOP controls a large share of the ownership. Congress has even considered mandating employee voting rights at companies in which an ESOP controls at least 30 percent of the stock. "In a time of deadly competition, a highly educated work force, and a tight labor market, labor-management cooperation should be an economic necessity for many companies," says Joseph Blasi, author of *Employee Ownership: Revolution or Ripoff?* in *Business Week* magazine.[41]

Of course, giving employees a voice in the management of ESOP companies doesn't give management an automatic guarantee against takeovers. Indeed, the employees' vote could be counted on as a mechanism for making takeovers possible when they are needed the most—to rid a faltering company of entrenched and incompetent management.

No discussion of the structural impediments to quality management would be complete without a mention of executive pay. As teamwork comes to be recognized as a necessary part of doing business in U.S. companies, management will eventually have to confront its most sacred management prerogative. Few would argue that the knowledge and responsibilities of corporate chieftains deserve to be well compensated. Yet the gluttonous size of many executive compensation packages is unfair by any logical standards, and may well contribute to morale and productivity problems at many companies. Some eighty years ago, J. P. Morgan observed that excessive salaries disrupt teamwork. Peter Drucker, the noted management expert, wrote in *The Frontiers of Management* of the fat compensation packages many U.S. executives enjoy: ". . . they offend the sense of justice of many, indeed of the majority of management people themselves."[42]

While corporations increasingly seek to link employee pay to measures of corporate performance, few boards of directors hold their executives to the same standards. Last year the average combined salary and bonus of the highest-paid CEOs totaled $1 million, according to *Business Week* magazine. The 17 percent pay rise of these CEOs was *triple* the average 5.1 percent gain of middle managers. Moreover, in the United States in the troubled 1980s, the gap between the average pay of CEOs and that of factory workers and engineers has *doubled* since the go-go 1960s. Today's CEO makes ninety-three times more than the average factory worker and forty-four times more than the average engineer. The differential balloons even more if you factor in the much higher tax rate applied to CEO salaries in the 1960s than today.[43] At the same time, U.S. CEOs make far more than their more successful Japanese counterparts, who in turn earn only about eight times the salary of the lowest-paid worker.[44]

Executives who are serious about teamwork will need to think about ridding their companies of the double standards that shape corporate compensation. If, as many executives contend, job satisfaction for their employees must come from more than just a paycheck and if money is indeed "a mere hygiene factor," shouldn't the same hold true for top management? If Deming and others are correct about the synergistic effects of teamwork, is it fair to give the bulk of the credit, in the form of multi-million-dollar bonuses and stock options, to the top executives alone? Ultimately, more companies might follow the example of the handful of pioneers who have linked the fortunes of the CEO to those of their employees. For example, Herman Miller, the innovative furniture maker, limited its CEOs' pay to no more than twenty times the income of its manufacturing employees.[45] Similarly, at ice cream maker Ben & Jerry's, the ceiling on executive pay is five times the level of its factory workers' pay.[46]

Deming's philosophy, as the preceding chapters have shown, embraces a mix of management practices and scientific theories that have helped companies such as Ford and Florida Power & Light become more productive and more competitive, and that have helped them serve their customers better. The underpinnings of quality management are based on both an obsession with the customer and the scientific observation that all things in life are variable and that long-term improvement comes from controlling and reducing the level of natural variation that plagues all processes. While the power of Deming's ideas are rooted in science, a great part of his appeal has nothing to do with science at all.

Deming's is a highly humanistic philosophy born of an intrinsically optimistic view of mankind and what working men and women can accomplish, if only they are given a chance. While Deming, especially in later years, has sometimes shown the common human frailties of egotism and impatience, he has been driven by a vision and an uncompromising belief in his convictions and values. For the thousands who have flocked to his seminars over the years, it is the principles of the man, every bit as much as his teachings, that have been the attraction. Workers come away from his lectures convinced that he understands their efforts and their frustrations. Managers recognize the help his ideas can lend them and appreciate being held to a higher standard. For most, the pursuit of quality, Deming's way, is a compelling challenge.

In the 1980s' pursuit of greed, glamour, and instant gratification, it has been intriguing to watch a grass-roots movement thrive on the ideals of quality, learning, and self-improvement. At a time when job security is as tenuous as the borders of Europe or the ownership of a takeover candidate, Deming created a new belief system that executives and workers in all industries could share. The workers who toiled on the Fiero and the managers who helped prepare FP&L for the Deming Prize share a common bond: While change will come faster than ever before, they are far better prepared to face it, not as a threat but as an opportunity for growth and improvement both for themselves and for their companies. And as Deming's principles are embraced by pioneers in government and education in the 1990s, they could give the United States powerful new tools for tackling the country's most pressing social problems.

Abegglen, James C., and George Stalk, Jr. *Kaisha: The Japanese Corporation*. New York: Basic Books, 1985.

"AFSC Chief Randolph Cites Value of CPAR." *Defense Daily*, February 2, 1989, p. 167.

Altschuler, Alan, Martin Anderson, Daniel Jones, Daniel Roos, and James Womack. *The Future of the Automobile: The Report of MIT's International Automobile Program*. Cambridge, Mass.: MIT Press, 1984.

Andrews, Walter. "Pentagon Adopts Japanese Production Techniques." United Press International, August 18, 1988.

Bingaman, Ron, and F. Alton Doody. *Reinventing the Wheels: Ford's Spectacular Comeback*. Cambridge, Mass.: Ballinger Publishing, 1988.

Bridgman, Percy Williams. *Reflections of a Physicist*. New York: Arno Press, 1980.

Brown, Warren. "Contract Talks Could Retool Auto Industry." *Washington Post*, July 19, 1987, p. H1.

———. "The Making of the All-New Thunderbird." *Washington Post Magazine*, November 6, 1988, pp. 43–67.

Buss, Dale D. "GM Radically Shifts Its Strategy to Match Output, Sales." *Wall Street Journal*, December 19, 1986, p. 6.

———, and Melinda Grenier Guiles. "GM Slows Big Drive for Saturn to Produce Small Car in Five Years." *Wall Street Journal*, October 30, 1986, p. 1.

Byrne, John A., Ronald Grover, and Todd Vogel. "Is the Boss Getting Paid Too Much?" *Business Week*, May 1, 1989, pp. 46–52.

Churchill, Beryl Gail. *People Working Together: A 75th Anniversary Salute to Powell*. Powell, Wyoming: Custom Printing, 1984.

Cohen, Stephen S., and John Zysman. *Manufacturing Matters*. New York: Basic Books, 1987.

Cole, Robert E. *Work, Mobility and Participation*. Berkeley: University of California Press, 1979.

Dedrick, Calvert L., and Morris H. Hansen. *Final Report on Total and Partial Unemployment: The Enumerative Check Census*, Vol. IV. Washington, D.C.: The U.S. Government Printing Office, 1938.

Deming, W. Edwards. *The Elementary Principles of the Statistical Control of Quality, a Series of Lectures.* Tokyo: Nippon Kagaku Gijutsu Remmei, 1951.

———. "The Merit System: The Annual Appraisal: Destroyer of People" (unpublished essay).

———. *Out of the Crisis.* Cambridge, Mass.: MIT Center for Advanced Engineering Study, 1986.

———. Personal diaries, 1946, 1947, 1950, 1952, 1965.

———. *Quality, Productivity and Competitive Position.* Cambridge, Mass.: MIT Center for Advanced Engineering Study, 1982.

Dertouzos, Michael L., Richard K. Lester, and Robert M. Solow. *Made in America: Regaining the Competitive Edge.* Cambridge, Mass.: MIT Press, 1989.

Drucker, Peter F. *Concept of the Corporation.* New York: New American Library, 1983.

———. *The Frontiers of Management.* New York: Truman Talley Books/E. P. Dutton, 1986.

Dubos, Rene. *Louis Pasteur: Free Lance of Science.* New York: De Capo Press, 1960.

Dwyer, Paula, and Dave Griffiths. "How the Pentagon Can Go to War Against Abuse." *Business Week,* July 4, 1988, p. 34.

Ealy, Lance A. *Quality by Design: Taguchi Methods and U.S. Industry.* Dearborn, Mich.: ASI Press, 1988.

Farrell, Christopher, and John Hoerr. "Employee Ownership: Is It Good for Your Company?" *Business Week,* May 15, 1989, pp. 116–23.

Fisher, Anne B. "GM Is Tougher Than You Think." *Fortune,* November 10, 1986, p. 55.

Fuji Xerox, edited by Japan Business History Institute. *Fuji Xerox: The First Twenty Years: 1962–1982.* Tokyo: Fuji Xerox, 1983.

Gabor, Andrea. "GM's Bootstrap Battle: The Factory-Floor View." *U.S. News and World Report,* September 21, 1987, pp. 52–3.

———. "The Leading Light of Quality." *U.S. News and World Report,* November 28, 1988, pp. 53–6.

———. "The Man Who Changed the World of Quality." *International Management,* March 1988, pp. 42–6.

———, Mary Lord, Peter Dworkin, Steve L. Hawkins, and Jack A. Seamonds. "What They Don't Teach You at Business School." *U.S. News and World Report,* July 13, 1987, pp. 44–6.

Garvin, David A. *Managing Quality: The Strategic and Competitive Edge.* New York: Free Press, 1988.

Gellerman, Saul W., and William G. Hodgson. "Cyanamid's New Take on Performance Appraisal." *Harvard Business Review,* May–June 1988, pp. 36–41.

Godfrey, A. Blanton. "The History and Evolution of Quality at AT&T." *AT&T Technical Journal,* March–April 1986, pp. 9–19.

Halberstam, David. *The Reckoning*. New York: William Morrow and Co., 1986.

Halliday, Jon. *A Political History of Japanese Capitalism*. New York: Pantheon Books, 1975.

Hampton, William J., and James R. Norman. "General Motors: What Went Wrong." *Business Week*, March 16, 1987, pp. 102–10.

Hayes, Robert H., and Steven C. Wheelwright. *Restoring Our Competitive Edge*. New York: John Wiley & Sons, 1984.

Holusha, John. "Detroit Experimenting with the Plastic Look." *New York Times*, November 29, 1985, p. D1.

———. "G.M. Chief Sees Profit Gain Soon." *New York Times*, February 12, 1987, p. D1.

———. "Raising Quality: Consumers Star." *New York Times*, January 5, 1989, p. D1.

Hopper, Kenneth. "Creating Japan's New Industrial Management: The Americans as Teachers." *Human Resource Management*, Summer 1982, pp. 13–34.

Imai, Masaaki. *Kaizen: The Key to Japan's Competitive Success*. New York: Random House Business Division, 1986.

Ingrassia, Paul. "GM 'Quality' Can Be Hazardous to Your Health." *Wall Street Journal*, December 2, 1987, p. 28.

Ishikawa, Kaoru, trans. David J. Lu. *What Is Total Quality Control? The Japanese Way*. Englewood Cliffs, N.J.: Prentice-Hall, 1985.

Jacobson, Gary, and John Hillkirk. *Xerox: American Samurai*. New York: Macmillan Publishing Co., 1986.

Juran, J. M. *Juran on Leadership for Quality*. New York: Free Press, 1989.

———. *Managerial Breakthrough*. New York: McGraw-Hill Book Co., 1964.

———, Frank M. Gyrna, Jr., and R. S. Bingham, eds. *Quality Control Handbook*. New York: McGraw-Hill Book Co., 1951.

Kamata, Satoshi, trans. Tatsuru Kamata. *Japan in the Passing Lane: An Insider's Account of Life in a Japanese Auto Factory*. New York: Pantheon Books, 1982.

Keller, Maryann. *Rude Awakening*. New York: William Morrow & Co., 1989.

Kilian, Cecelia S. *The World of W. Edwards Deming*. Rockville, Md.: Cee Press Books/Mercury Press, 1988.

Kleinfeld, N. R. "Wntd: C. F. O. with 'Flair for Funk.'" *New York Times*, March 26, 1989, p. D4.

Kobayashi, Koji. *Computers and Communications*. Cambridge, Mass.: MIT Press, 1986.

———. "Quality Management at NEC Corporation." *Quality Progress*, April 1986, pp. 18–23.

Lacey, Robert. *Ford: The Men and the Machine.* Boston: Little Brown and Co., 1986.

"Leaky Water Law." Editorial, *Los Angeles Times*, April 15, 1987, Metro section, p. 4.

Lee, Albert. *Call Me Roger.* Chicago: Contemporary Books, 1988.

Levin, Doron P. "GM Falls Below Rivals in Auto Profit Margins." *Wall Street Journal*, June 22, 1986, p. 1.

"The Little Engine That Could." *Fortune*, February 15, 1988, p. 39.

Lowenstein, Louis, and Ira M. Millstein. "The American Corporation and the Institutional Investor: Are There Lessons from Abroad?" *Columbia Business Law Review*, Vol. 3, 1988, pp. 739–49.

Manchester, William. *American Caesar.* New York: Dell Publishing Co., 1978.

Mann, Nancy R. *The Keys to Excellence: The Story of the Deming Philosophy.* Los Angeles: Prestwick Books, 1985.

———. "Profile: Dr. W. Edwards Deming." *Road & Track*, February 1984, pp. 14–6.

Markoff, John. "Xerox vs. Apple: Standard 'Dashboard' Is at Issue." *New York Times*, December 20, 1989, p. D7.

Mayo, Elton. *The Human Problems of Industrial Civilization.* New York: Arno Press, 1977.

Meyer, H. H., E. Kay, and J. R. P. French, Jr. "Split Roles in Performance Appraisal." *Harvard Business Review*, January–February 1965, pp. 123–9.

Mooney, Marta, and Marek Hessel. "Deming's Philosophy: A Manager's View" (unpublished article).

Morrison, David C. "Right at the Start." *National Journal*, April 8, 1988, p. 978.

———. "Up in Arms." *National Journal*, July 11, 1987, pp. 1782–6.

Morrocco, John D. "GAO Warns of Potential Risks in Major New Weapons Programs." *Aviation Week and Space Technology*, April 13, 1987, pp. 98–102.

"Nashua Corp.: How Selling Copiers Again May Save It from Disaster." *Business Week*, May 2, 1983, pp. 54–5.

Nashua History Committee. *The Nashua Experience: History in the Making, 1673/1978.* Canaan, N.H.: Phoenix Publishing, 1978.

Norman, E. H., *Origins of the Modern Japanese State: Selected Writings of E. H. Norman*, John W. Dower, ed. New York: Random House, 1975.

"Nuclear Construction—Doing It Right." *Engineering News Record*, April 21, 1983, pp. 26–9.

Orsini, Joyce Nilsson. "Bonuses: What Is the Impact?" *National Productivity Review*, Spring 1987, pp. 187–93.

Peters, Tom, and Nancy Austin. *A Passion for Excellence*. New York: Warner Books, 1985.

Port, Otis. "Developments to Watch." *Business Week*, December 12, 1988, p. 82.

Prahalad, C. K., and Gary Hamel. "The Core Competence of the Corporation." *Harvard Business Review*, May–June 1990, p. 79.

Reich, Cary. "The Innovator." *New York Times Magazine*, April 21, 1985, p. 29.

Risen, James. "GM's Revolution in Auto Design." *Los Angeles Times*, April 2, 1989, p. 1.

———. "GM Taking Back Seat to Rival Ford." *Los Angeles Times*, December 6, 1986.

Roethlisberger, Fritz J., and William J. Dixon, with Harold A. Wright. *Management and the Worker: An Account of a Research Program Conducted by the Western Electric Company, Hawthorne Works, Chicago*. Cambridge, Mass.: Harvard University Press, 1939.

Rohan, Barry. "Poletown: The Price, the Promise." *Detroit Free Press*, September 8, 1985, p. 24.

Scherkenbach, William W. *The Deming Route to Quality and Productivity*. Rockville, Md.: Mercury Press, 1986.

Schlesinger, Jack M. "GM's New Compensation Plan Reflects General Trend Tying Pay to Performance." *Wall Street Journal*, January 26, 1988, p. 39.

Segalas, H. A. "Special Focus on Sucrose Polyester." Drexel Burnham Lambert Research Report, March 1987.

Shewhart, Walter. *Statistical Method from the Viewpoint of Quality Control*, W. Edwards Deming, ed. Washington, D.C.: Graduate School of the Department of Agriculture, 1939.

Sloan, Alfred P. *My Years with General Motors*. New York: Anchor Books, 1972.

Smith, Douglas K., and Robert C. Alexander. *Fumbling the Future: How Xerox Invented, then Ignored, the Personal Computer*. New York: William Morrow & Co., 1988.

"Sports Car Drivers Start Your Engines." *Newsweek*, June 9, 1986, p. 51.

Stertz, Bradley A. "GM Will Discontinue the Fiero, Citing Slump in 2-Seater Market." *Wall Street Journal*, March 2, 1988, p. 3.

Strickland, Jack. "Total Quality Management." *Army Research Development and Acquisition Bulletin*, March–April 1988, pp. 1–4.

Sullivan, L. P. "Quality Function Deployment." *Quality Progress*, May 1986, p. 77.

Tanur, Judith, M., Frederick Mosteller, William H. Kruskal, Richard F. Link, Richard S. Pieters, and Gerald R. Rising. *Statistics: A Guide to the Unknown*. San Francisco: Holden-Day, 1972.

Thurow, Lester C. *The Zero Sum Solution*. New York: Simon & Schuster, 1985.

Toyoda, Eiji. *Toyota: Fifty Years in Motion*. Tokyo and New York: Kodansha International, 1985.

Treece, James B., Mark Maremont, and Larry Armstrong. "Will the Auto Glut Choke Detroit?" *Business Week*, March 7, 1988, pp. 54–62.

Tribus, Myron. "Deming's Redefinition of Management," report for MIT Center for Advanced Engineering Study.

Wadsworth, Harrison M., Kenneth S. Stephens, and Blanton A. Godfrey. *Modern Methods for Quality Control*. New York: John Wiley & Sons, 1986.

Wallis, W. Allen. "Statistical Research Group, 1942–1945." *Journal of the American Statistical Association*, June 1980, pp. 320–1.

Walton, Mary. *The Deming Management Method*. New York: Dodd Mead & Co., 1986.

Whiteside, David, Richard Brandt, Zachary Schiller, and Andrea Gabor. "How GM's Saturn Could Run Rings Around Old-Style Carmakers." *Business Week*, January 28, 1985, pp. 126–8.

Witzenberg, Gary. *Fiero*. Tucson: HP Books, 1986.

Wood, Robert Chapman. "A Lesson Learned and a Lesson Forgotten." *Forbes*, February 6, 1989, pp. 70–8.

Wright, J. Patrick. *On a Clear Day You Can See General Motors: John Z. DeLorean's Look Inside the Automotive Giant*. New York: Avon Books, 1979.

NOTES

In the case of published materials, only short forms are given here; full citations are given in the Bibliography.

INTRODUCTION

1. Interview conducted with Donald E. Petersen by Claire Crawford Mason, provided by Ford.
2. Interview with Larry Sullivan.
3. Myron Tribus, testimony before the U.S. House of Representatives, Committee on Science and Technology, June 24, 1986, p. 7.
4. Interview with John Whitney.
5. Peters and Austin, *Passion for Excellence*, pp. 119–21.
6. Tribus, "Deming's Redefinition of Management."
7. Ibid. Also, Mooney and Hessel, "Deming's Philosophy."
8. Deming, Indianapolis Deming Seminar, February 1989.
9. Drucker, *Frontiers of Management*, p. 224.
10. Deming, Indianapolist Deming Seminar, February 1989.
11. Segalas, "Special Focus on Sucrose Polyester." Also, Prahalad and Hamel, "The Core Competence of the Corporation."
12. Mooney and Hessel, "Deming's Philosophy.
13. Ibid. Also, notes from Peter Drucker.
14. Interview with Tatsuro Toyoda.
15. Interview with Jim Miller, Dow Chemical.
16. Mann, *Keys to Excellence*, p. 3.
17. Discussion with Marta Mooney and Maryann Gould.
18. Interview with W. Edwards Deming.
19. Deming, *Elementary Principles*, p. 9.
20. Deming, *Out of the Crisis*, p. 71.
21. Ibid., pp. 103–6.
22. Ibid.
23. Interview with Ichiro Miyauchi.
24. Deming, *Out of the Crisis*, p. 59.
25. Ibid., p. 23.

26. Scherkenbach, *The Deming Route*, p. 131.
27. Deming, *Out of the Crisis*, p. 33.
28. Marta Mooney, undated letter to the author, 1989.
29. Scherkenbach, *The Deming Route*, p. 128.
30. Ibid., pp. 91–93.
31. Bridgman, *Reflections of a Physicist*, pp. 85, 97, 113. Recommended by Scherkenbach as favorite of Deming's.
32. Deming, *Out of the Crisis*, p. 24.
33. Ibid., p. 28.
34. Ibid., p. 12.
35. Discussion with W. Edwards Deming.
36. Scherkenbach, *The Deming Route*, p. 22.

CHAPTER ONE

1. Deming, *Out of the Crisis*, p. 20.
2. Interview with W. Edwards Deming.
3. Interview with George Kuper.
4. Off-the-record interview. Also, interview with W. Edwards Deming.
5. Interview with W. Edwards Deming.
6. Kilian, *World of W. Edwards Deming*, pp. 44, 116.
7. Interview with W. Edwards Deming.
8. Walton, *Deming Management Method*, pp. 3–4. Also, interview with W. Edwards Deming.
9. "Leaky Water Law."
10. Churchill, *People Working Together*, p. 9.
11. Walton, *Deming Management Method*, pp. 4–5.
12. Kilian, *World of W. Edwards Deming*, p. 40.
13. Interview with W. Edwards and Elizabeth Deming. Also, Walton, *Deming Management Method*, pp. 4–5.
14. Interview with Ronald Moen. Also, interview with J. W. Perkins.
15. Interview with Linda Deming.
16. Walton, *Deming Management Method*, p. 6. Also, conversation with Cecelia Kilian.
17. Kilian, *World of W. Edwards Deming*, p. 46.
18. Mayo, *Human Problems*, p. 99.
19. Ibid., p. 96. Also, Roethlisberger and Dixon, *Management and the Worker*, pp. 153, 88.
20. Walton, *Deming Management Method*, p. 6.
21. Ishikawa, *What Is Total Quality Control?*, p. 25.
22. Notes from W. Edwards Deming and Peter Drucker.

23. Deming, *Out of the Crisis*, p. 71.
24. Godfrey, "History and Evolution of Quality at AT&T."
25. Tanur, Mosteller, Kruskal, Link, Pieters, and Rising, p. 146–47.
26. Interview with Morris Hansen.
27. Ibid.
28. Dedrick and Hansen, *Final Report on Total and Partial Unemployment*, pp. 1, 9.
29. Interview with Morris Hansen.
30. Ibid.
31. Ibid.
32. Interview with W. Edwards Deming.
33. Godfrey, "History and Evolution of Quality at AT&T," p. 10.
34. Shewhart, *Statistical Method*, pp. 2–4.
35. Ibid., p. 4.
36. Garvin, *Managing Quality*, p. 5.
37. Ibid., pp. 6–7.
38. Phone conversation with Ronald Moen.
39. Godfrey, "History and Evolution of Quality at AT&T," p. 11.
40. Ealy, *Quality by Design*, p. 75.
41. Ford videotape, furnished by Larry Sullivan.
42. Ibid.
43. Ibid.
44. Interview with W. Edwards Deming.
45. *Encyclopaedia Britannica*, 1985. Also, interview with W. Edwards Deming.
46. Interviews with Morris Hansen and W. Edwards Deming.
47. Interview with W. Allen Wallis.
48. Lacey, *Ford*, pp. 421–22.
49. Wallis, "Statistical Research Group."
50. Ibid. Also, Walton, *Deming Management Method*, p. 8. Also, Deming, *Elementary Principles*, p. 12.
51. Wright, *On a Clear Day*, p. 163.
52. Deming, *Elementary Principles*, pp. 9–12.
53. Ibid., p. 7.
54. Mooney and Hessel, "Deming's Philosophy."
55. Imai, *Kaizen*, p. 6.
56. Interview with Myron Tribus.
57. Myron Tribus, testimony before the U.S. House of Representatives, Committee on Science and Technology, June 24, 1986, p. 7.
58. Ford videotape, furnished by Larry Sullivan.
59. Interview with Hal Tragash.

60. Deming, Indianapolis Deming Seminar, February 1989.
61. Deming, *Out of the Crisis*, p. 327.
62. Ibid., p. 327.
63. Deming lecture at JUSE, October 1988.
64. Interview with W. Edwards Deming.
65. Ibid.
66. Ibid. Deming attributes this analogy to Myron Tribus.
67. Deming lecture at JUSE, October 1988.
68. Interview with W. Edwards Deming.
69. Deming lecture at JUSE, October 1988.
70. W. Edwards Deming, unpublished paper, September 17, 1988.
71. Ecclesiastes 3:22.
72. Deming lecture at JUSE, October 1988.

CHAPTER TWO

1. Interviews with W. Edwards Deming and Eizaburo Nishibori.
2. Halberstam, *The Reckoning*, p. 311.
3. Notes from JUSE.
4. JUSE, *Deming Prize 35*, p. 11.
5. JUSE, *Deming Prize 35*, p. 17.
6. Walton, *Deming Management Method*, p. 10.
7. Deming, diaries, 1947.
8. Ibid.
9. Ibid.
10. Ibid.
11. Ibid.
12. Engineer's Club journal, August and September 1950.
13. Norman, *Origins of the Modern Japanese State*, p. 232.
14. Ibid., p. 242.
15. Halliday, *Political History of Japanese Capitalism*, p. 177.
16. Halberstam, *The Reckoning*, p. 311.
17. Manchester, *American Caesar*, p. 383.
18. Kobayashi, "Quality Management at NEC Corporation."
19. Garvin, *Managing Quality*, p. 180. Also, Wood, "A Lesson Learned."
20. Civil Communications Section Management Lectures, p. 165.
21. Civil Communications Section Management Lectures, p. 137.
22. Kobayashi, *Computers and Communications*, pp. 19–20. Also, Kobayashi, "Quality Management at NEC Corporation."
23. Deming, *Elementary Principles*, editor's preface by Kenichi Koyanagi, pp. 2–3.

24. Deming, diaries, 1950.
25. Ibid.
26. Mann, "Profile: Dr. W. Edwards Deming."
27. Deming, *Elementary Principles*, p. 1.
28. Ibid., pp. 1–2.
29. Ibid., p. 6–7.
30. Ibid., p. 9.
31. Ibid., p. 7.
32. Interview with Zenzaburo Katayama, October 1988.
33. Letter from Kenichi Koyanagi to Joseph Juran, June 22, 1964.
34. Ishikawa, *What Is Total Quality Control?*, p. 90. Also, interview with Ichiro Miyauchi.
35. Imai, *Kaizen*, pp. 5–9.
36. Ibid., p. 7.
37. Interviews at Fuji Xerox, October 1988.
38. Deming, lecture at JUSE, October 1988.
39. Garvin, *Managing Quality*, p. 187. Also, interview with Junji Noguchi.
40. Interview with Eizaburo Nishibori.
41. Engineer's Club journal, August and September 1950.
42. Ishikawa, *What Is Total Quality Control?*, p. 17.
43. Cole, *Work, Mobility and Participation*, p. 142.
44. Conversations at the Esquire Club, Tokyo, October 1988.
45. Ishikawa, *What Is Total Quality Control?*, p. 5.
46. Cole, *Work, Mobility and Participation*, p. 142.
47. Reporting by Amy Saltzman.
48. Ibid.
49. Interview with Larry Sullivan.
50. Norman, *Origins of the Modern Japanese State*, p. 13.
51. Halliday, *Political History of Japanese Capitalism*, pp. 62, 67–68.
52. Imai, *Kaizen*, p. 5.
53. Interview with Eizaburo Nishibori, October 1988.
54. Hopper, "Creating Japan's New Industrial Management."
55. Norman, *Origins of the Modern Japanese State*, essay by John W. Dower, p. 19.
56. Interview with Junji Noguchi.
57. Ford videotape.
58. Off-the-record interview.
59. Interview with Junji Noguchi. Also, interview with Kent Sterett.
60. Ishikawa, *What Is Total Quality Control?*, pp. 94–95.
61. Interviews by Michael Berger.
62. Off-the-record interview.

63. Interview with Yōtaro Kobayashi.
64. Interviews by Michael Berger.
65. Ibid.
66. Interview with Junji Noguchi.
67. Gabor, "The Leading Light of Quality." Also, additional notes by Jim Impoco.
68. Interview with Junji Noguchi.
69. Off-the-record interview.
70. Interview with Ichiro Miyauchi.
71. Port, "Developments to Watch."

CHAPTER THREE

1. Interview with Larry Sullivan.
2. Ibid.
3. Conway videotape, "Nashua Seminar—Short Version."
4. Ibid.
5. Ibid.
6. Ibid.
7. Interview with Larry Sullivan.
8. Deming, *Out of the Crisis*, p. 28.
9. Interview with Lloyd S. Nelson.
10. Ibid.
11. Interview with Larry Sullivan.
12. Ibid.
13. Interview with Lloyd S. Nelson.
14. Nashua History Committee, *The Nashua Experience*, pp. 95–113.
15. "Nashua Corp."
16. Interview with Lloyd S. Nelson.
17. Ibid.
18. Interview with J. W. Perkins.
19. Interview with Charles Clough.
20. Interview with Ed Johnson.
21. Interview with Robert Amberg.
22. Ibid.
23. Ibid.
24. Ibid.
25. Interview with Lloyd S. Nelson.
26. Interview with Ed Johnson.
27. Interview with William Conway.
28. Interviews with W. Edwards Deming and Charles Clough.

29. Interview with Frank Faticanti.
30. Interview with Walter J. Powers.
31. Interview with Lloyd S. Nelson.
32. Interview with Bill Masuda.
33. Ibid.
34. Ibid.
35. Ibid.
36. Ibid.
37. Gabor, "The Man Who Changed the World of Quality."
38. Off-the-record interview.
39. Interviews with Charles Clough and John Montesi.
40. Interview with Lloyd S. Nelson.
41. Interview with Frank Faticanti.
42. Interview with John Montesi.
43. Ibid.

Chapter Four

1. Interview with Donald Petersen by Claire Crawford Mason, provided by Ford.
2. Interview with Larry Sullivan.
3. Interview with William E. Scollard.
4. Letter from John Manoogian, March 15, 1988.
5. Interviews with Larry Sullivan and Louis R. Ross.
6. Bingaman and Doody, *Reinventing the Wheels*, p. 75.
7. Letter from Don Peterson to Deming, February 28, 1990.
8. Interview with William E. Scollard.
9. Ibid.
10. Ibid.
11. Interview with Donald Petersen by Claire Crawford Mason, provided by Ford.
12. Interview with James Bakken.
13. Interview with Larry Sullivan.
14. Interviews with Larry Sullivan and James Bakken.
15. Off-the-record interviews.
16. Interview with James Bakken.
17. Interview with Larry Sullivan.
18. Halberstam, *The Reckoning*, pp. 236–45.
19. Interview with William E. Scollard.
20. Bingaman and Doody, *Reinventing the Wheels*, p. 33.
21. Ibid., p. 40.

22. Halberstam, *The Reckoning*, p. 461.
23. Ibid., pp. 499–500. Also, interview with Larry Sullivan.
24. Lacey, *Ford*, pp. 575–76, 583.
25. Ibid., pp. 578, 581–2.
26. Ibid., pp. 575–58.
27. Bingaman and Doody, *Reinventing the Wheels*, p. 47.
28. Ibid., pp. 47–8.
29. Interview with Louis R. Ross.
30. Ibid.
31. Ibid.
32. Ibid.
33. Ibid.
34. Ibid.
35. Interviews with James Bakken and Lionel (Bud) Chicoine.
36. Dertouzos et al., *Made in America*, p. 117.
37. Interview with Larry Sullivan.
38. Brown, "The Making of the All-New Thunderbird."
39. Interview with Louis R. Ross.
40. Brown, "The Making of the All-New Thunderbird."
41. Interview with Ronald Moen.

CHAPTER FIVE

1. Lacey, *Ford*, pp. 157, 170–71.
2. Altschuler et al., *Future of the Automobile*, pp. 147–48.
3. Interview with David Cole.
4. Ibid.
5. Deming, *Out of the Crisis*, pp. 31–32.
6. Deming, *Elementary Principles*, pp. 3–4.
7. Interview with Akikazu Kida.
8. Interview with Maryann Keller.
9. Altschuler et al., *Future of the Automobile*, p. 34.
10. John Whitney, unpublished paper.
11. Interview with Larry Sullivan.
12. Ibid.
13. Interview with William E. Scollard.
14. Conversation with Burt Serre.
15. Ford Motor Company, *Q 101 Quality System Standard Handbook*.
16. Halberstam, *The Reckoning*, pp. 536–37.
17. Bingaman and Doody, *Reinventing the Wheels*, p. 47. Also, interview with Larry Sullivan.

18. Interview with Larry Sullivan.
19. Interview with J. L. French.
20. Interviews with Mel Rowe and Jim Fullerton.
21. Ibid.
22. Ibid.
23. Interview with Leo Brown.
24. Ibid.
25. Interview with Mel Rowe.
26. Interviews with Mel Rowe and Jim Fullerton.
27. Interview with Leo Brown.
28. Interview with Mel Rowe.
29. Interview with Jim Fullerton.
30. Interviews with Mel Rowe and Jim Fullerton.
31. Interview with J. L. French.
32. Ibid.
33. Interview with Brad King.
34. Interview with Charles Walden.
35. Interview with J. L. French.
36. Ibid.
37. Ibid.
38. Ibid.
39. Sullivan, "Quality Function Deployment."
40. J. L. French, "Design of Experiments Manual," October 1, 1987.
41. Interview with J. L. French.
42. J. L. French, "3.8 liter, 4–6 Front Cover Quality/Analysis," October 1, 1987.
43. Interview with J. L. French.
44. Ibid.
45. Ealy, *Quality by Design*, p. 68. Also, unpublished Ford paper, November 11, 1987.
46. Ealy, *Quality by Design*, p. 70.
47. Ibid., pp. 55–57.
48. Ibid., p. 59.
49. W. H. Moore, "Ford Has a Better Idea," unpublished paper. Furnished by Larry Sullivan.
50. Interview with Louis R. Ross.
51. Interview with Donald P. Clausing. Also, Ealy, *Quality by Design*, p. 105.
52. Interviews with Donald P. Clausing and S. Jefferson Kennard.
53. Interviews at Toyota.
54. Interviews with Donald P. Clausing and Larry Sullivan.

55. Holusha, "Raising Quality: Consumers Star."
56. Ibid. Also, interview with William E. Scollard.

CHAPTER SIX

1. Interview with Frank Thompson.
2. Off-the-record interview.
3. Interview with John Hudiberg.
4. Ibid.
5. Interview with Norman Rickard.
6. Interview with Kent Sterett.
7. Interview with Marshall McDonald.
8. Ibid.
9. Ibid.
10. Interview with Kent Sterett.
11. "Nuclear Construction—Doing It Right." Also, interview with Kent Sterett.
12. "Nuclear Construction—Doing It Right."
13. Interview with Ronald Moen.
14. Interview with Kent Sterett.
15. Ibid.
16. Ibid.
17. Internal FP&L documents regarding service reliability indicators.
18. Interview with Harry Hansen.
19. Ibid.
20. Ibid.
21. Interview with Kent Sterett.
22. Interviews with members of the Stuart team. Also, interviews with Frank Thompson. Also, FP&L's QI Story documents.
23. Interview with John Hudiberg.
24. Interview with Kent Sterett.
25. Interview with John Hudiberg. Also, interview with Kent Sterett.
26. Interview with Junji Noguchi.
27. Interview with Kent Sterett.
28. Interview with Frank Thompson.
29. Interview with Earl Conway.

CHAPTER SEVEN

1. Interview with Donald P. Clausing.
2. Dertouzos et al., *Made in America*, p. 270.
3. Remarks by David Kearns.

4. Smith and Alexander, *Fumbling the Future*, pp. 119–20.
5. Off-the-record interview. Also, Xerox press release on 1989 financial performance and Xerox Corporation 1987 annual report.
6. Smith and Alexander, *Fumbling the Future*, p. 129.
7. Ibid., pp. 159–60.
8. Ibid., p. 42.
9. Ibid., pp. 30, 128.
10. Ibid. p. 126.
11. Ibid., pp. 14, 49.
12. Ibid., pp. 154–56. Also, interviews with Myron Tribus and off-the-record interviews.
13. Jacobson and Hillkirk, *Xerox: American Samurai*, p. 3.
14. Interviews with Pauline Brody and Donald P. Clausing. Also, speech by Barry Rand.
15. Interview with Robert Graham.
16. Off-the-record interview.
17. Off-the-record interview.
18. Xerox, "Leadership Through Quality," August 1983, p. 17.
19. Interview with Hal Tragash.
20. Off-the-record interview.
21. Interview with Philip Crosby. Also, off-the-record interviews.
22. Off-the-record interview.
23. Ibid.
24. Xerox, "Leadership Through Quality," August 1983, p. 19.
25. Interview with Donald P. Clausing.
26. Ibid.
27. Interview with Norman Rickard.
28. Interview with Hal Tragash. Also, off-the-record interview.
29. Interview with Donald P. Clausing.
30. Interview with Barry Rand.
31. Interview with Donald P. Clausing.
32. Speech by Barry Rand.
33. Interview with Robert Graham.
34. Interview with Robert Graham.
35. Interview with Barry Rand.
36. Interview with Robert Graham.
37. Ibid.
38. Interview with Carolyn McZinc.
39. Interviews with Donald P. Clausing and S. Jefferson Kennard.
40. Fuji Xerox, *Fuji Xerox*, p. 220.
41. Ibid., pp. 177–82, 299–300. Also, interviews at Fuji Xerox.

42. Ibid., pp. 263–64. Also, off-the-record interview.
43. Interview with Donald P. Clausing.
44. Fuji Xerox, *Fuji Xerox*, pp. 203–5. Also, interview with Yōtaro Kobayashi.
45. Interview with Yōtaro Kobayashi.
46. Fuji Xerox, *Fuji Xerox*, p. 250.
47. Ibid., p. 266.
48. Fuji Xerox, *Fuji Xerox*, pp. 268–71.
49. Interview with Takamichi Hatanaka.
50. Ibid.
51. Ibid.
52. Ibid.
53. Ibid.
54. Ibid. Also, internal Fuji Xerox documents.
55. Demonstration at Fuji Xerox, October 1989.
56. Interview with Donald P. Clausing.
57. Site visit at Fuji Xerox, October 1989.
58. Interview with Takamichi Hatanaka.
59. Internal documents regarding reviews for the 5026/5030 copiers.
60. Ibid.
61. Interview with Yōtaro Kobayashi.
62. Ibid.
63. Interview with S. Jefferson Kennard. Also, interview with David Kearns.
64. Off-the-record interview. Also, interview with David Kearns.
65. Ibid.

CHAPTER EIGHT

1. Interview with Robert Stempel.
2. General Motors Annual Report, 1981.
3. Rohan, "Poletown."
4. Note from Maryann Keller.
5. Treece et al., "Will the Auto Glut Choke Detroit?"
6. Fisher, "GM Is Tougher Than You Think."
7. Whiteside et al., "How GM's Saturn Could Run Rings."
8. Buss and Guiles, "GM Slows Big Drive for Saturn to Produce Small Car in Five Years." Also, off-the-record interviews.
9. Holusha, "G.M. Chief." Also, Buss, "GM Radically Shifts." Also, Risen, "GM Taking Back Seat." Also, notes from Steve Hagarty at GM.

10. Hampton and Norman, "General Motors: What Went Wrong."
11. Wright, *On a Clear Day*, pp. 226–27. Also, Sloan, *My Years with General Motors*, pp. 505–6.
12. Interview with Roger Smith.
13. Wright, *On a Clear Day*, pp. 60, 155, 169, 231, 251.
14. Keller, *Rude Awakening*, pp. 101–3.
15. Hampton and Norman, "General Motors: What Went Wrong."
16. Reich, "The Innovator."
17. Ibid.
18. Interviews with Roger Smith and Jim Perkins.
19. Interview with Bob Stempel.
20. Interview with Maryann Keller.
21. Wright, *On a Clear Day*, pp. 63–6. Also, Keller, *Rude Awakening*, pp. 101–4.
22. Interview with Ronald Moen.
23. Witzenberg, *Fiero*, p. 53.
24. Internal Pontiac document.
25. Speech by William Hoglund, August 25, 1982, p. 24.
26. Holusha, "Detroit Experimenting."
27. Interview with Maryann Keller.
28. Hampton and Norman, "General Motors: What Went Wrong."
29. Interview with Maryann Keller.
30. Ibid. Also, Keller, *Rude Awakening*, pp. 215–17.
31. Speech by William Hoglund, August 25, 1982.
32. Interview with William Hoglund. Also, interview with Ernest P. Schaefer.
33. Interview with William Hoglund.
34. Internal Pontiac document.
35. Ron Moen's résumé.
36. Internal Pontiac document.
37. Ibid.
38. Ibid.
39. Ibid.
40. Interview with William Hoglund.
41. Ibid.
42. Ibid. Also, interview with Ron Moen.
43. Interview with William Hoglund.
44. Internal Pontiac document.
45. Ibid.
46. Interview with Bob Dorn.
47. Off-the-record interview.

48. Witzenberg, *Fiero*, p. 53.
49. Ibid., p. 29.
50. Ibid.
51. Interview with Ernest P. Schaefer.
52. Witzenberg, *Fiero*, p. 46.
53. Ibid., p. 53.
54. Ibid., p. 50.
55. Interview with Ernest P. Schaefer.
56. Ibid.
57. Gabor, "GM's Bootstrap Battle."
58. Witzenberg, *Fiero*, p. 49.
59. Interview with Maryann Keller.
60. Interview with Ernest P. Schaefer.
61. Ibid.
62. Off-the-record interview.
63. Interview with Ronald Moen. Also, Witzenberg, *Fiero*, p. 59.
64. Witzenberg, *Fiero*, pp. 65, 71, 80. Also, interview with Ernest P. Schaefer.
65. Interview with Maryann Keller.
66. Ingrassia, "GM 'Quality.' " Also, interview with Maryann Keller.
67. Interview with Maryann Keller. Also, GM press release, March 1, 1988.
68. Stertz, "GM Will Discontinue the Fiero." Also, "Sports Car Drivers Start Your Engines." Also, interview with Maryann Keller.
69. Interview with Thomas J. Donnan.
70. Gabor, "GM's Bootstrap Battle."
71. Interview with Ernest P. Schaefer.
72. Gabor, "GM's Bootstrap Battle."
73. Interview with David Cole.
74. Interview with Ernest P. Schaefer.
75. Gabor, "GM's Bootstrap Battle."
76. Ibid.
77. Brown, "Contract Talks Could Retool Auto Industry."
78. Gabor, "GM's Bootstrap Battle."
79. Off-the-record interview.
80. Gabor, "GM's Bootstrap Battle."
81. Interview with Maryann Keller.
82. Interview with Arvin F. Mueller.
83. Off-the-record interview.
84. Phone conversation with Laura Joseph.
85. Ibid.

86. "The Little Engine That Could."
87. Interview with Beth Hubbard.
88. Interview with N. L. Keller. Also, phone conversation with Laura Joseph.
89. Interview with Beth Hubbard.
90. Ibid.
91. Ibid.
92. Ibid.
93. Ibid.
94. Schlesinger, "GM's New Compensation Plan."
95. Deming, unpublished essay on performance appraisal.
96. Interview with Mary Jenkins.
97. Keller, *Rude Awakening*, pp. 216–17. Also, interview with Bunkie Knudsen.
98. Keller, *Rude Awakening*, pp. 216–17.
99. Interviews with Rosetta Reilly, Gary Cowger, and Bob Dorn.
100. Interviews at Hamtramck.
101. Interview with Rosetta Reilly.
102. Risen, "GM's Revolution in Auto Design."
103. Interview with Mike McCurdy.
104. Interview with Maryann Keller.
105. Interview with Ed Czapor.
106. Ibid.
107. Ibid.
108. Interview with Dick Donnelly.
109. Notes from Maryann Keller.
110. Interview with William E. Hoglund.
111. Interview with Roger Smith.

Chapter Nine

1. Interview with Marc Wallace.
2. Off-the-record interview.
3. Gellerman and Hodgson, "Cyanamid's New Take on Performance Appraisal."
4. Deming, "The Merit System."
5. Interview with Michael Beer.
6. Interview with Mary Jenkins.
7. Deming, "The Merit System."
8. Ibid.
9. Ibid. Also, interview with W. Edwards Deming.

10. Interview with William Hodgson.
11. Meyer et al., "Split Roles in Performance Appraisal."
12. Interview with Michael Scott Morton. Also, interview with Michael Beer.
13. Interview with William E. Hoglund.
14. Schlesinger, "GM's New Compensation Plan."
15. Interview with Michael Beer.
16. Interview with Mary Jenkins.
17. Ibid.
18. Ibid.
19. Internal Powertrain document, "BOC Powertrain's compensation philosophy."
20. Interview with William Hodgson.
21. Interview with Saul Gellerman.
22. Interview with William Hodgson.
23. Off-the-record interview.
24. Interview with William Hodgson.
25. Interview with Richard Donnelly.
26. Interview with William Hodgson.
27. Ibid.
28. Interview with Tom Laco.
29. Interview with R. Peter Mercer.
30. Interview with James Bavis.
31. Interview with David Barash.
32. Interview with William Hodgson. Also, interview with Louis R. Ross.
33. Interview with R. Peter Mercer.
34. Interview with David Barash.
35. Orsini, "Bonuses: What Is the Impact?"
36. Ibid.
37. Ibid.
38. Ibid.
39. Interview with Saul Gellerman. Also, interview with David Barash.
40. Interview with Tom Laco.
41. Interview with David Barash.
42. Interview with Louis R. Ross.
43. Interview with Mary Jenkins.
44. Interview with William E. Hoglund.
45. Ibid.

Chapter Ten

1. Interview with Kenneth Hopper.
2. Gabor et al., "What They Don't Teach You at Business School."
3. Ibid.
4. Interview with Marta Mooney.
5. Letter from IBM, April 21, 1989.
6. Interview with Robert Mosbacher.
7. Interview with Thomas Murrin.
8. Malcolm Baldrige National Quality Awards, Application Guidelines, 1989.
9. Interview with Ken Sayers, Motorola.
10. Interview with Curt Reimman. Also, Port, "Developments to Watch."
11. Interview with Thomas Murrin.
12. Speech by Richard Cheney, July 11, 1989.
13. House Republican Research Committee, Task Force on High Technology and Competitiveness, "Quality as a Means to Improving Our Nation's Competitiveness," July 12, 1988.
14. Morrocco, "GAO Warns of Potential Risks."
15. Off-the-record interview.
16. Interview with Gordon Keefe.
17. Strickland, "Total Quality Management."
18. Dwyer and Griffiths, "How the Pentagon Can Go to War Against Abuse."
19. "AFSC Chief Randolph Cites Value of CPAR."
20. Strickland, "Total Quality Management."
21. Andrews, "Pentagon Adopts Japanese Production Techniques."
22. Off-the-record interview.
23. House Republican Research Committee, Task Force on High Technology and Competitiveness. "Quality as a Means to Improving Our Nation's Competitiveness," July 12, 1988.
24. Interview with Lou Schultz.
25. Morrison, "Right at the Start."
26. Public Affairs Division, Internal Revenue Service, news release, June 2, 1988. Also, interview with Brian Joiner.
27. Morrison, "Up in Arms." Also, off-the-record interview.
28. Speech by Richard Cheney, July 11, 1989.
29. Morrocco, "GAO Warns of Potential Risks."
30. Bureau of National Affairs, Daily Report for Executives, January 25, 1988.

31. Interview with Thomas Murrin.
32. Ibid. Also, interview with Lou Schultz.
33. Interview with Lou Schultz.
34. Walton, *Deming Manufacturing Method*, pp. 199–201.
35. Lowenstein and Millstein, "The American Corporation and the Institutional Investor."
36. Ibid.
37. Speech by Ira Millstein, May 22, 1989.
38. Ibid.
39. Drucker, *Frontiers of Management*, p. 246.
40. Farrell and Hoerr, "Employee Ownership: Is It Good for Your Company?"
41. Ibid.
42. Drucker, *Frontiers of Management*, pp. 140–41.
43. Byrne et al., "Is the Boss Getting Paid Too Much?"
44. Drucker, *Frontiers of Management*, pp. 140–141.
45. Byrne et al., "Is the Boss Getting Paid Too Much?"
46. Kleinfeld, "Wntd: C.F.O. with 'Flair for Funk.' "

INDEX

Abernathy, William, 268
Acceptable Quality Levels (AQL),
  275–76
Adams Harkness & Hill, 122
after-the-fact grading system, 243
Agriculture Department, U.S., 52
Air Force Logistics Command, U.S.,
  274
Aisin Seiki, 142
Akiba, Kojiro, 211
Alcoa, 100, 186
Aldikacti, Hulki, 227–28, 230–31
Alexander, Robert, 191
Allaire, Paul, 213
Allante (Cadillac), 223, 244
Allied Signal Aerospace, 89
Alto (computer), 192
Amberg, Robert, 115–17
Ambler, Ernest, 99
American Assembly of Collegiate
  Schools of Business, 268
American Cyanamid, 27, 250, 251,
  253, 257–59, 260, 262
American Society for Quality Control,
  55
American Supplier Institute (ASI), 24,
  130, 161, 269, 274
  creation of, 144–45, 156, 269
  QFD popularized by, 160

Taguchi methods as basis of, 154–
  55, 156, 160–61
analysts, auto, 142, 220, 222, 229, 231,
  237, 244, 247
annual reviews, *see* reviews, annual
Antarctica, 71
antitrust legislation, 34, 144, 194
Apple, 192
appraisals, performance, 18–19, 26, 130
  bell curves in, 27, 251, 255
  criticisms of, 58, 242–43, 250–54,
    258, 259, 260, 263–64
  forced-distribution systems of, 242,
    254–56, 257, 258–59, 261
  pass-fail system of, 239, 243, 256–
    57, 265–66
  quotas in, 15, 21–22, 27, 42, 242,
    255–56, 258–59
  social responsibility as factor in,
    262–63
  team approach to, 243, 256–57, 262,
    265–66
  top management and, 252–53, 254,
    255, 258, 259
  traditional U.S. approach to, 18–19,
    26, 186, 254
  variation and, 27, 58–63, 252
Asaka, Tetsuichi, 95, 183–84, 197,
  206–7, 211, 213

311